PROPERTY Vs SHARES

DISCOVER YOUR KNOCKOUT INVESTMENT STRATEGY

PETER KOULIZOS & ZAC ZACHARIA

Wrightbooks
A Wiley Brand

Zac would like to dedicate this book to his wonderful wife, Kelly, for her incredible encouragement, love and support, and also to his late father and mother, who have inspired him to become the best he can be — and also taught him the importance of helping others to change their lives for the better.

First published in 2013 by Wrightbooks,
an imprint of John Wiley & Sons Australia, Ltd
42 McDougall St, Milton Qld 4064

Office also in Melbourne

Typeset in 11/13.5 pt Bembo Std

© Petraki Pty Ltd and ZIZ International Pty Ltd 2013

The moral rights of the authors have been asserted

National Library of Australia Cataloguing-in-Publication data:

Author:	Koulizos, Peter, author.
Title:	Property Vs Shares: discover your knockout investment strategy / Peter Koulizos and Zac Zacharia.
ISBN:	9781118613139 (paperback)
Notes:	Includes index.
Subjects:	Real estate investment.
	Stocks.
	Investments.
Other authors/contributors	Zac Zacharia, author.
Dewey Number:	332.6

Cover design by Paul McCarthy

Cover image: © iStockphoto.com/Viktor Kitaykin

Printed in Singapore by C.O.S Printers Pte Ltd

10 9 8 7 6 5 4 3 2 1

CONTENTS

About the authors		*iv*
Acknowledgements		*v*
Introduction		*vi*
Disclaimer		*viii*
Round 1	The basics of investment	1
Round 2	Why invest?	9
Round 3	History of the property and share markets	23
Round 4	Investment cycles	39
Round 5	Where to do your research	52
Round 6	Understanding the tables and statistics	64
Round 7	The risks of investment	79
Round 8	Return on investments	90
Round 9	Costs of investing	101
Round 10	Market participants and facilitators	111
Round 11	Managed investments	124
Round 12	Trading vs investing	134
Round 13	Financing your investment	149
Round 14	Investment structures	161
Round 15	Self managed superannuation funds	172
Round 16	Tax and investments	184
Round 17	Legal issues	195
Round 18	Overseas investments	206
Round 19	Schemes and scams	216
Round 20	Top questions to ask	231
Round 21	Case studies	242
Round 22	Advanced investment opportunities	254
Round 23	Conclusion: and the winner is...	271
Glossary		*281*
Index		*288*

ABOUT THE AUTHORS

Peter Koulizos

Peter 'The Property Professor' Koulizos is coordinator of the property and share investment courses for TAFE SA. He also teaches in the Victoria University property investment workshop in Melbourne, Sydney and Brisbane. In addition to his teaching in property investment, he teaches property, valuation and property economics at the University of South Australia. Peter holds a teaching degree, a graduate diploma in property and a master of business (property). Peter also personally invests in property and currently holds several investment properties. Peter's previous book is entitled *The Property Professor's Top Australian Suburbs*.

Zac Zacharia

Zac Zacharia is founder and managing director of a financial services business, the Centra Wealth Group, through which he provides financial planning, investment advice and education services to his clients. Before founding Centra Wealth, Zac had worked as a senior private client adviser at one of Australia's most respected financial services businesses. He lectures to students of the share investment course at TAFE SA as well as providing training services to students and members of Kaplan. He is a sought-after speaker and regularly contributes articles and investment opinions to numerous publications.

Zac's qualifications, together with his personal investment and trading experience have provided him with the street smarts and intuition to understand how global investment markets interact, so as to provide dynamic investment strategies for his clients and fulfil his passion for helping people change their lives financially for the better.

ACKNOWLEDGEMENTS

This book would not have been possible without the help of a number of specialists that we consulted. A big thank you to:

- Dom Cosentino, Partner, Kennedy & Co Chartered Accountants, for his contribution to the chapters on tax.

- Matt Davis, licensed mortgage broker, Property Planning Australia, for his input into the property finance section.

- Steve Russo, Partner, Kennedy & Co Chartered Accountants, for his specialist knowledge of self managed superannuation funds.

- Sean Ryan, Director, FBR Law, for his contribution to the discussion of legal issues in relation to property and the advanced property investment strategies.

INTRODUCTION

Finally, here is *one* comprehensive book that covers *both* property and share investment! Many books deal with property *or* shares, but this is the first to provide the facts about both of these asset classes, side by side, in a tell-all, no-holds-barred style.

Is one kind of investment better than the other? Does one provide more capital growth? Is one better for income? What about the risks? This book will dispel the myths and break through the misinformation about both of these asset classes. You will learn the facts, benefits, risks and much more about each of these investments so that you can decide for yourself which, if not both, is good for you.

Our motivation behind writing the book is to help answer the endless stream of questions we are asked regularly that boil down to: Which is the better investment—property or shares?

We believe that a lot of people have a vested interest in promoting either property or shares—but we would like to present the facts on both so that people can formulate their own opinions.

This book:

- is set out in an easy-to-read format
- is divided into succinct chapters, covering issues related to both property and shares
- is written by professionals who not only teach but also personally invest
- provides helpful tips on what to buy, and when to buy
- includes details on what to look out for, such as property and share investment scams
- provides an unbiased point of view on both asset classes

- includes case studies that aim to provide guidance to readers on their investment strategies
- is supported by our website at www.propertyvsshares.com.au.

Property Vs Shares is intended to serve as a reference guide to potential and existing investors in each asset class. Whether you have already invested in shares or property, or you are just starting to consider investing in these assets and want to find out about the risks and benefits of each, this book provides the necessary information to help you make an educated and informed decision based on your own investment goals.

Our website

We have created an exclusive website for readers of *Property Vs Shares* to supplement your learning beyond your reading and study of this book. The website address is www.propertyvsshares.com.au.

It includes a bonus chapter available for you to download that contains our top picks for property and shares until 2020. Through our website we will keep the material in this book up to date and relevant—and continue the debate about which is best: property or shares!

Our website will also keep you updated as to our current opinions on the property and sharemarket, as well as provide you with a wealth of resources and helpful hints and tips.

DISCLAIMER

The information presented in this work is general in nature and of an educational and informative nature. It has been prepared without taking into account your objectives, financial situation or needs; therefore, before you decide to act on any of the suggestions and strategies that are contained in this book, you should consider their appropriateness having regard to your objectives, financial situation and needs. This work is sold with the understanding that neither the authors nor the publisher are engaged in rendering legal, financial, accounting, tax, or other professional services. If professional assistance is required, the services of a competent professional person should be sought.

The authors certify that all of the views expressed in this book accurately reflect their personal views about any and all of the subject securities or issuers. Although the authors believe that the information contained in this book is accurate and reliable and is based on their skills, knowledge and experience and obtained from reputable websites, research organisations and published works, neither the authors nor the publisher make any representations or warranties with respect to the accuracy or completeness of the contents of this work and specifically disclaim all warranties, including without limitation warranties of fitness for a particular purpose. The advice and strategies contained herein may not be suitable for every situation. The fact that an organisation or Website is referred to in this work as a citation and/or a potential source of further information does not mean that the authors or the publisher endorses the information the organisation or Website may provide or recommendations it may make. Further, readers should be aware that Internet Websites listed in this work may have changed or disappeared between when this work was written and when it is read. Except to the extent that liability cannot be excluded, neither authors nor the publisher nor contributing writers nor any associated entities, shall be liable for any loss or damage arising from this here Work for any reason including if caused by any error in, or omission from the material presented in the work.

Please remember that past performance is not a reliable indicator of future results. The forecasts used in this work are intended as a guide only. They are predictive in character and as such may be affected by inaccurate or incomplete assumptions or by known or unknown risks and uncertainties and therefore may differ materially from the results that individual investors ultimately achieve.

Information concerning taxation is of a general nature and does not constitute advice. Please consult a qualified accountant or financial adviser who will be able to provide you with reliable advice for your individual situation.

Round 1

THE BASICS OF INVESTMENT

Investing requires you to give up the opportunity to spend money you have *today* in order to earn more money (that will be available for you to spend) *in the future*. In other words, you are making a sacrifice of a *certain amount* today for the potential to receive an *uncertain amount* and benefit from the investment at some point in the future. An investment in a growth asset does not carry a guarantee of how much money you will receive in the future, but you can expect that it will be more than you initially invested.

When you make an investment, you do so because you expect the investment to grow in value, or to provide you with a regular income, or both.

Asset classes

Investors can generally choose to allocate their money to any of four types of investments, or asset classes. Two of these have defensive characteristics, which means that they provide guaranteed and virtually certain returns, but they do not provide you with opportunities for growth, or increase in the capital value of the investment. The other two types of asset have growth characteristics: they do not provide a guarantee of what your return will be, but they do offer the potential for capital growth. Each asset class therefore has unique advantages and disadvantages for the investor, and also unique characteristics and influences. Importantly, each type of investment also has a different risk–return profile—in other words, a different level of potential return on your investment that rises as the level of risk rises. This is shown in figure 1.1 (overleaf).

Figure 1.1: the different types of investments and their risk–return profiles

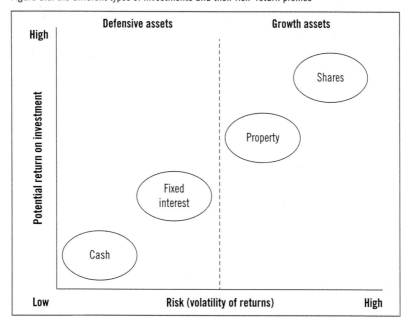

The four asset classes and their characteristics are as follows.

Cash

This asset class includes any investment that is essentially cash-based or that can easily be converted to cash. It has the lowest risk of a capital loss. Cash includes physical notes and coins, but more commonly the term is used to refer to short-term interest-bearing investments, such as bank bills, commercial bills and fixed term deposits and cash management accounts.

The most common way for people to invest in this asset class is to put money away in a bank account. Compared with the other asset classes, you will receive a relatively low return (currently around 3 per cent per year), but cash is considered to be a very low risk investment: you are virtually guaranteed that not only will you get your money back but you will also earn 3 per cent interest on the money you invested. Your cash deposit won't grow in value: you'll just receive the income based on how much you invested, how long you invested for, and the interest rate. You have very good access to your money, as you can generally walk into a bank or make a phone call or access your account on the internet and have your money in a matter of minutes.

Fixed interest (including bonds)

This asset class is also defensive and includes securities such as bonds. Bonds are like an IOU. You are in effect lending money to a government or corporation such as a bank (also known as the issuer). In return for your money, the issuer promises to pay you a fixed rate of interest for the life of the bond and pay back the original amount, known as principal.

The returns you receive will be relatively low (currently around 4.5 per cent per year). Fixed interest is also considered a low risk investment: your money is guaranteed by the government or corporation issuing the bond. You should get all your money back in addition to receiving interest earned at periodic intervals. But the safety of your investment will always depend on who the issuer is: your money is safer in a government bond or bank term deposit than it is in a corporate bond issued by a small company. Your initial investment might not grow in value (if you hold it to maturity) but you will receive income from the interest earned. You have reasonably good access to your money, as you should be able sell your bond on the market within a day.

Property

This asset class is a growth asset, just like shares. However, it carries a lower level of investment risk than shares, as you will see in Round 7. Property investment can be direct — which means that you buy the investment yourself (such as houses, offices or factories) — or indirect — which means that you buy an investment in an entity, such as a property trust, which in turn buys and holds one or more properties. These property trusts can be listed on a stock exchange or unlisted.

Compared with the other asset classes, property has a moderate return, which is accompanied by a moderate risk. Historically it has been shown that the capital growth in property (about 9 per cent per year) is slightly less than the capital growth from shares, but so is the associated risk. Investors and owner-occupiers are often attracted to property because of the security it offers. People can make a profit from holding property if it is well located and they are willing to hold onto it for a period of time. However, some people have lost money on property; this is generally because they bought the wrong type of property, at the wrong time, in a poor location. Property buyers generally find that the value of their property increases over time and, if they are investors, they also receive income in the form of rent. On the negative side, property has low liquidity, meaning that you can't sell it and access the funds quickly as you can with the other asset classes, and you have to sell the whole investment, even if you only need a smaller amount of cash.

Shares

This asset class is also a growth asset, but depending on the shares you invest in, carries the highest level of investment risk. When you buy shares in a company, you become a part-owner of that company. As a part-owner, you are eligible to a proportionate share in the company's performance. This includes a share in profits (that you take as dividends) as well as capital growth (that you earn through the value of your shares increasing). Shares can be bought as a direct investment in companies listed on the Australian Securities Exchange and international sharemarkets, or as an indirect investment through a managed fund that invests in shares.

People are attracted to the sharemarket because of the relatively high returns. Compared with the other asset classes, shares have the highest potential to provide you with capital growth (on average investors can expect growth of 7–10 per cent per year from a portfolio of blue chip shares), but they are also accompanied by the highest level of investment risk. Share investors expect their shares to grow in value (capital growth) and they will earn a dividend (income) while they hold onto the shares. While this is the case most of the time, it is not a certainty. People can lose money on the sharemarket when the value of their shares drops or dividends are reduced or no longer paid. On some occasions, companies go broke and investors can lose most, if not all, of their money. On the positive side, you have very good access to your assets, as you can generally sell all or just some of the shares on the sharemarket within a day. This makes shares more liquid than property.

Why does the sharemarket exist?

Sharemarkets exist to provide businesses with a source of funds (called capital) with which they can expand and grow their business. It also exists to facilitate a way for existing owners of the business (the shareholders) to sell their shares to new buyers, and vice versa.

One of the ways that a company can raise money to finance its business is to 'go public'—that is, to become listed on a stock exchange. It does this by issuing shares in the company to the general public. Investors receive shares in the company in exchange for their money, effectively becoming part-owners, or shareholders, of the company. Money raised in this way is called equity capital. This differs from debt capital (such as corporate bonds), which is borrowed money—equity capital does not need to be repaid to the investor, while debt capital (raised through bonds, for instance) does have to be repaid. Equity capital represents continuous ownership of the company.

In return for the funds investors provide, the business issues shares in the business. As shareholders, investors effectively become a part-owner of the business—and they can share in the benefits of being an owner of the company, including distributions of profits (through dividends), and of course through the increase in the value of the company (through the share price of the company increasing).

It is important for an investor to understand the difference between the primary market and the secondary market (see figure 1.2, overleaf).

The primary market facilitates the raising of capital for a company—for example, through the issue of shares directly to shareholders. This is during the IPO (initial public offering) phase, where a company lists on the market for the first time; or after a listing, where a company goes to the market again to raise funds (for example, through share purchase plans, rights issues and other forms of equity issues, such as bond or preference share issues). Funds raised in the primary market go directly to the company, where they are used by the company according to the plans the company set out in the prospectus issued for the capital raising.

The secondary market is where most people buy and sell shares, and it is the market that facilitates the buying and selling of shares between shareholders. As a general rule, investors are trading with each other in this market, rather than providing funds for the benefit of the company.

Figure 1.2: the primary and secondary markets

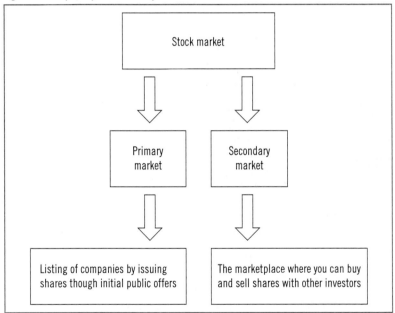

Before you make the decision to invest, you also need to consider the following points, and this is where a good financial adviser can help you.

- Why are you investing—what are your investment goals?
- What types of investments should you consider?

- What is your investment time frame—when will you require the use of your investment funds?

- How much money (capital) can you afford to invest?

- How much risk are you willing to take with your investment— how much can you afford to lose without the loss affecting your lifestyle?

- How will you diversify your investments to minimise your risk—will you allocate your investment funds across different asset classes?

- Will you use the concept of compound interest—will you add to your investments regularly and also reinvest your income or dividends from your investment?

- What investment structure will you use for your investments— your own name, a partnership, a trust, a company, a super fund?

- Should you consider borrowing funds to use for investment?

 ## Peter's property insights

Property has proven to be a relatively safe way of making money in the long term. The threat that the value of your property will plummet overnight is minimal, and you will receive frequent and regular income through rental payments.

Zac's share insights

There is no doubt that you can make more money by investing in shares than any other asset class—but with higher potential returns comes higher risk (or volatility). You can also lose much more money if you invest in the wrong shares at the wrong time.

Conclusion

Table 1.1 summarises the relationship between the asset classes—including their similarities and differences in terms of return, risk, capital growth, income and liquidity.

Table 1.1: the asset classes and their characteristics

Asset	Return	Risk	Capital growth	Income	Liquidity
Cash	Very low	Very low	No	Yes	Excellent
Fixed interest	Low	Low	No	Yes	Good
Property	Moderate	Moderate	Yes	Yes	Poor
Shares	High	High	Yes	Yes	Good

To be a smart investor you need to create wealth, but also to minimise the associated risk.

So far as property is concerned, success is about buying the right type of property in the right location in order to maximise your profits.

When it comes to shares, success is about buying the right share at the right time—and, importantly, selling it at the right time. Ultimately, an investor should hold a diversified investment portfolio that is allocated across all asset classes in accordance with their investment profile, needs and tolerance for risk. Therefore, holding some shares, some property and some cash in a portfolio is the formula for successful investment.

Round 2

WHY INVEST?

Do you dream of becoming financially independent? That is, to reach a point in your life when your lifestyle and living expenses are more than covered by the income you earn, *without* you having to physically work for it.

A few people may be lucky enough to achieve financial independence by receiving an inheritance, others from winning the lottery—but for most of us, the only way to achieve financial independence is through saving as much of our income as we can, and investing it in growth assets that will significantly increase in value over a long period of time.

Investing can therefore be thought of as the process of making your money work for you, rather than you having to work for your money. There are two ways to make your money work for you:

- Make your money earn money and provide you with income.
- Use your money to buy something that should increase in value, providing you with capital growth.

One secret to investing successfully is compound interest. Compound interest is where you earn interest on the money you save or invest, and then when that interest is paid to you, it is added to the amount you reinvest, and it earns interest too. This results in you earning interest on a higher amount of money which includes interest already earned, so the interest compounds and increases exponentially instead of at a fixed rate over time.

Reasons for investing

People invest their money for many reasons. These include:

- to retire richer
- to retire earlier

9

- to supplement their income
- for lifestyle reasons—so they can just work part time
- to give up their day job.

Retire richer

Most investments are targeted at retirement. This includes contributing to superannuation and buying property or shares. This is a passive strategy with minimum risk, which basically involves buying assets and holding onto them until retirement when they can be used to finance your lifestyle in lieu of your salary.

Retire earlier

This is a more aggressive strategy than just buying and holding for the long term. Being able to retire earlier can be achieved using a number of strategies, including trading property or shares or both, rather than simply holding them.

Supplement income

To be able to make some extra income will generally require the investor to sell part or all of their assets from time to time. In property, this is most commonly achieved through renovating property. In the sharemarket, this can done by periodically selling a portion of your portfolio.

Work part time

This is an extension of the previous strategy. This requires making enough extra income so you can cut back from full-time employment to working two, three or four days per week. Most people will use the same strategy outlined for supplementing your income, but will need to do it on a consistent or regular basis.

Give up your day job

This is the most aggressive and riskiest strategy of all. Investing in property to achieve this goal will require people to renovate or develop property on a regular basis. In the sharemarket, some people have given up their daytime employment as they have been able to successfully trade shares or derivatives. Share traders watch the market closely, and buy and sell on a short-term basis to generate income.

Investment options

As outlined in Round 1, there are really only four areas to invest your money:

- save it in cash
- invest it in fixed interest products such as term deposits or bonds
- invest it in property
- invest it in shares.

Cash and fixed interest won't grow in value. At best, they will earn you interest — or income.

Property and shares can and do grow in value, over time. These investments will often also provide you with regular income while you are invested in them. So, which is better? Let's look at the benefits of investing in each of these growth assets.

★ ★ ★ ★ ★ ★ ★ **PROPERTY** ★ ★ ★ ★ ★ ★ ★

Why invest in property?

Property is a very popular investment as it is familiar to everyone: everyone lives in one! But how does property perform as an investment?

Potential for significant capital growth

Putting your money in the bank or investing in fixed interest doesn't provide you with any capital growth. If you purchase property, however, you are anticipating that your property will grow in value. While this happens in most cases, you need to ensure that you buy property in the right location to maximise your capital growth. For example, a $400 000 brand new house bought on the outskirts of the metropolitan area might grow at 5 per cent per year whereas a period or character-style property in a top suburb, bought for the same price, could grow at 10 per cent per year. In ten years' time, the property on the outskirts won't even have doubled in value, whereas the older style, well-located property is worth over $1 million! If you had bought the well-located property, you could possibly retire in 12 years' time, based on your increased net wealth. There is less chance of being able to retire using the funds from the poorer performing, outer suburban property. Even though properties increase in value over time, it is crucial that you buy the *right* property in the *right* location so as to maximise your returns.

Regular rental income

One of the benefits of being the owner of investment property is that you can collect an income almost straight away. You can often settle on a property during the week and by the weekend have a tenant who has paid you some rent in advance. With other assets, you often have to wait for the end of the term of the investment (for example, in the case of a term deposit) or when your periodic payments or dividends are due, which is commonly only twice a year.

Secure hedge against inflation

An inevitable part of modern day life is inflation. Inflation means that the prices of goods and services increase over time. The rate of inflation varies according to the strength of the economy. One great advantage of holding property is that property values increase at a greater rate than inflation. In other words, property prices increase at a greater rate than most other goods and services. This is great news if you already own property, but not such great news if you are looking to buy property. The important thing to keep in mind is to buy the right property in the right location sooner rather than later.

Numerous tax benefits

Many tax benefits may be available for property investors, in particular tax deductions and depreciation (both on the building itself, and on the fixtures and fittings within the building).

Any legitimate expense incurred in running your investment property should be tax deductible. For example, if you travel to the property to collect the rent, you are able to claim a deduction. Money paid to a property manager to manage your property is also a tax deduction.

Depreciation of the building may be claimed as a tax deduction (whether you built it or not). The age of the building or item will determine if you can claim any depreciation and at what rate you can depreciate it. Buying a new or relatively new property (built after 17 July 1985) allows for the highest level of depreciation. Claiming building depreciation is a smart way to increase your cash flow.

It should be noted that you should never buy property just for tax purposes. Getting a tax benefit should be an added benefit to investing in property, not the only benefit.

Greater degree of control

Owning property allows for a greater degree of control than if you owned shares. For example, as an individual shareholder you cannot do anything to improve the value of your shares. However, if you own property, you can add value by painting, landscaping or upgrading. For a few thousand dollars, you can get much more than that in return in added capital value or rent or both.

Lower volatility

As property doesn't fluctuate in price as much as shares, there is greater security in purchasing property. You can sleep well at night knowing that your property won't plummet in price in a day, which can happen to shares, especially in a bear market (a bear market is where share prices fall significantly, by around 20 per cent or more, and investor sentiment turns to pessimism). Lower volatility is one of the best advantages of owning property over shares. The US subprime mortgage crisis, which led to the global financial crisis (GFC), illustrated the volatility that can exist in property markets, but thankfully the Australian property market is structured differently to the one in the US due to our stronger and safer banking and finance sector.

High demand for property

Everyone needs a place to live. Property, especially well located, period or character-style property, will always be in demand. As the number of households increases with more migrants coming to Australia to start a new life, and with the number of overseas students coming here to study, demand for property is increasing.

No margin calls

Providing your property is worth more than your loan and you can continue to make the minimum mortgage repayments, the bank will not call on you to pay off more of your loan than your scheduled repayments, or worse, force you to sell your property.

When you use a margin loan to purchase shares, you are obligated to maintain a specific loan-to-value ratio (LVR). LVR is the proportion of the loan to the market value of your asset. Should the value of your shares plummet, you may be asked to deposit some more money into the account (usually this is required within 24 hours) to reduce the LVR, or you may be forced to sell some, or all, of your shares to reduce your borrowings. This is the case even if your share portfolio is still worth more than your debt and you can still make the repayments on your margin loan!

Cheaper finance

A loan for a home can be obtained at a much cheaper rate than a margin loan to buy shares. In early 2013, for instance, the cheapest margin loan rates were around 8.5 per cent, whereas the cheapest variable rate home loans were about 5.5 per cent.

Higher leverage

This is one of the greatest advantages of investing in property rather than shares. You can get higher leverage.

Using property as security to borrow money allows you to leverage (borrow against the security) to a greater extent than if you were using a share portfolio as security. Most lenders may lend up to 95 per cent of the value of the property being purchased, as compared with 75 per cent if you were purchasing top quality shares. Let me illustrate this with an example.

If you had $40000 in cash, you could buy a $400000 property. Half of your cash will go towards the deposit for the house and the other half towards the purchasing fees. Alternatively, if you had $40000 in cash, you could buy a portfolio of blue-chip shares valued at only $160000. If we assume that both assets will grow at about their long-term average, it would take more than 100 years for a $160000 share portfolio growing at 10 per cent per year to be worth more than a $400000 property growing at 9 per cent per year!

★ ★ ★ ★ ★ ★ ★ ★ SHARES ★ ★ ★ ★ ★ ★ ★ ★

Why invest in shares?

Almost every working Australian owns shares, be it directly (through shares that they have personally bought), or indirectly (through their super funds or managed funds). Shares fluctuate in value every moment of every trading day, but how does share investment perform over the long term compared with property?

Potential for the greatest capital growth

Investing in shares provides you with the greatest potential for an increase in the value of your investment. That is because shares, just like property, are a growth asset. But that doesn't mean that any and every share you buy will increase in value. There are many things to consider when it comes to deciding what shares to buy, and when to buy them. As a general rule, you should look to buy good quality shares—that is, shares in companies that have strong management, a healthy balance sheet, a good business model and the potential to grow earnings—and buy when those shares are undervalued.

Potential for regular dividend income

An investment in shares may provide you with regular income (in addition to capital growth). This income is in the form of dividends, paid to investors from the profits that the company makes. Some companies, such as Telstra and the larger banks, usually pay a higher dividend (in percentage terms relative to your investment) than other shares (such as CSL or News Corporation). Other companies may not pay dividends at all. Be aware though, that a company can change its dividend policy depending on what its management decides.

Ability to outpace inflation

Just like property, shares have the potential to increase in value faster than the rate of inflation, as they are a growth asset. It is important, though, to ensure you buy the right shares at the right time and to sell them at the right time to reap the benefits of this potential.

Tax benefits

Shares provide numerous tax benefits to investors just as property investment does.

- Interest on investment loans is tax deductible. Any interest that you pay on an investment loan used to purchase shares is tax deductible. The same can also be said for property.

- Any losses you make can generally be used to offset gains. A general rule is that any *capital losses* that are made from selling your shares can be used to offset any *capital gains* that you make when you sell your shares at a profit. These tax loss benefits can be carried forward. This is also true of property. However, trading in shares is more common than trading in property.

- Franking credits on dividend payments can be used to reduce your tax. When a company pays a dividend, the dividend can be sourced from the company's pre-tax income or post-tax income. Where a company has paid tax first (at the company tax rate of 30 per cent) and paid a dividend from after-tax income, then that dividend carries with it a franking credit. This franking credit is used to reduce the amount of tax you have to pay on the dividend income that you have earned—with the effect that you end up paying only the difference between your marginal tax rate and the tax rate paid by the company at 30 per cent. Retired investors who pay no tax on earnings (because they hold their investments in a superannuation fund in pension phase) can claim these credits as a refund from the ATO—effectively increasing their dividend income by a further 30 per cent!

Higher potential returns

Shares have on average, historically provided the highest percentage of total returns over the long term when compared with property. However, shares have also been the highest in terms of volatility—that is, the range of returns has also been the widest of all the asset classes. This is consistent with the adage that higher returns are usually linked to higher risk.

Lower holding costs

Shares have significantly lower holding costs than property. The only holding costs that may be incurred for share ownership are:

- management or advisory fees that can range between 0.1 per cent and 1.5 per cent or more of your investment funds under advice. This is paid to your financial adviser for managing your portfolio.

- administration fees of up to 1 per cent or more may be payable to the administrator of your investment portfolio.

Lower entry and exit costs

Shares have significantly lower entry and exit costs than property. The only entry and exit costs that may be incurred are:

- *No stamp duty.* Unlike property, no stamp duty is payable on share purchases and sales. This has been the case since July, 2000.

- *Lower brokerage and transaction fees.* The cost of buying shares (brokerage or commission) is a lot lower than the cost of buying property. Discount stockbrokers charge brokerage fees ranging from just $9.95 per trade, and it is rare these days to find transaction fees, even with full-service brokers, that exceed 1.5 per cent of the value of the transaction.

Need less money to start buying

Unlike property, you can start investing in shares with as little as $500.

Liquidity and quicker settlement (access to cash)

Shares have a significant advantage over property when it comes to buying and selling, because (depending on the share) there is usually a steady supply of sellers or buyers to transact with—and the price at which they are willing to transact is always provided and known.

Settlement of transactions happens in three days, so if you need to sell your investment quickly to get cash, you will have your money in as little as three or four days!

With shares, you can also sell a portion of your shares at any time if you need access to cash. With a property, you have to sell the whole property—you cannot sell only a bedroom, for example.

Leverage

Using a margin loan, an investor can purchase a large parcel of shares with as little as 25 per cent 'deposit'. This means that you control 100 per cent of the value of your shares using only 25 per cent of your equity. Of course, while this means you have the potential to make larger profits because you are holding a larger position, and a smaller favourable move in price will result in a larger percentage move in your profit, the opposite is also true for losses.

Availability, speed and immediacy of information

The internet has given investors immediate access to a large amount of timely information about companies, the economy and research opinions. In addition, the price of a share is constantly changing, reflecting investor sentiment at every minute, so you always know what the market value is for an investment.

Diversification

Shares allow an investor to diversify their investment portfolio, and therefore reduce risk, much more easily than with property investment. This is due to the fact that you can spread your investment dollars across a larger number of different companies in different sectors or industries.

Less need for legal involvement and costs

Unlike buying and selling property, a share transaction is very straightforward and doesn't require the use of expensive and specialist professional services, such as solicitors or conveyancers.

No tenants

A benefit of investing in shares is that you don't have to find tenants or manage the property. It can take some time to find a tenant to rent your property, and there is always a risk of having a tenant who may damage your property. In addition, you will need to manage the tenant and the property, which can be costly. This is not the case with shares.

Make money from the market going up or down

With property investment, you can easily make money if the property market is increasing in value. But with shares, you can make money as the share price goes up — but also as they go down in value. This is achieved through a process called short selling. Investors make a profit when they buy an investment at a low price, and sell it at a higher price. Usually, the buying step is done first (at a low price, and then selling later at a higher price). However, if you think the price of your share is going to fall, you can still profit from the buying low and selling high concept—the only difference is what step you do first. When short selling, you are able to borrow shares from your broker, sell them first (at the higher price) and then when the market falls, buy them later (at the lower price). When the position is closed, you return the shares to your broker. In this example, you have still bought low and sold high and made money—the only difference being what you did first.

Hedging

You can hedge your share investment portfolio by buying insurance using derivatives such as options, futures or CFDs (contracts for difference). This allows you to protect a share portfolio when the market is falling, because the value of the derivative will increase to offset any unrealised loss incurred in your share portfolio.

So which is best: property or shares?

Table 2.1 provides a summary of the benefits of investing in both shares and property.

Table 2.1: reasons for investing in property and shares

Why you should invest in property	Why you should invest in shares
Potential for significant capital growth	Potential for the greatest capital growth
Regular and frequent rental income	Potential for regular dividend income
Secure hedge against inflation	Ability to outpace inflation
Numerous tax benefits	Tax benefits
Greater degree of control	Higher potential returns
Lower volatility	Lower entry, holding and exit costs

Why you should invest in property	Why you should invest in shares
High demand for property	Need less money to start buying
No margin calls	High liquidity and quick access to cash
Cheaper finance	Availability and speed of information
Higher leverage	Ability to leverage
	Diversification
	Less need for legal advice or costs
	No tenants or maintenance issues
	Can profit from market going up or down
	Hedging through the use of derivatives

 ## Peter's property insights

Property is the perfect asset if you are aiming to create wealth in a relatively secure manner. There is less likelihood of your asset plunging in value overnight compared with investing in the sharemarket. Tax benefits, such as depreciation allowances, can also reduce your tax liability and provide you with extra cash so you can either pay off your loan more quickly or spend as you wish. The higher leverage and lower interest rates that are possible with property can fast-track your path to a comfortable lifestyle and retirement.

Zac's share insights

Investing in the sharemarket is ideal if you are seeking higher returns and potentially higher capital growth. In the short term, the capital value of your share investment is likely to fluctuate, sometimes significantly, but in the long term, good quality blue-chip shares have been proven to outperform property. The biggest attractions to share investment are the ability to sell a small portion of your portfolio when it suits you, settlement for purchases and sales is much faster than for property, and you will never have to worry about the 'tenant from hell'.

 ## Conclusion

To achieve your financial goals and become financially independent, you have to create wealth. One way to do this is to invest in growth assets such as property or shares.

Owning property *or* shares can help you achieve the goals mentioned at the beginning of the chapter:

- to retire richer
- to retire earlier
- to supplement your income
- for lifestyle reasons — so you can just work part time
- to give up your day job.

A balanced approach to investment includes owning property *and* shares. In this manner, you can diversify your risk. Diversification also allows you to take advantage of the potential capital growth that shares offer, and also provides the combined income, capital growth and security that property offers.

Successful investing requires that you understand the risk associated with each investment you make, as well as how to manage that risk. It also requires an appreciation that some types of investments tend to perform better at certain times. We will discuss this in greater detail in Round 7.

The question you should be asking yourself is not which asset should I buy, but how much of each asset will I hold in my investment portfolio at any time. The answer to this will depend on how much risk you're willing to take and how quickly you wish to increase your wealth.

Round 3

HISTORY OF THE PROPERTY AND SHARE MARKETS

It is important that we first look at what has happened in the property and share markets in the past, as history can provide a guide (but not a guarantee) to what might happen in the future. The property and share markets have been operating in Australia for a very long time and there is a plethora of information that we can use to help determine what might be in store for both of these markets in future.

★ ★ ★ ★ ★ ★ ★ **PROPERTY** ★ ★ ★ ★ ★ ★ ★

History of the property market

The property market has been around since the beginning of time. Ever since the first cave-dwellers staked claim to their first home, the notion of owning property has been a highly sought ideal through the ages.

In modern Australian history, the property market was established as soon as the first settlers arrived. Many wealthy individuals and companies staked claims to large allotments of land and then proceeded to subdivide them into smaller allotments for housing and commercial buildings.

In the early days it was mainly the wealthy who could afford to own more than one property. They leased out additional properties to poorer households who could not afford to buy their own home, but the Second World War brought many changes to the Australian property market, including public housing, housing for migrants, and the flow-on effects of women entering the workforce.

Soon after the Second World War, many states and territories around Australia formed housing commissions and trusts. They were set up to provide housing for low-income families. In the 1950s, these bodies built many houses and blocks of flats, many of which still stand today. At the same time, many Europeans migrated to Australia and this flood of people created a huge demand for property, both to rent and to own.

In the 1950s it was becoming easier for middle-income earners to buy rental property. Friendly societies, building societies and some investment banks were lending money to people who had the capacity to borrow, but often at a very high interest rate. It was also at this time that many more women entered the workforce, which meant there was more money coming into the household, so it was easier to borrow money for a home and pay off the mortgage.

The deregulation of the banking system in the 1980s brought many mum and dad investors into the property investment market. Deregulation brought with it more lending institutions, which offered interest rates and loans that many moderate-income families could afford. Deregulation also brought more competition into lending.

This increased capacity to borrow money in the 1980s resulted in an increased demand for property, which caused some significant price rises.

Property prices

Property prices can be very difficult to measure due to changes in the nature of the properties over time. This is explained in depth in Round 6, but suffice to say for now that it is difficult to make a comparison between a house built, say, in the 1950s, and one built today. A typical 1950s house had three bedrooms, one bathroom, one living area and a carport, and was originally built on a 700 square metre block of land. A house built today will often be built on a 400 square metre block of land and consist of four bedrooms, two bathrooms, two living areas and a double garage. Houses built today are bigger, but the blocks of land are smaller.

Partly due to the complexity involved in making comparisons over time, there is at present no single continuous set of historical property price data. Tables 3.1 and 3.2 (overleaf) show data from two different sources to illustrate growth in property prices.

Table 3.1 shows median Australian house prices from 1913 to 2003. Table 3.2 (overleaf) provides more detail and shows increases in established house prices for all capital cities, and a weighted average of all capital cities. The median price is the middle price when house prices are placed in order from lowest to highest. The weighted average for all capital cities is derived from combining the data from each of the eight capital cities. Please note that table 3.1 shows house *prices*, whereas table 3.2 (overleaf) shows an *index* (not prices), which illustrates the increase in house prices over time.

Table 3.1: Australian property prices, 1913 to 2003 (measured at the June quarter)

Year	Price	Year	Price
1913	$1070	1963	$9530
1918	$1290	1968	$11920
1923	$1790	1973	$21380
1928	$1890	1978	$37680
1933	$1260	1983	$60750
1938	$1570	1988	$99640
1943	$2030	1993	$145130
1948	$2030	1998	$175510
1953	$5370	2003	$312910
1958	$7170		

Source: Stapledon N. (2007) 'Long Term Housing Prices in Australia and Some Economic Perspectives', PhD thesis, School of Economics. Sydney: UNSW pp 64–65.

Table 3.2: Australian property price indexes, 2003 to 2012

Year	Price index of established houses Sydney	Price index of established houses Melbourne	Price index of established houses Brisbane	Price index of established houses Adelaide	Price index of established houses Perth	Price index of established houses Hobart	Price index of established houses Darwin	Price index of established houses Canberra	Price index of established houses; weighted average of 8 capital cities
Jun–2003	93.7	94.9	83.1	90.5	90.2	79.7	91.3	90.9	92.0
Jun–2004	97.7	99.4	103.8	102.4	104.9	107.8	103.0	100.3	100.0
Jun–2005	94.2	103.4	105.5	107.8	122.5	114.5	122.6	100.0	101.9
Jun–2006	94.3	110.0	110.9	113.8	169.6	124.6	150.3	107.0	109.3
Jun–2007	98.2	125.1	128.1	126.9	192.1	135.4	166.3	118.5	120.3
Jun–2008	101.1	143.2	146.1	147.0	190.8	143.1	177.7	126.7	129.9
Jun–2009	100.3	144.3	142.2	149.0	185.3	145.0	197.5	126.4	129.1
Jun–2010	117.3	177.2	154.3	162.8	208.3	156.2	223.6	146.6	149.8
Jun–2011	116.6	172.2	147.7	157.1	194.5	155.1	213.2	147.7	145.8
Jun–2012	115.6	164.6	143.3	155.2	198.3	147.9	233.4	144.5	143.1

Source: 6416.0 House Price Indexes: Eight Capital Cities, Australian Bureau of Statistics.

Prices have increased over time, due mainly to the demand for property, but also due in part to the increasing size and improving quality of new homes.

Since the Second World War, the median house price has increased by approximately 8.5 per cent per year. However, there have also been some significant price movements over the last 100 years.

- The best year for property over this time was 1950, when the median price increased by 132.5 per cent. This marked growth was caused largely due to the federal government having placed a halt on prices for the previous six years, immediately after the Second World War. This interference by the government caused property prices to spike as soon as the halt was lifted.

- The worst year for property was 1930, which experienced a drop in median price of 18 per cent. This was the beginning of the Great Depression. The stock market crash of 1929 caused the economy to suffer greatly, which in turn led to massive job losses, which meant many people were unable to make repayments on their mortgages.

- The best 20-year period was from 1969 to 1989, when property prices increased from $12 930 to $134 670, an annual increase of 12.4 per cent.

- In the worst 20-year period, from 1920 to 1940, property prices did not increase at all. This lack of growth is mainly due to the drop in prices as a result of the Great Depression: property prices dropped by a total of 35 per cent over four years.

★ ★ ★ ★ ★ ★ ★ ★ **SHARES** ★ ★ ★ ★ ★ ★ ★ ★

History of the stock market

The earliest stock market is believed to have been established by Muslim and Jewish merchants living in Cairo, Egypt, at the start of the 11th century. It was only in the 13th and 14th centuries, however, that a central and organised financial institution for trading was established to administer the trading process. Historians agree that the Van der Beurze family is responsible for setting up the first exchange in a building in Antwerp, Holland. These *beurzen* (or *bourses*) soon expanded to neighbouring areas through Europe

In the early 17th century, the first official stock exchange opened in Amsterdam. The first company to be listed on this stock exchange was the Dutch East India Company in 1602, and these were also the first company shares ever released. In fact, the Dutch have been credited for pioneering modern trading and banking methods—so much so that Wall Street (where the New York Stock Exchange is located) was actually founded in the New Amsterdam settlement in New York.

Wall Street itself derived its name from the fortified walls of timber and earth that were put up in New York to ward off attacks from American Indian tribes. Eventually, the wall was removed and government surveyors mapped out the actual street, naming it Wall Street.

All major industrialised nations have a stock market—some countries even have more than one. According to the World Federation of Exchanges, the biggest stock exchanges in the world are as shown in table 3.3.

Table 3.3: top stock markets in the world

	Exchange	Sharemarket capitalisation or value ($)	Total world sharemarket value (%)
1	NYSE Euronext (US)	13 613 345.3	26
2	NASDAQ OMX (US)	4 576 855.0	9
3	London SE Group (UK)	3 571 896.4	7
4	Tokyo SE Group (Japan)	3 334 918.8	6
5	NYSE Euronext (Europe)	2 752 856.0	5
6	Hong Kong Exchanges	2 714 201.7	5

Exchange	Sharemarket capitalisation or value ($)	Total world sharemarket value (%)
7 Shanghai SE (China)	2 219 896.8	4
8 TMX Group (Canada)	2 034 211.5	4
9 Deutsche Börse (Germany)	1 428 806.0	3
10 Australian Securities Exchange (ASX)	1 349 206.1	3
Others	16 527 769.3	31
WFE Total	**52 701 900.8**	**100**

Source: World Federation of Exchanges, November 2012.

History of the Australian stock market

In Australia, the stock market dates back to 1861, when the country's first stock exchange was established in Melbourne in the midst of the gold rush that brought hundreds of thousands of people to Victoria. Other cities soon opened stock exchanges of their own, including the Sydney stock exchange (1871), the Hobart stock exchange (1882), the Brisbane stock exchange (1884), the Adelaide stock exchange (1887) and the Perth stock exchange (1889). This created a total of six stock exchanges on the Australian stock market.

These state-based stock exchanges held informal meetings from 1903, but soon after the US stock market crash in 1929 and the Great Depression that followed in the 1930s, there was seen to be a need for a more formalised structure to manage the six state-based exchanges according to uniform rules and regulations. This led to the establishment of Australian Associated Stock Exchanges (AASE) in 1937 that would make common trading rules for all the exchanges.

Years later, in 1960, the derivatives market was born in Australia. Derivatives are financial products whose prices are *derived* from the price of another asset, such as a share or a commodity (like wool). The opening of the Sydney Futures Exchange allowed wool traders to hedge their transactions by providing financial products that they could buy to guarantee a selling price for their wool, rather than having to wait until they were ready to sell their wool and accept whatever market price prevailed at the time. This was followed by the opening of the options market in 1976, and the warrants market in 1990.

In 1985, however, all the state-based stock exchanges and the AASE met to discuss the future of the Australian stock market, with the objective of creating a single national Australian stock exchange. This was approved by Parliament, so the exchanges amalgamated and were operational in 1987.

At the same time, computer-based trading was introduced with a system known as the Stock Exchange Automated Trading System (SEATS). Trading slowly transitioned to this electronic system—resulting in the trading floor and open outcry system of trading being closed in Australia in 1990. SEATS was eventually replaced by a system called CLICK XT in 2006, a system that the derivatives market had used to match trades since 1997. CLICK was superseded by a cutting-edge trading platform called ITS (Integrated Trading System) that brought together equities and derivatives trading on one platform.

Australia was also one of the first countries in the world to introduce an electronic settlement system called FAST in 1993. This brought with it streamlined settlement processes, but it was replaced in 1996 by the Clearing House Electronic Sub-register System (CHESS), which is still used today.

In 1996, the stock exchange members (brokers) voted to demutualise and the exchange became an incorporated entity known as ASX Limited, and it listed on the exchange two years later in 1998.

In 2006, financial reforms eventually led to a world-first merger between any two listed exchanges: the Sydney Futures Exchange and the Australian Stock Exchange. As a result, the new entity was called the Australian Securities Exchange (ASX).

In November 2011, a rival to the ASX was born, ending the monopoly of trading in Australia. The new exchange is called CHI-X. The new exchange provides brokers with a choice of trading venue for the major stocks initially, with more shares to be dual-listed on CHI-X and the ASX over time. This competition has provided brokers (and traders) with a reduction in trading fees and also better trading services — including lower buy-sell spreads (the difference between the highest buy price and the lowest sell price of a share at any given moment).

All securities trading in Australia is regulated by ASIC — the Australian Securities and Investments Commission — which seeks to ensure that the market trades fairly and that there is transparency in reporting and trading.

How shares have performed over time

The most common measure of the performance of the Australian sharemarket is the All Ordinaries index (All Ords). Think of this as a mathematical average of the market capitalisation of the Top 500 companies on the Australian sharemarket. The index is regularly reviewed so that it will always include the Top 500 companies by market capitalisation and liquidity.

Table 3.4 shows the value of the All Ordinaries Index since 1938.

Table 3.4: value of the All Ordinaries Index since 1938

Year	Index value	Year	Index value
Jun-1938	66.8	Jun-1978	342.3
Jun-1943	67.6	Jun-1983	605.3
Jun-1948	98.1	Jun-1988	1554.9
Jun-1953	97.4	Jun-1993	1738.1
Jun-1958	148.6	Jun-1998	2668.4
Jun-1963	222.6	Jun-1903	2998.9
Jun-1968	418.6	Jun-1908	5332.9
Jun-1973	388.1		

Source: Data sourced from IRESS, www.iress.com.au (1937 to 1982), and HUBB Financial, www.hubb.com (1982 to December 2012).

How properties and shares have performed over time

The problem with statistics is that results can usually be interpreted in such a way as to support any specific argument. We therefore decided to conduct our own research on the performance of the sharemarket against the property market so as to draw our own conclusions.

Growth

As shown in table 3.5, we used the All Ordinaries index as a proxy for owning a portfolio of blue-chip shares, and the Median House Price index as a proxy for owning an average property and compared the annual change as at 30 June each year in percentage terms.

Table 3.5: comparison of the returns from shares and property, June 1937 to December 2012

Year	Shares (%)	Property (%)	Year	Shares (%)	Property (%)
Jun–1937	8.5	3.4	Jun–1951	32.8	16.7
Jun–1938	−10.1	1.9	Jun–1952	−30.7	−1.3
Jun–1939	−3.9	2.5	Jun–1953	−1.6	−1.3
Jun–1940	−10.6	2.5	Jun–1954	11.7	3.0
Jun–1941	6.7	7.9	Jun–1955	7.1	2.7
Jun–1942	−13.6	8.4	Jun–1956	−10.1	10.7
Jun–1943	19.9	5.2	Jun–1957	16.9	10.8
Jun–1944	3.7	0.0	Jun–1958	6.7	2.9
Jun–1945	4.6	0.0	Jun–1959	18.5	2.8
Jun–1946	14.8	0.0	Jun–1960	20.5	14.1
Jun–1947	10.5	0.0	Jun–1961	−9.9	−9.4
Jun–1948	6.8	0.0	Jun–1962	−4.4	11.3
Jun–1949	−10.6	0.0	Jun–1963	10.3	12.4
Jun–1950	22.9	132.5	Jun–1964	8.5	4.2

Year	Shares (%)	Property (%)	Year	Shares (%)	Property (%)
Jun–1965	−19.4	4.2	Jun–1990	−1.3	1.6
Jun–1966	3.0	3.7	Jun–1991	0.4	0.6
Jun–1967	9.7	3.7	Jun–1992	9.9	2.5
Jun–1968	52.9	7.1	Jun–1993	5.7	2.8
Jun–1969	−4.1	8.5	Jun–1994	14.4	3.6
Jun–1970	1.7	10.4	Jun–1995	1.6	1.7
Jun–1971	−15.0	12.9	Jun–1996	11.2	1.2
Jun–1972	25.3	10.2	Jun–1997	21.6	3.2
Jun–1973	−3.3	20.4	Jun–1998	−2.1	9.9
Jun–1974	−31.3	20.8	Jun–1999	11.3	6.5
Jun–1975	12.1	12.2	Jun–2000	9.7	10.0
Jun–1976	29.9	12.9	Jun–2001	5.1	8.3
Jun–1977	−9.8	9.2	Jun–2002	−7.6	20.5
Jun–1978	11.9	5.4	Jun–2003	−5.2	16.7
Jun–1979	12.3	6.8	Jun–2004	17.7	8.7
Jun–1980	57.7	18.0	Jun–2005	19.8	1.9
Jun–1981	10.1	14.9	Jun–2006	19.0	7.3
Jun–1982	−34.4	5.8	Jun–2007	25.4	10.1
Jun–1983	28.3	5.3	Jun–2008	−15.5	8.0
Jun–1984	8.9	12.8	Jun–2009	−26.2	−0.6
Jun–1985	30.6	9.3	Jun–2010	9.9	16.0
Jun–1986	37.2	7.2	Jun–2011	8.1	−2.7
Jun–1987	49.6	4.5	Jun–2012	−11.3	−1.9
Jun–1988	−11.9	18.7	Dec–2012	12.8	1.5
Jun–1989	−2.1	35.2			

Source: Data sourced from IRESS, www.iress.com.au (1937 to 1982), and HUBB Financial, www.hubb.com (1982 to December 2012).

You can clearly see from table 3.5 (pp. 32–33) and figure 3.1 that the sharemarket has historically been more volatile than the property market, with large swings in returns (both positive and negative).

Figure 3.1: comparison of the annual returns from property and shares, June 1937 to June 2012

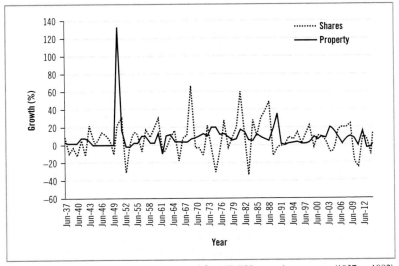

Source: Data sourced from IRESS, www.iress.com.au (1937 to 1982), and HUBB Financial, www.hubb.com (1982 to December 2012).

Figure 3.2 shows the distribution of sharemarket returns by financial year ending June for every year since 1937. This chart is called a bell curve because it shows the number of times that the market has posted returns within a price range over the last 77 years.

Figure 3.2: distribution of sharemarket returns by financial year, 1937 to 2012

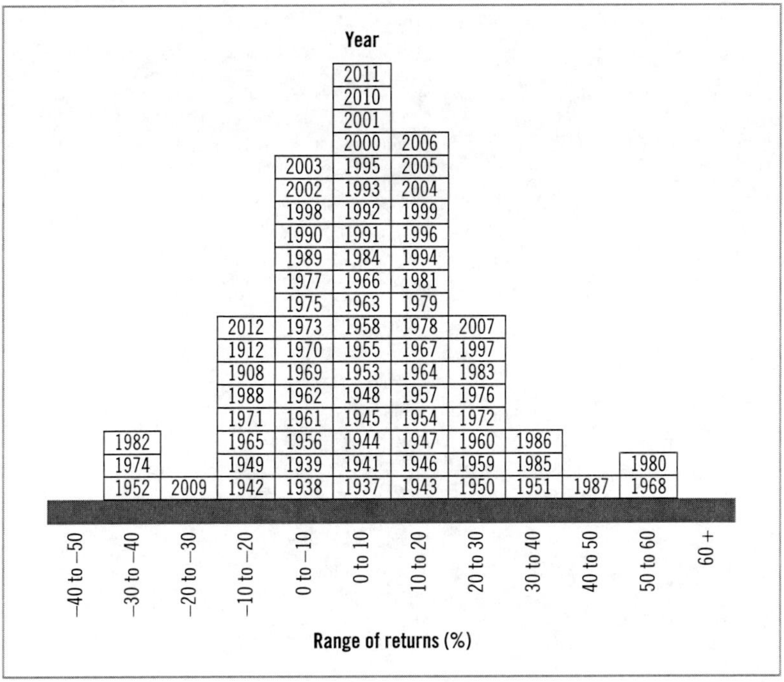

Year

−40 to −50	−30 to −40	−20 to −30	−10 to −20	0 to −10	0 to 10	10 to 20	20 to 30	30 to 40	40 to 50	50 to 60	60 +
				2011							
				2010							
				2001							
				2000	2006						
			2003	1995	2005						
			2002	1993	2004						
			1998	1992	1999						
			1990	1991	1996						
			1989	1984	1994						
			1977	1966	1981						
			1975	1963	1979						
		2012	1973	1958	1978	2007					
		1912	1970	1955	1967	1997					
		1908	1969	1953	1964	1983					
		1988	1962	1948	1957	1976					
		1971	1961	1945	1954	1972					
1982		1965	1956	1944	1947	1960	1986				
1974		1949	1939	1941	1946	1959	1985			1980	
1952	2009	1942	1938	1937	1943	1950	1951	1987	1968		

Range of returns (%)

Source: Data sourced from IRESS, www.iress.com.au (1937 to 1982), and HUBB Financial, www.hubb.com (1982 to December 2012).

Figure 3.3 (overleaf) shows that the distribution of growth returns from the property market for every financial year ending June since 1914 is much less volatile than the returns from the sharemarket.

Figure 3.3: distribution of growth returns from the property market by financial year, 1914 to 2012

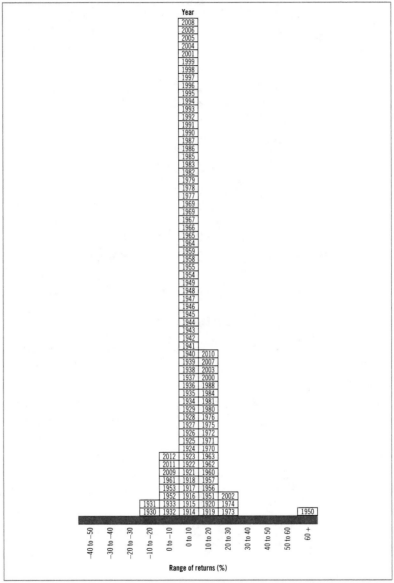

Source: Data sourced from IRESS, www.iress.com.au (1937 to 1982),
and HUBB Financial, www.hubb.com (1982 to December 2012).

Peter's property insights

The property landscape has changed over time and prices have increased. There is no guarantee that property prices will increase every year but, as an asset held for the long term, property's performance has been relatively steady in comparison with sharemarket performance.

Zac's share insights

The sharemarket has provided investors with a significant amount of volatility, over the last few years in particular. So much so that if you had invested in the All Ordinaries index in November 2007, by March 2009 you would probably have lost around 55 per cent of your capital. While the global financial crisis was an unusual event in the world's economic history, you should expect an unusual event such as this to occur every 20 or so years. But investors shouldn't be afraid of the potential volatility: instead you should use risk management strategies and sufficiently diversify your investment portfolio to navigate through these unusual events when and if they happen.

 ## Conclusion

As investors, our objective is to make a positive return on our capital, in an attempt to beat the effects of inflation and to grow our wealth.

A positive return on capital can be achieved in two ways:

- through capital growth (an increase in the value of your investment)
- through income generated by investment.

A truly powerful boost to your return on capital is the effect of compounding—in other words, using the income from the investment to reinvest so that it generates more income. This compounds that growth! This can easily be achieved in the sharemarket by reinvesting your dividends (and buying more shares).

The statistics we compiled, and the comparisons that we have made, have shown that if you want to outperform property investment, in growth terms, with a share investment, your ally and also your biggest enemy is the volatility of the sharemarket. You should not adopt a buy-and-forget approach to share investment if your priority is capital growth. In this case, capital depreciation during periods when the market posts negative growth will set you back significantly. Adopting a framework of timing your investments (both entry and exit) in the sharemarket is critical.

Timing is not as critical for property investment because this asset class has traditionally been less volatile than shares, and has usually posted positive returns.

Round 4

INVESTMENT CYCLES

Every investor needs to be aware that all investment markets are interrelated, like a big financial jigsaw puzzle. We will examine these relationships later on in this chapter, but first it is important to understand the impact that the business (also called the economic) cycle will have on investment returns.

It is generally accepted by economists that the health of any country's economy is measured by an economic indicator known as gross domestic product (GDP). Put simply, GDP is the value of all the goods and services that are produced by a country. In Australia, this data is compiled and released quarterly by the Australian Bureau of Statistics (ABS).

If a country produces more and more goods, GDP grows and the quarterly trend is up. As the trend in GDP rises, it can be concluded that the economy is getting stronger—businesses are likely to be making profits; unemployment is likely to be low; consumer confidence is likely to be high and consumers are increasing the amount and value of the products they are purchasing. Business confidence and investment is also likely to be high. Investors in turn are also confident that economic growth will continue, and so they continue to invest in growth assets, such as property or shares, in search of higher returns.

The opposite is true when the trend in GDP starts to decline. A decline implies that there is a slowdown in the economy, and if that slowdown continues for too long, businesses are likely to be making lower profits (or worse, some may fail), unemployment may start to rise; consumers may become less confident and start saving rather than spending; and investors are likely to hold off on making further investments due to a lack of confidence that the economy will continue to grow.

Economists have long recognised that there is a cyclical relationship in this economic activity—that the cycle goes from good to bad, and back to good. All economies will experience periods of expansion as the economy grows, and periods of contraction as the economy slows. We have to expect that there will be some degree of economic slowdown in any economy every so often, but it is the overall *trend* of economic growth that is of interest to investors. An upward trend in economic activity, as indicated by GDP, is good for most investment markets. A slowdown (or downtrend) of this duration for two consecutive quarters is what economists call a technical recession.

Despite the occasional slowdown, GDP should continue to grow over time in a developing or developed economy.

In figure 4.1 you can see Australia's GDP growth since 1965 and that GDP has now reached nearly US$1.5 trillion.

Figure 4.1: Australia's GDP value since 1965

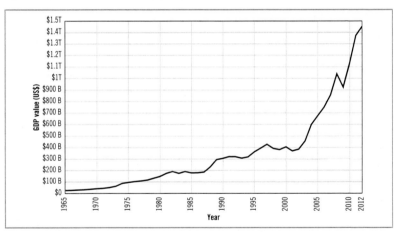

Source: www.tradingeconomics.com.

Around 68 per cent of Australia's annual GDP is provided by the services sector (which includes, property and business services, construction, finance and insurance, retail trade, health and community services, wholesale trade and education), while the mining sector contributes only 19 per cent of GDP.

The business cycle can be measured by the direction of the trend in GDP on a quarterly basis.

Figure 4.2 shows a chart of Australia's GDP growth rate illustrating the percentage change in Australia's GDP since January 2007. It is apparent that Australia escaped a technical recession twice during the global financial crisis, experiencing GDP negative growth for just two quarters, but not consecutively.

Figure 4.2: quarterly growth rate (percentage change) of Australian GDP since 2007

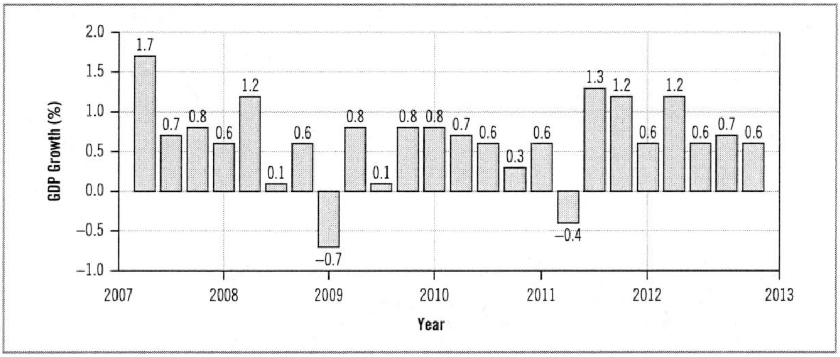

Source: www.tradingeconomics.com.

In an ideal world, the pace of economic growth would happen at a steady rate and within a defined range. The pace of growth is maintained and managed by a country's central bank (in Australia, this is the Reserve Bank of Australia, or RBA). The RBA regulates the speed of economic growth through its monetary and fiscal policies, including using interest rates to stimulate or slow down economic activity, as appropriate, with the goal of managing economic growth to avoid wild swings in growth and slowdown.

On occasion, however, and usually because of external influences beyond the control of the RBA, the economy will get ahead of itself, experiencing what is known as a bubble (where growth rises too high, and too fast); or the economy will slow down too much, experiencing either a correction or, if it slows down for too long, a recession. It is these peaks and troughs that we use to define the extreme levels in what is known as the business cycle.

The business cycle is, therefore, the periodic and irregular movement of economic activity (from peak to trough), as it is measured by changes in economic growth of a country. Unfortunately, though, the business cycle does not behave in a predictable or sequential cycle, so one stage does not necessarily always lead to the next expected stage of the cycle.

A very popular way to describe the business cycle is by using an analogy to an analogue clock. This economic clock, as it is known, is an economic theory that attempts to describe the interaction of the markets and how interest rates affect property and share markets. The theory states that the business cycle should progress sequentially around the clock, with the impacts on the economy as noted in figure 4.3.

Figure 4.3: the economic clock

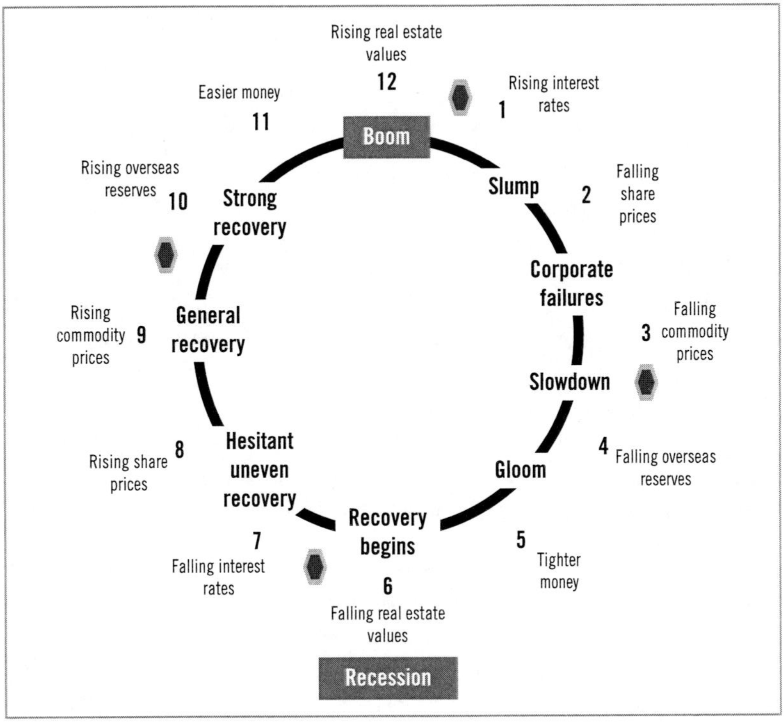

Over time, as the level of GDP rises, the business cycle will go through periods of expansion and contraction, from peak to trough and back again. Figure 4.4 demonstrates the cycle

Figure 4.4: the business cycle

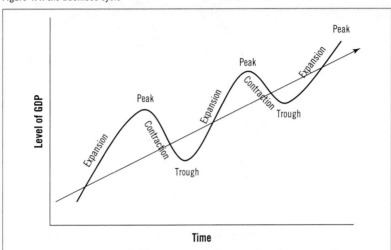

Stages within the business cycle

In July 2007 a research paper by Jeffrey Stangl, Ben Jacobsen and Nuttawat Visaltanachoti entitled 'Sector rotation over business-cycles' provided some insightful analysis of a sector rotation theory that was originally published by research house, Standard & Poors, 12 years earlier in a book entitled *Sector Investing*. That research paper identified that certain sectors consistently outperform other sectors during various stages of the business cycle. The conclusion was that investors can use the business cycle to determine what sectors to invest in.

It can be demonstrated that five stages exist within the business cycle (three during an expansion phase, where the economy is growing, and two during the contraction phase, when the economy is slowing down) as it moves from peak to trough (see figure 4.5, overleaf). The problem is that no-one knows for sure what stage the economy is in until *after* it has entered the next stage.

Figure 4.5: the five stages of the business cycle

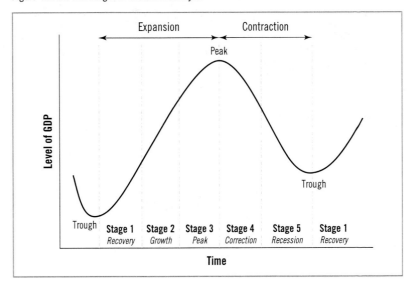

Let's now examine each phase of the business cycle in more detail, and note the distinctions between the various stages.

The expansion phase

In this phase of the business cycle, economic activity (and GDP) is trending up (see figure 4.5) because people are employed, earning money and accumulating wealth. Demand for goods and services increases beyond the supply, leading to a rise in prices, or inflation.

There are three stages during this phase:

1 *Recovery.* This stage follows the lowest point of a recession and is the level at which the downtrend in GDP has turned (to start moving upwards again). Economic activity starts trending higher after a sustained period of decline, as measured by GDP. Lower prices and low interest rates are the catalyst of demand for goods and services. New jobs are created; credit becomes available for investors wanting to borrow; and the economy starts to grow again.

2 *Growth.* This is the second stage during the expansion and is where the economy grows strongly as prices rise, and wages increase. Unfortunately, rising labour costs drive prices ever higher, fuelling inflation.

3 *Peak.* This is the third stage of economic expansion, which ends with a peak and is where the uptrend in GDP is broken. This is largely due to companies and individuals having reached the limits of their financial means—forcing companies to scale back spending and cut jobs. Consumers become more conservative and reduce their spending, hurting corporate profits further. Banks reduce the amount they are willing to lend as corporations and consumers start to feel financially burdened. This causes the social mood to change from optimism to pessimism.

The contraction phase

In this phase, economic activity (and GDP) has started to trend down (see figure 4.5). There are typically two stages in this phase—with a possible third that may eventuate if the correction is severe enough.

1 *Correction.* This stage follows the highest peak in the business cycle, and is the point after which the uptrend in GDP has been broken. Economic activity starts trending lower due to slowing demand as consumers and businesses cut their spending on goods and services that have become too expensive. Unemployment usually starts to trend upwards as businesses cut costs and reduce output. It continues downwards until any economic excesses from the previous expansion are unwound.

2 *Recession.* This stage eventuates if economic activity slows down far enough and for long enough to create a technical recession—where the economy has two consecutive quarters of negative growth.

3 *Depression.* This stage of contraction is rare, but it is where the economy experiences a prolonged period of recession (lasting more than two years) or where GDP falls by more than 10 per cent.

The challenge is to know and identify what stage of the business cycle we are in at any point in time (or what time it is on the economic clock), and also whether the cycle is likely to progress sequentially to the next stage. We use several indicators to help us do this.

The trend in quarterly GDP is one indicator of what stage of the cycle the economy is in, and is shown in table 4.1.

Table 4.1: quarterly GDP and the business cycle

GDP trend		Likely stage of the cycle
Previous quarter	This quarter	
Negative	Positive	Stage 1 — Recovery
Positive	More positive	Stage 2 — Growth
Positive	Less positive	Stage 3 — Peak
Positive	Negative	Stage 4 — Correction
Negative	More negative	Stage 4 — Correction
Negative	Less negative	Stage 5 — Recession

To further confirm the stage of the business cycle we are in, we also look at the following indicators:

- trends in interest rates
- trends in consumer and business confidence
- the shape of the bond yield curve.

The bond yield curve is a graph of a specific bond's interest rates at a fixed point in time, to show the different interest rates of a specific bond series at different maturity dates. The shape of the graph gives investors an indication of future interest rate changes.

A normal yield curve is one that has longer maturity bonds delivering a higher yield than shorter term bonds.

An inverted yield curve is one that has shorter term yields being higher than longer term yields—often a sign of an upcoming recession.

A flat (or humped) yield curve is one where short-term and longer term yields are very close to each other—also a predictor of economic transition.

★ ★ ★ ★ ★ ★ ★ ★ **SHARES** ★ ★ ★ ★ ★ ★ ★ ★

The relationship between the sharemarket and the business cycle

The sharemarket is generally believed to predict the business cycle trend by between six and 12 months. This is due to the fundamental reason why share prices go up in the first place.

A company's share price is a reflection of the consensus of investors' *expectations* of a company's earnings (and therefore its value) in the future. Therefore, it is safe to assume that a share investor will take the risk to make an investment in a share only if they believe that the company will be worth more in future than it is now. The only way a company can increase its value to shareholders (and therefore its share price) is through increasing its earnings (or revenue) by selling more goods and services, or investing in itself with the aim of increasing its revenue and value—indicating an increase in consumer and business spending. If this happens, we would expect that it would be the result of an improving economy (see figure 4.6, overleaf).

While this is a causal relationship, it has generally been accepted that the sharemarket is a barometer for the economy between six and 12 months ahead of time, largely because of the lag in obtaining economic data to support the fact that the economy has in fact followed suit.

Figure 4.6: the relationship between the sharemarket and the business cycle

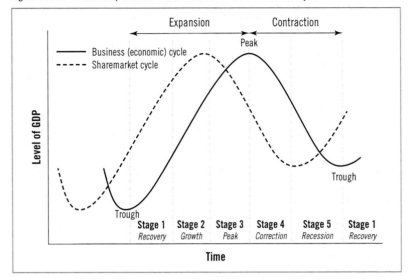

★ ★ ★ ★ ★ ★ ★ PROPERTY ★ ★ ★ ★ ★ ★ ★

The relationship between the property market and the business cycle

While the sharemarket generally leads the economic cycle by between six and 12 months, we believe the property market follows, or perhaps slightly lags behind, the economic cycle by between three and six months (see figure 4.7). This is because property values are a factor of demand and supply. Demand is driven by things such as location, employment, affordability and consumer confidence.

For example, if a country goes into recession, if jobs are lost and banks become averse to the risk of lending money, demand for property will fall. In these circumstances a formerly healthy property market cannot survive. This is because capital investment is the key cyclical driver of economic growth, and therefore new development is a key influence on the business cycle.

Of course, demand for property is also linked to people's employment—if people are confident and are employed, they are more likely to invest in property. House price rises have traditionally occurred during periods of economic expansion and prosperous growth. They have also typically fallen during periods of significant contraction and deep recession (see figure 4.7).

Figure 4.7: the relationship between the property market and business cycle

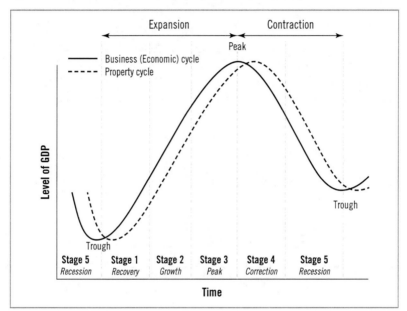

 Peter's property insights

Property investors can maximise their opportunity to make money by timing the purchase and sale of their asset(s). Obviously buying at the bottom of the market and selling at the peak is ideal, but to the untrained eye the peaks and troughs of a cycle are only evident after they have occurred. However, if you study the business cycle, you can anticipate both the increase and slowdown in housing demand, giving a clue as to when you should be buying and selling.

Zac's share insights

Successful share investing relies on *timing*. The volatility of the sharemarket in the last 10 to 20 years has proven to investors that the traditional view of 'buy and hold' is no longer the most efficient way of making money in the sharemarket.

Timing your share investment decisions therefore relies on using economic data and investing in accordance with the sector investment roadmap (see figure 4.8) that is based on Standard & Poors *Guide to Sector Investing 1995*. Understanding what stage and phase of the business cycle that the economy is in will help guide you as to whether to be invested in the sharemarket—and also what sectors and industries you can expect to outperform during each stage of the cycle.

Figure 4.8: sector investment roadmap

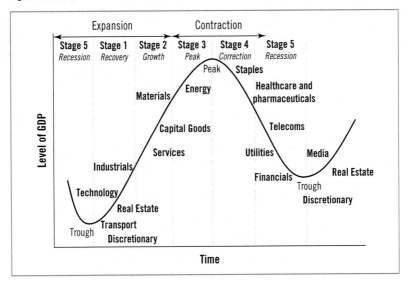

Conclusion

As the business cycle progresses, specific sectors and industries will tend to perform better in one stage than another as there is more demand for products and services for that sector or industry during that stage of the economy.

The investment roadmap (see figure 4.8) provides a broad summary of what sectors tend to outperform during each stage of the business cycle and can serve as a guide as to what sectors to invest more in during each stage of the economic cycle to achieve the highest probability of success in your growth investments.

★ ★

Round 5

WHERE TO DO YOUR RESEARCH

Research, research, research. Research is vital in making any successful investment decision. There is a never-ending number of sources of information. You can get caught up in the plethora of information that is available, but in this chapter we will discuss the top websites and popular magazines where you can access vital data and analysis that will help you make informed and educated investment decisions. These are sound sources that provide accurate information that we recommend. There are plenty of other sources of information, but the ones listed here are a good start. Be careful: there are plenty of spruikers who promote their products and offerings rather than give independent advice!

Websites

Table 5.1 offers a summary of our recommended property and share investment websites, which then are described in more detail.

Table 5.1: useful websites for property and share research

Property	Shares
www.abs.gov.au	www.asx.com.au
www.domain.com.au	www.asic.gov.au
www.google.com	www.moneysmart.gov.au
www.myrp.com.au	www.finance.yahoo.com.au
www.news.com.au	www.afr.com.au

Property	Shares
www.onlinenewspapers.com.au	www.morningstar.com.au
www.pricefinder.com.au	www.tradingeconomics.com
www.realestate.com.au	www.investors.asn.au
www.reia.com.au	www.sharedividends.com.au
www.rpdata.com.au	www.investogain.com.au
	www.delisted.com.au

★ ★ ★ ★ ★ ★ ★ PROPERTY ★ ★ ★ ★ ★ ★ ★

Property research websites

This section describes the type of property information that you will find at each website.

Australian Bureau of Statistics — www.abs.gov.au

This is the official website for Australian statistics. There is far more information on this website than you will ever need if you are looking for data to help you with your property investment decisions. You can conduct a wide variety of research and analysis just using this one website. Of particular interest to property investors is the demographic and housing data which is gathered every five years through the census.

For example, to help determine if a suburb is worth investing in for capital growth, the following indicators are just some of the positive signs I look for:

- *Occupation.* The number of people in professional positions should be increasing. The higher people's income, the more they can spend on buying or renting property.

- *Median income.* The pace of growth of incomes in the suburb should be greater than that of the state or nation. This indicates a wealthier demographic moving into the area.

- *Education.* The percentage of university- or tertiary-qualified people is increasing at a faster rate than the state average. University-qualified people generally earn a higher salary than those who don't have a higher education qualification. This is another sign that a wealthier demographic is moving in.

- *Landlord type.* You should be looking for areas where the percentage of homes rented from the state or territory housing authority is either below the state average or the rate of decrease in this type of housing is faster than that of the state.

Fairfax Media — www.domain.com.au

This is the real estate website for Fairfax Media. It is used by people mainly when they are looking to buy or rent property, but this site also offers a wide variety of data for the property investor, such as free reports, videos and tips on buying, improving, managing and maintaining property.

Google Maps — www.google.com.au

The Google Maps facility can provide you with a bird's-eye view of an area from the comfort of your own home. You can also use the Street View function and get a better perspective of an area. I also like to use the satellite map as, at a glance, this can give me an indication of where an industrial estate might be, and the location of shopping centres, schools, parks and so on. When using Google maps, some of the attributes I search for are:

- not too many industrial buildings in the suburb, or at least not too close to the property I wish to buy

- location of schools and major shopping centres

- location of train lines and stations (you don't want to be too close to a train line but being in the vicinity of a train station is advantageous)

- distances to the city or sea or major facilities (the closer you are to these facilities the greater the potential for capital growth)

- flight path (you don't want to be directly under the flight path, but being close to the airport can be a bonus as it is a hub of employment).

My RP Data — www.myrp.com.au

RP Data has two main websites. The website nominated here is for the general public. You can download free reports, as well as some which you will have to pay for. The free reports include a suburb profile, which provides a demographic snapshot of a particular suburb, and median house and unit property values tracked over time. Reports that you can buy range from a suburb sales report, which provides all sales in a suburb for the past 12 months, to a rental insight report, which presents detailed current rental information for when you're considering buying a rental property.

News Ltd — www.news.com.au

Not only can you get your daily news from this website but there are also many real estate articles written by property experts that are freely available. Topics range from buying property and taking out mortgages to property market updates and forecasts. These articles are updated regularly, which means you can quickly build a library of useful information.

Online Newspapers — www.onlinenewspapers.com

I regard local knowledge as critical when purchasing property. It can be hard to gain that knowledge if you are not a local or don't live near the area. Solution? Check out the Online Newspapers website, which has many newspapers not just from Australia but also from all over the world. Want to invest in Whyalla (SA) but live in Victoria? No problem. Check out the *Whyalla News*. Live in Manly or Manhattan but want to find out what is happening in Blacktown (NSW)? No problem. Read the *Blacktown Sun*. There are well over 100 national and local newspapers that you can access from this website, which will keep you up to date with local news and views.

PriceFinder — www.pricefinder.com.au

You can access some free information from this website, but to gain access to the most comprehensive data and analysis you need to pay and subscribe to become a member. If you become a member, you will have unlimited access to a wide variety of information, including sale price estimates, titles and plans.

www.realestate.com.au

As the name suggests, this website deals with all things real estate. From searching for property to buy or rent, through to articles written by property specialists, this website has it all. The best way to stay up to date is to subscribe to email alerts and the newsletter. Email alerts will automatically be sent to you when a property is listed that meets your criteria. The newsletter will keep you up to date with what is happening in the world of property.

Real Estate Institute of Australia (REIA) — www.reia.com.au

The Real Estate Institute of Australia is the national association for Australia's real estate profession. Even though this website is mainly for real estate salespeople and agents, it does have very useful consumer information, including buying, selling, renting property and median price statistics. It also has links to its members, which are the state and territory real estate institutes.

RP Data — www.rpdata.com.au

This RP Data website is mainly for the real estate industry, but some information is also available at no cost to buyers, sellers and investors. Of particular interest is the RP Data-Rismark Daily Home Value Index, which tracks movements in property prices on a yearly, quarterly, monthly and daily basis. You can also stay up to date by reading the capital market reports and regular press releases.

★ ★ ★ ★ ★ ★ ★ ★ **SHARES** ★ ★ ★ ★ ★ ★ ★ ★

Share and investment research websites

With so much information freely available to share investors on the internet, it can be daunting to know where to find reliable and quality information. To help you, this section describes the websites that we use ourselves and that we have found to be reliable sources of information.

Australian Securities Exchange — www.asx.com.au

The ASX website is an absolute treasure trove of information. Not only can you find current and historical share price data, a history of all company announcements, details on financial products traded on the ASX and also the way that markets work, but the site also hosts a wealth of education courses and tools—aimed at everyone from beginners to seasoned investors.

Australian Securities and Investments Commission (ASIC) — www.asic.gov.au

The ASIC website is a government website from which you can do company searches, ensure financial advisers and companies are licensed, and also read about how ASIC regulates the markets and companies in Australia.

Moneysmart — www.moneysmart.gov.au

This is ASIC's consumer website — and is a very good reference tool to bookmark and check regularly. The information on this website is honest, objective and very relevant, with no jargon: it is aimed at people who don't have a financial background. Find out about managing your money, how to borrow money, details about superannuation, and how to spot a scam and use the online calculators and tools to help you manage your money.

Yahoo! Finance — www.finance.yahoo.com.au

Yahoo! Finance is a handy website that provides a one-stop shop for financial news and information about companies. It carries the latest business and market news, charts and market updates, as well as editorials and features on investing.

Australian Financial Review (AFR) — www.afr.com.au

The *AFR* is Australia's premier business newspaper. It is read by virtually everyone who invests in the market — including professional advisers and money managers. The *AFR* provides a good mix of company news and editorial opinions — and regularly features special articles on investment-related topics.

Morningstar/Aspect Huntley — www.morningstar.com.au

Morningstar/Aspect Huntley is one of Australia's oldest and most respected financial newsletter services. It provides comprehensive data and objective information on more than 12000 managed funds and 2000 stocks available to individual investors, including proprietary Morningstar analyst research on 250-plus individual stocks and 300 investment strategies distributed through 4000 individual funds. The site also offers independent editorial content produced by Morningstar analysts and journalists based in Sydney and around the world.

TradingEconomics — www.tradingeconomics.com

This website is noteworthy to bookmark as a reference source for economic data from Australia and almost every country in the world. You can find information about almost every economic indicator over almost any time frame, such as GDP, unemployment levels, consumer confidence, business confidence and interest rates.

Australian Investors Association (AIA) — www.investors.asn.au

The AIA is a nonprofit organisation that helps its members become more successful long-term investors. It educates and exposes the interests of Australian investors across all types of investments and asset classes by providing self-directed investors with education and networking opportunities.

Share Dividends — www.sharedividends.com.au

Share Dividends is a handy website to bookmark for keeping up to date with what dividends companies are paying, and also when they are paying them.

Invest to Gain — www.investogain.com.au

This is a useful website run by volunteers, and it features tools to help you make investment decisions. It also has a lot of free educational information on investing.

Delisted — www.delisted.com.au

This website provides valuable information on corporate actions, and new company listings and existing company delistings. Delisted companies are those that have been removed from the ASX. Delisting can occur for numerous reasons, such as a company being taken over by another company, changing its name, going out of business, or through its own decision to privatise.

Magazines

Table 5.2 provides a summary of our recommended property and share investment magazines.

Table 5.2: recommended property and share investment magazines

Property	Shares
Australian Property Investor	*AFR Smart Investor*
Smart Property Investment	*Money*
Your Investment Property	

★ ★ ★ ★ ★ ★ ★ **PROPERTY** ★ ★ ★ ★ ★ ★ ★

Property magazines

This section provides a brief description of each of the property magazines we recommend.

Australian Property Investor (API)

This is a monthly publication full of articles, news and views on property and investment. Regular features include the opportunity for readers to ask questions through columns such as 'API connect' and 'bricks and mortar'. Of particular interest are the updates on each state and territory. A very comprehensive databank outlining information on auction clearance rates, property market indicators and median prices can be found at the back of the magazine. The website for the magazine can be found at www.apimagazine.com.au and includes a very informative blog.

Smart Property Investment (SPI)

Smart Property Investment is the newest of the three national property magazines. It promotes itself as 'the magazine *by* investors *for* investors', as many of its contributing writers are property investors. As is the case with the other two property magazines, readers are able to ask questions, and it includes comprehensive research and analysis of property markets in the Data Centre section. The online version of this magazine is at www.spionline.com.au. The statistics on suburbs include tables of information, maps and graphs, which are well set out and easy to understand.

Your Investment Property (YIP)

This is a monthly magazine based in Sydney but covering news and views from all over the country. Readers are able to ask questions of property experts through Property Q&A, Tax Q&A and Legal Q&A. Suburb highlights are a popular feature of this magazine. *Your Investment Property* also has a wide-ranging database of information, including demand versus supply statistics, vacancy rates, capital growth and rental yield. The *YIP* website is www.yourinvestmentpropertymag.com.au and it offers enlightening videos on the best suburbs to invest in.

★ ★ ★ ★ ★ ★ ★ ★ **SHARES** ★ ★ ★ ★ ★ ★ ★ ★

Share investment magazines

Australia is fortunate to have several high-quality share investment magazines. The following are the standouts.

AFR Smart Investor Magazine

The *Australian Financial Review's Smart Investor* magazine is a useful tool for active Australian investors seeking information and analysis aimed at wealth creation and financial security. It features independent commentary and strategies from Financial Review Group experts, in-depth coverage of all asset classes and analysis of emerging trends.

Money

Money magazine helps you manage your finances by cutting through the jargon to deliver clear and precise information. Each issue features well-researched reports and advice from some of Australia's respected financial writers, including Paul Clitheroe and Ross Greenwood, Australia's own financial commentating gurus and successful share investors in their own right.

 ## Peter's property insights

You could easily suffer from information overload from the abundance of data and analysis that is available. However, if you are interested in saving time and money, I suggest the following:

- Most of the data in the free suburb reports originates from the Australian Bureau of Statistics (ABS) census information. If you are the type of person who likes detail, just use the ABS website. However, if you like your information well set out and in an easy-to-read format, select the free suburb report that most suits your needs.

- Google Maps is an exceptional tool but I strongly encourage you to also visit the area and property that you are interested in. The maps are not always 100 per cent accurate and street view vision can often be two or three years old.

- Subscribe to one of the property magazines, but also visit all of their websites regularly, as they each have something different to offer.

Zac's share insights

When it comes to shares, everyone has an opinion—that's what makes the sharemarket so interesting and so volatile. The fact is that the sharemarket values and re-values a company every single second that the market is open. Short term, this can cause significant changes (up and down) to the share prices, so it is important to know what you are doing when it comes to making share investment or trading decisions. An astute financial adviser is often a useful resource to help you make the right investment decisions and can provide you with a lot of research. Be careful about relying too much on adviser or broker research—always consider the independence of the research provider first, and also their track record.

 ## Conclusion

Knowledge is power and nowhere is this truer than when it comes to investing. By understanding what you are investing in, you are more likely to become more astute, confident and successful as an investor.

We strongly encourage you to do your research but, in the end, you need to act upon it. You won't achieve your investment goals if you just think and read about investment: you actually have to invest!

Round 6

UNDERSTANDING THE TABLES AND STATISTICS

A famous person once said: 'There are three kinds of lies: lies, damned lies and statistics'. This phrase highlights the point that numbers and statistics can be manipulated to suit either side of a particular argument. For this reason, statistics need to be considered carefully so that you can gain a greater understanding of what is actually happening.

It is easy to calculate statistics for the sharemarket, as all shares are basically the same. One BHP share is exactly the same and worth the same as any other BHP share. It doesn't matter who owns it, how long they have owned it or where the shareholder lives: the two shares can easily be compared, as they are identical.

The same cannot be said for property. The problem with property and statistics is that property is heterogeneous. In other words, there is no single property on this planet that is exactly the same as another.

★ ★ ★ ★ ★ ★ ★ PROPERTY ★ ★ ★ ★ ★ ★ ★

Understanding property statistics and data

Even in a brand new block of apartments, one apartment is not exactly the same as another. There can be differences in size, number of bedrooms, number of bathrooms, quality of fittings and fixtures, building level, car parks, views—and the list goes on. However, the most important difference between the properties is their location. It is impossible for one apartment to be exactly the same as any other apartment because they cannot possibly share the exact same geographical location.

Even if there are two brand new apartments that are identical in size, quality, number of car spaces, and they are positioned next to each other, they are not exactly the same as they are in slightly different positions within the apartment tower.

This is one of the reasons that the quality of information is so important in property and you need to take great care when interpreting property data.

In table 6.1, we have included some data to illustrate a couple of points. The table shows the hypothetical performance of six suburbs in Melbourne. The top row includes terms that are explained immediately following the table, and the rest of the table has some indicators based on price, rent and the general health of the property market.

Table 6.1: sample of annual property statistics for six Melbourne suburbs, December 2012

Suburb	No. sold	Median house price ($000)	12-month growth (%)	10-year growth (%)	Gross rental yield (%)	Vendor discount (%)	Average days on market	Vacancy rate (%)
Carrum	70	440	−2.8	6.3	4.1	−9.18	86	4.84
Chelsea	140	450	−0.3	6.7	4.1	−8.92	80	2.97
Coburg	280	570	−4.7	6.4	3.9	−7.46	80	4.18
Collingwood	77	670	−5.2	6.6	3.8	−8.59	54	2.13
Cremorne	10	665	−15.6	6.5	4.2	SNR	38	SNR
Flemington	70	620	−2.4	6.3	3.7	−3.66	57	3.35

The terms used in table 6.1 are those you will see in most analyses of investment property. Here they are explained.

- *Suburb.* Name of the suburb.
- *No. sold.* The total number of properties sold in the suburb in the previous 12 months.

- *Median house price.* All house sales are ranked in order of magnitude. The median price is the one that is in the middle of the list. For example, in the total of 77 sales in the suburb of Collingwood, the median price of $670000 is the 39th sale in the list. Median price should not be confused with average price, as the average is calculated in a different way. The median price is a better indicator of property values as it makes allowances for unusually very low and very high prices, which can distort the figures if you were to just use the average price.

- *12-month growth (%).* The change in median price over the last 12 months.

- *10-year growth (%).* The average annual growth in median price over the past 10 years.

- *Gross rental yield (%).* An indication of the estimated gross rental return on property in the listed suburb. It is calculated by dividing the advertised rent by the median price. The higher the number, the higher the rent as a proportion of the sale price, and the better a cash-flow investment it is likely to be.

- *Vendor discount (%).* The difference between the initial advertised price and the final sale price. If this number is high, it can be an indication that it is a buyers' market and the vendor (owner) has needed to drop their price significantly in order to secure a sale. The level of discount can also show whether owners have unrealistic expectations of what their property is really worth.

- *Average days on market.* The average number of days it takes to sell a property by private treaty. This statistic is measured from the initial listing date to the sales date. A low number can indicate that property in the suburb is particularly sought after.

- *Vacancy rate (%).* The proportion of all rental properties in the listed suburb that are not tenanted at a particular time. If there are many vacant properties, it might mean that there is an oversupply of investment property in this suburb.

- *SNR (statistically not reliable).* There is not enough data to make a calculation that can be relied upon. As mentioned earlier, property is heterogeneous and you need a relatively high number of properties to make a reliable calculation.

Discussion

Of particular note for table 6.1, (see p. 65) is the data for the suburb of Cremorne. With only 10 sales, this data is not very reliable. Each of the 10 houses could be very different from the others. One might be brand new, another a period-style home; one single storey, another double storey; one in poor condition, another in pristine condition; one may have two bedrooms, another four bedrooms. All 10 houses could have sold in 10 different streets. It is very difficult to come to a viable conclusion with so few houses sold.

Coburg, on the other hand, is completely different. Here 280 houses were sold in the past 12 months. The statistics in this suburb are far more reliable than they are in Cremorne, due to the volume of data.

★ ★ ★ ★ ★ ★ ★ ★ **SHARES** ★ ★ ★ ★ ★ ★ ★ ★

Understanding share price data

Share prices on the sharemarket are the result of an auction process—the price at which a buyer and a seller are willing to transact.

An overwhelming amount of information about every share is available to investors. During market trading hours, shares are revalued by investors every second of the day—so the price in the morning may not be the same as the price in the afternoon. The following section explains some of the common statistics presented in analysis of share investments.

Share price quotes

An investor will use a share price quote to obtain current share price information. Almost all sources of share price information will provide you with a table that looks similar to table 6.2 (overleaf), from the ASX.

Note: A lot of the freely available share price quotes (for example through the ASX website or through Yahoo! Finance) are delayed by at least 20 minutes during the trading day.

Table 6.2: data available on shares, using CBA as an example

Code	Last	$+/–	Bid	Offer	Open	High	Low	Volume
CBA	63.250	0.010	63.130	63.280	63.340	63.350	63.010	1 342 457

Source: ASX.

A typical share price quote will include the following information.

- *Last (or close).* This describes the last traded price paid or received for a share transaction.

- *Change (or +/–).* This is the change in price from the previous day's closing price

- *Bid.* This is the highest price that an investor is willing to pay to buy a share.

- *Offer (or ask).* This is the lowest price than an investor is willing to sell their shares for.

- *High.* This is the highest price that the share traded at during the day's trading period.

- *Low.* This is the lowest price that the share traded at during the day's trading period.

- *Volume.* This is the number of shares that have traded in the current trading session. The number of shares traded is only counted once per transaction, so if Investor A is buying 5000 shares and trades with Investor B, then only 5000 shares will be counted towards the day's traded volume, not 10 000.

Market depth (see table 6.3) is a listing of price and the number of shares that buyers are bidding at and those that sellers are offering to sell their shares at. Market depth is a statistic used by investors to see where to place their order if they want to buy or sell their shares immediately, or to analyse where most buyers and sellers are clustered.

A transaction is made only when a seller lowers their price to meet the highest bidding buyer, or if buyers raise their prices to meet the lowest-offering seller. This is dependent on there being sufficient volume at each price level at which the buyer or seller is willing to transact.

Table 6.3: a market depth screen showing buyers and sellers at various price levels

Buyers			Sellers		
No. of buyers	Volume	Price ($)	Price ($)	Volume	No. of sellers
1	411	63.13	63.20	2700	1
2	500	63.12	63.21	1635	2
1	2000	63.08	63.25	2000	5
1	250	63.05	63.26	1000	2
2	350	63.02	63.30	1500	1

Other share price information may include the company's listing information, as shown in table 6.4.

Table 6.4: company listing information, using CBA as an example

Issuer code	CBA
Securities	ASX Code, Security Description
Official listing date	12 September 1991
GICS Industry Group	Banks
Exempt Foreign	No
Internet Address	www.commbank.com.au
Registered Office Address	Ground Floor, Tower 1, 201 Sussex Street, Sydney, NSW, Australia

(continued)

Table 6.4: company listing information, using CBA as an example *(cont'd)*

Head Office Telephone	(02) 9378 2000
Head Office Fax	(02) 9118 7192
Share Registry	Link Market Services Ltd Level 12, 680 George Street, Sydney NSW, Australia 2000
Share Registry Phone	1800 022 440

Explanation of terms

The terms used in table 6.4 are explained here.

- *Issuer code.* This is usually a three-letter code that is used to identify the share on the exchange. For example, Commonwealth Bank of Australia has the code 'CBA'.

- *Official listing date.* This is the first date that the share was listed on the exchange.

- *GICS industry group.* Every share listed on the sharemarket is categorised into an industry group according to the main business activity it is involved in. This is known as a global industry classification standard (or GICS) and is the methodology used across stock exchanges all around the world. This makes it easy to identify which companies are similar, or likely to be competing in the same sector or industry

- *Share registry.* Listed shares must maintain a registry of their shareholders, and the registry administers all changes of ownership, payments of dividends, and so on. Some companies maintain their own registry, while others outsource the registry to one of the bigger registry businesses, such as Computershare or Link Market Services.

Share price charts are graphical representations of share price history over a selected period of time. Figure 6.1 is a line chart showing the closing prices and the volume (being the number of shares traded each day) for CBA over six months.

Figure 6.1: closing prices and volume of CBA shares traded over a period of six months

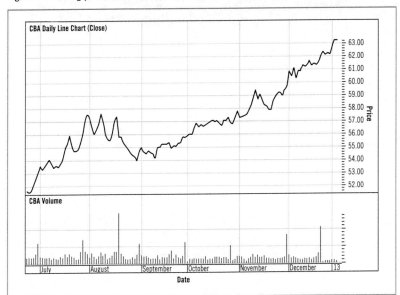

Source: Hubb Investor charting software, www.hubb.com.

There are other ways of representing share price history, and these provide additional information to the analyst. These include bar and candlestick charts, which show the daily, open, high, low and close price ranges for each day (see figure 6.2, overleaf).

We can use price charts to identify trends in share prices over time. This trend analysis is called technical analysis, and it can help alert us as to when the time is right to buy or to sell a share. You can find out more about how to use technical analysis to time your share investments by downloading an exclusive ebook from our website at www.propertyvsshares.com.au.

Figure 6.2: daily open, high, low and close price ranges and volume of CBA shares traded over a period of six months

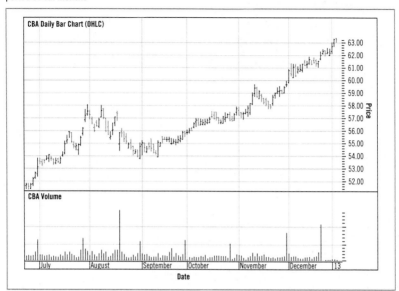

Source: Hubb Investor charting software, www.hubb.com.

Company fundamental analysis

You don't need a degree in accounting to read, compare and understand financial information about a company in order to make an investment decision. From all the financial information and ratios available, you need to know what to look for to make an objective assessment of a company's financial position.

We usually look at the following categories of financial information to help us make a judgement as to the current and future prospects of a company.

How cheap is the company — value analysis

Value analysis (see table 6.5) is one aspect of fundamental company analysis.

Table 6.5: value analysis

Value	Company	Market	Sector
P/E ratio	14.20	14.30	11.20

The terms used in value analysis include the following.

- *P/E ratio.* This is the price-to-earnings ratio: it is a calculation of the share price divided by earnings per share (EPS). It represents a multiple of how expensive the company is relative to its earnings. Investors use P/E as a relative measure of how cheap or expensive a company is, compared with its peers, or the market. Table 6.5 shows that Commonwealth Bank of Australia (CBA) has a P/E ratio of 14.20, whereas its peers (companies in the same sector—the banks) have P/E ratios of 11.20. This means that other banks' price is 11.20 times their earnings, which indicates that CBA is therefore significantly more expensive than its competitors.

- *Valuation.* Many brokers will provide a price valuation (or target) for a share as part of their research. This valuation can be calculated using a variety of methods, such as discounted cash flow, net asset valuation and others. It is also based on several assumptions about the future expectations of the company, which may or may not eventuate. As a result, this valuation should be considered a guide only, rather than cast in stone.

How much income will you get—income analysis

Just as a tenant will pay you a regular rental for the use of your property, most profitable companies will pay their shareholders regular dividends on their investment holdings. Dividends are a distribution of residual profits made by the company during the period, and these are generally paid out to shareholders twice a year, following the company presenting its investors with its financial results.

The terms used in income analysis (see table 6.6) are:

- *Dividend yield.* This is a calculation that shows how much a company pays out in dividends each year relative to its share price. The dividend yield is expressed as a percentage, and a higher dividend yield implies a higher income stream. When using this data, be aware of whether it is calculated using historical dividend data or forecast data of future dividend payments. Also, be aware that companies can cut or even stop dividend payments to shareholders at will if business conditions decline, or the company cannot afford it.

- *Franking.* The franking percentage shows how much of the dividends have been paid out of a company's post-tax income. A shareholder is entitled to claim back the franking credits attached to dividends, which means they will pay tax on their dividends at their individual marginal tax rates, but they can claim a rebate (or credit) for the tax already paid by the company. The reason franking credits exist is to prevent double taxation of dividends: if a company pays out dividends from its post-tax income, it has already paid tax on the dividend paid to shareholders, at the corporate tax rate (currently 30 per cent). It would be unfair to tax that dividend again in the hands of the shareholder, and the tax office therefore allows taxpayers to claim back the tax paid by the company.

- *Dividend stability.* This measure refers to the probability that a company will continue to pay its dividends. It is calculated based on the company's history of paying consistent dividends: the higher this number is, the more likely it will be that the company will pay its shareholders a dividend.

Table 6.6: income analysis

Income	Company	Market	Sector
Dividend yield (%)	5.3	4.9	6.9
Franking (%)	100.0	3.4	4.4
Dividend stability	99.3	90.8	98.5

What are the company's growth expectations — growth analysis

Investors purchase shares in companies primarily because they expect that the share price will increase in value over time. Share prices will increase when investors expect that the company will improve its sales and its profit. Table 6.7 shows an example of growth analysis.

Table 6.7: growth analysis

Growth rates	10-year	5-year	1-year	2 year forecast
Sales	6.3%	0.9%	−2.3	1.7%
Cash flow	−0.4%	−183.5%	−115.4%	55.0%
Earnings	12.0%	5.0%	−1.2%	5.9%
Dividends	9.0%	5.5%	4.4%	3.8%
	2012	2013	2014	2015
EPS (cents)	434.3	472.5	499.4	538.6
DPS (cents)	334.0	357.0	377.5	407.0

The terms used in growth analysis are as follows.

- *Sales growth rates.* This refers to how much the company has increased its revenue over time, and the forecast growth rate in future.

- *Cash flow growth rates.* This refers to how much the company has increased its cash flow over time, and the forecast growth rate in future.

- *Earnings growth rates.* This refers to how much the company has increased its profits over time, and the forecast growth rate for profit in future.

- *Dividend growth rates.* This describes how much the company has increased the dividend it pays its shareholders over time, and the forecast growth rate for dividends in future.

- *EPS.* This refers to earnings per share and represents the company's earnings (or profit) divided by the number of shares on issue. It effectively provides a measure of how much profit the company generates for each share in the company.

- *DPS.* This refers to dividends per share and represents the company's dividend payment for each share. The difference between EPS and DPS represents the amount of money that a company will not distribute to shareholders.

What is the risk of investing in the company — risk analysis

Risk is the possibility that you will lose your money due to a fall in a company's share price. Beta is a statistic that indicates the tendency of a share price's movements to respond to swings in the market. It can be calculated mathematically, although some brokers will provide it to you in their company research databank.

A beta of 1 indicates that the share's price will move with the market. A beta of less than 1 means that the share price will be less volatile than the market. A beta of greater than 1 indicates that the share's price will be more volatile than the market. Table 6.8 shows that Commonwealth Bank has a beta of 0.77; it is theoretically 23 per cent less volatile than the sharemarket as a whole.

Table 6.8: risk of investing in CBA shares versus the market and sector

Risk	Company	Market	Sector
Beta	0.77	1.00	0.93

Peter's property insights

I find studying the statistics helps with my property investment decision, but I also conduct other research, as outlined in the previous chapter. Unlike the sharemarket, the reality of the property market is not revealed primarily in the numbers. Numbers and statistics help, but the big picture can only be seen by using several research tools.

If I were studying table 6.1 (see p. 65), there are a few points that would be of interest to me.

- Every suburb has dropped in value in the last 12 months, which is reflective of the whole property market in 2012.

- As most investors hold property for the long term, the rise in house prices over the past 10 years has been quite good, especially when you consider the effect of the global financial crisis (GFC).

- The gross rental yield on houses is relatively low. However, if the table included flat/unit/townhouse data, the gross rental yield would be higher.

- Even though I believe all six suburbs listed in the table are great investment suburbs, I would need to do more research to help determine which particular property in any of these suburbs suited my investment needs.

Zac's share insights

It is easy to get carried away and overwhelmed by the sheer amount of statistical, fundamental and economic information, and the volume of research and opinions that are available to share investors through brokers and other information providers. As with everything in life, keeping it simple is always best. Value is really based on what the majority of investors are perceiving and expecting. I believe that there is more value in analysing trends in data rather than the data in isolation. Analysing price and volume trends and interpreting what the majority of investors are actually doing can yield greater results than relying on research opinions and valuations that are reliant on a multitude of assumptions.

 ## Conclusion

Studying numbers and analysing statistics should be a vital part of your due diligence before you make an investment. Ensure that you are looking at quality data provided by an independent organisation and that you have enough data to make an educated and informed decision.

Round 7

THE RISKS OF INVESTMENT

Whenever you invest in property or shares, there is a risk involved. The risks are many and varied, and some are common to both of these asset classes. An outline of these risks is detailed later in this chapter.

This risk–reward relationship is largely a result of a phenomenon called volatility. Volatility can be thought of as the potential range of returns you can expect to get (both positive and negative). Figure 7.1 shows the relevant risk and returns for each of the four main asset classes.

Figure 7.1: levels of risk and return for the four main asset classes

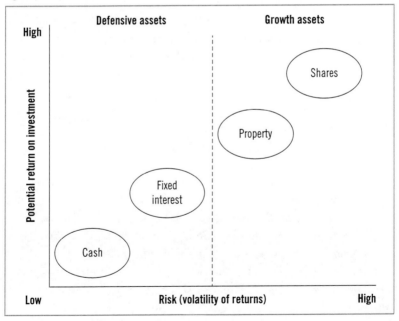

We can see that the trade-off for the opportunity to make high returns is taking on a proportional degree of risk. Most inexperienced investors fear volatility—but without volatility there isn't much potential for return. The secret, therefore, is to manage your investment risk.

The amount of risk you take in investing will depend on the type of investment you make. For example, if you invest money in a defensive asset, such as a fixed term deposit in the bank, there is virtually no risk of you losing your money. When your fixed deposit matures, you will get your original investment back along with the interest payable on that investment. It's important to be aware that the return you will get on your investment can be higher or lower than if you invested in a growth asset such as property and shares.

What is your attitude towards risk?

Before you consider investing, one of the first things you should understand is your approach and attitude to risk. Ask yourself, how comfortable are you with the possibility of losing your money? How do you feel about the prospect of the return on your investment fluctuating? There's more about working out your own risk profile later in this chapter.

★ ★ ★ ★ ★ ★ ★ PROPERTY ★ ★ ★ ★ ★ ★ ★

The most common risk property investors face is vacancy. That is, your property has no tenant, but you still have to pay all the bills, including interest on the mortgage during this vacancy period. If you are risk averse, you should focus on buying residential property. If you are willing to take on a little more risk (and potentially more reward in the form of higher rent), consider purchasing commercial property. Or, if you have a large appetite for risk, consider becoming involved in renovation or property development.

One of the first steps in minimising risk is to select the right property. In residential property, this generally means selecting a property in a good location and in reasonable condition so as to attract a reliable tenant. A good location doesn't mean it has to be in an expensive suburb. You have a better chance of getting a decent tenant in a $400 000 property that is in a clean state and in good condition than a $1 000 000 property that is dirty and full of cracks and termites.

The risks in property investment can be divided into two categories: controllable and non-controllable risks.

Controllable risks

As the name suggests, a controllable risk is one the investor has some power or control over, such as the choice of what to buy and how much to spend.

What to buy

As mentioned earlier, residential property is less risky than commercial property. This is because the chance of long-term vacancy is almost nil. You will probably find a tenant within a week or two for a residential property, but it can take months or even years to find tenants for some types of commercial property. If you don't mind taking on extra risk for the potential of a higher rental return, you might consider purchasing commercial property; in other words, retail, office or commercial buildings.

When to buy

If you consider that the market is too hot and that people are paying ridiculously high prices for property, you can choose to opt out and wait for the property market to slow down. Alternatively, if you feel that the property market is at or near the bottom of its cycle, you might choose to buy sooner rather than later.

How much to spend

If you are risk averse, a lower priced property may help you worry less and sleep better at night, as you have less of your money invested. An investment of $300 000 in a unit or flat could be more suited to your risk profile than buying a $600 000 property.

How much you will borrow

Many property investors are willing to borrow the maximum amount, usually 95 per cent of the value of the property, whereas others feel more comfortable with borrowing 80 per cent or less and not having to pay lender's mortgage insurance (LMI).

When to sell

If you think you can anticipate a downturn in the property market and want to get out before prices fall, you can choose to sell the property when it suits you and your investment goals. If you don't need to sell and the property market is flat, you may choose to hold on until property prices increase again.

Non-controllable risks

A non-controllable risk is a risk over which an investor has no direct control. Non-controllable risks can include risks of interest rates changing or of the broad economy changing.

Economic risk

If the economy falters, as it did as a result of the global financial crisis (GFC), property prices can fall. Eventually property prices will rise again, but you need to consider the potential effects of fluctuations in the value of your property.

Business risk

This is relevant mainly to owners of commercial property. Imagine if you owned one commercial building and it was purpose-built for the occupant who ran a photo processing business. With the advent of digital cameras, the demand for film and photo processing has diminished. This means his business will suffer as revenues and profits drop, which in turn will probably affect his capacity to pay your rent.

Legislative risk

If the government decides to increase first home buyer grants or provides incentives to residential property investors, such as tax breaks or changes in self managed superannuation fund rules, this can increase the demand for property and, as a result, increase the price of houses and units. The opposite is also true when state or federal governments withdraw or reduce first home buyer incentives.

Interest rate risk

If interest rates go up, this will increase mortgage repayments, which can place stress on cash flow. A couple of simple ways to mitigate this risk is to have spare cash available to make increased mortgage payments, or consider fixing the interest rate for a period of time. There are other issues related to fixing your interest rate, which are discussed in Round 13.

★ ★ ★ ★ ★ ★ ★ ★ SHARES ★ ★ ★ ★ ★ ★ ★ ★

Growth assets provide investors with two ways of creating wealth: income (through dividends or rental returns) and growth (an appreciation in the value of the investment). If you invest in growth assets like shares or property, however, the risk of losing your money goes up — and so does your potential return. It's important to note that there are differing risk levels within growth assets too — for example, investing in a share such as BHP is not as risky as investing in a smaller company with a low market capitalisation, one that has just been listed and has no income. The latter would be a significantly more risky investment!

As we saw from figure 7.1 (see p. 79), the higher the potential return, the higher the level of risk you are taking. This is an accepted law of investing. Shares have the highest level of risk of all the asset classes. But it is important to understand that within this asset class there are differing levels of volatility (and hence risk) between the various types of shares that you can invest in.

For example, a company such as Woolworths (WOW) has lower risk than a speculative share such as Geodynamics (GDY). A well-diversified portfolio can therefore reduce volatility overall and reduce the risk within a share portfolio.

Controllable risks

As an investor, you can control specific risks associated with an investment, but there are also risks that you cannot control.

As we have seen in the property section, controllable risks are those for which you can make decisions, such as:

- *when* to make the investment
- *how much* to invest
- *when* to exit the investment
- *who* to invest with
- *what* to invest in
- *diversification* across different asset classes, and also within asset classes.

Non-controllable risks

Non-controllable risks are those that no amount of effort can prevent; however, by managing the controllable risks, you can minimise the impact of the non-controllable risks.

Inflation risk

This is the risk that inflation may exceed the return on your investment.

Market risk

This is the risk of losing money on your investments due to the market falling as a result of market sentiment. Market sentiment—which is the current attitude of investors to investment across all investors—may be influenced by economic, technology, political or legal reasons.

Currency risk

If you are investing overseas, you are usually required to pay for your investment in the overseas currency. This means you have to buy the currency of the overseas exchange using Australian dollars. Currency risk is the risk that rates will fluctuate over time, for political and economic reasons. Depending on when you sell your investment and bring your money back to Australia, the exchange rate is likely to be different, whether higher or lower, than when you originally made your investment. If it is higher, then you will receive fewer Australian dollars than you would otherwise have at the same exchange rate as you bought, which would erode any capital gains or income you have made on your investment.

Legislative risk

This is the risk of losing money on your investments because of the effect of a government policy change For example, the government's minerals resource rent tax (MRRT), which was introduced on 1 July 2012, had a significant impact on the profits of some mining companies exploring for, or producing, iron ore or coal.

Interest rate risk

Interest is the expense you pay when you borrow money to invest. Therefore, interest rates will affect your profitability: higher interest rates mean that you have to repay more on your borrowings.

Performance risk

This is the risk of losing money on your investments due to underperformance of your investment fund manager, investment adviser or even your own underperformance. Many first-time investors look at the previous year's (or quarter's) performance of a fund and mistakenly assume that that is the best fund to invest in. The problem is that a fund manager can underperform at any time—for example, due to their not adapting to a changing market, with the result that high performers in one year may be low performers in another year. Past performance should never be used as an indicator of future results.

Counterparty risk

A counterparty is the person who you deal with at the other side of your transaction. When you are buying shares, a counterparty is usually your broker, or the broker who is acting on behalf of the buyer or seller you are dealing with. There is always a small risk that the counterparty you are dealing with is not able to fulfil their obligations. For shares traded on the ASX through an Australian market participant, however, all trades are guaranteed to be settled through the National Guarantee Fund, which is a compensation fund available to meet certain claims arising from dealings with market participants.

To be a successful investor, you need to understand the risk–reward relationship—and importantly how you feel about risk. This is an important step in helping you decide what types of investments are best suited to you.

What is your investment time frame?

Strictly speaking, the money you use for investment should be money that you will not need in the short term (for example, over the next few weeks, months or even years). Higher risk strategies and investments can offer the potential for higher returns, but they usually deliver these over a longer period of time. The benefit of a longer period of time also allows a quality investment that performs poorly in the short term to recover if you happen to invest in it at the wrong time.

If you have a shorter term need for your funds, then you are better off considering investments that have historically lower levels of volatility, such as fixed deposits, bonds or even holding your money in a bank account, where its value is unlikely to fluctuate wildly.

Working out your risk profile

To help you understand your own tolerance to risk, you can use a risk profile questionnaire that asks you several questions to help you determine how you respond to uncertainty and risk, and also your expectations in terms of returns. You can find a questionnaire on our website (www.propertyvsshares.com.au), and various other websites, such as FinaMetrica (www.finametrica.com.au). The best way to establish your own risk profile, however, is to speak to a licensed financial adviser who can help you work it out.

At the end of the questionnaire you aggregate your score to determine your risk profile. Table 7.1 provides a summary of the investment characteristics of five investor risk profiles.

Table 7.1: investment characteristics for five investor risk profiles

| Characteristic | Investor risk profile | | | | |
	Conservative	Moderate	Balanced	Growth	High growth
Investment time frame	2–3 years	3–5 years	5–7 years	7–10 years	10+ years
Short-term risk	Low to moderate	Moderate	High	High	Very high
Investment return	Low to moderate	Moderate	High	High	Very high

Your investor risk profile will provide you with a guide as to how to allocate your investment funds among the major asset classes (see table 7.2, overleaf).

Table 7.2: typical allocation of growth and defensive assets for five investor risk profiles

Asset class	Investor risk profile				
	Conservative (%)	Moderate (%)	Balanced (%)	Growth (%)	High growth (%)
Growth assets (property, shares)	10	30	50	70	90
Defensive assets (cash, fixed interest)	90	70	50	30	10

To manage the investment risk according to your own investor risk profile, you should make asset allocations between the four asset classes—shares, property, fixed interest and cash—in accordance with the investment profiles shown in table 7.2. The asset allocations are designed to diversify risk across the various asset classes in an attempt to minimise risk (that is, reduce the probability of losing money) according to the investor's tolerance for risk.

Peter's property insights

In the short term, property development and renovating are two of the riskiest ventures in property. If you want to buy and hold for the long term and you have the appetite for risk (with the potential for higher returns), commercial property could be the ideal vehicle for you. Alternatively, if the thought of possible long-term vacancies scares you, stick to leasing out residential property.

Zac's share insights

Managing investment risk is the single most important thing an investor can do to ensure they achieve long-term success with their investment portfolio. Understanding your own risk profile and making investment decisions based on that will protect you from unwanted volatility. Also, be aware of the risks that you cannot control, and manage the risks that you can control by making prudent decisions on how much to invest, when to invest, what to invest in and, importantly, when to get out of your investment. I suggest that you develop an exit strategy for every investment you make.

 ## Conclusion

Investing in property and shares can be risky. If you are not prepared to accept risk, you should just leave your money in a defensive asset, such as in the bank. However, if you are willing to consider and mitigate your risks, the rewards in investing in property and shares can be bountiful.

Round 8

RETURN ON INVESTMENTS

The main reason for making an investment in a growth asset is because you are seeking a return on your investment. As has already been shown in this book, one of the great advantages of both property and shares is that you can create wealth through two types of return: income and capital growth.

Income

The income from shares is called a dividend. This is basically your share of the profits from the company, which, as a part-owner of the company, you are entitled to receive. Dividends are generally paid every six months to shareholders.

Let's imagine you invested in a company called Levendy Lemonade Company and it made an annual profit of $1 000 000. Let's also assume that Levendy Lemonade issued 10 000 000 shares and you bought 20 000 of them. If the profits are to be split evenly, each share would attract $0.10 profit ($1 000 000 profit ÷ 10 000 000 shares). As you own 20 000 Levendy Lemonade shares, your total income from dividends would be $2000 (20 000 shares × $0.10).

The income from property is called rent. If you have a tenant in your investment property, you are entitled to the payment of rent from them. This is money they pay you, the owner, for the privilege of occupying your property. Rent is generally paid weekly, fortnightly or monthly. If you owned a property and the tenant paid you rent of $385 per week, this would equate to an annual rental income of $20 020 ($385 × 52 weeks).

Income is only one form of return that is earned by an investor in a growth asset; the other is known as capital growth.

Capital growth

In the previous example, you bought 20 000 Levendy Lemonade shares. Let's suppose you bought them for $2 each (that is, $40 000). Let's also suppose that it has been a particularly hot summer and Levendy Lemonade sold many bottles of lemonade. Potential investors think that Levendy Lemonade is a great company to invest in and the price of its shares increases to $2.20 each. As you originally bought them for $2.00 and they are now worth $2.20 (your investment is worth $44 000), you have made a capital gain of 20c for each share you own, which equates to 10 per cent growth on your original investment.

In the property example, you own an investment property that generates rental income. Let's assume that you originally bought the property for $400 000. Due to low interest rates, banks being keen to lend money and high consumer confidence, demand for property has increased and your property is now worth $440 000. You have just made a capital gain of $40 000, an increase of 10 per cent.

Yield or return

In each of the investment examples just discussed, you made money from dividends and rent (income) and from the original asset growing in value (capital growth). The common way to measure returns is to compare how much you earned in relation to the original price.

This is commonly referred to as a yield or return. The term 'yield' is generally applied to the income, but both of these terms are interchangeable. The return or yield is commonly expressed as a percentage.

The equations to determine yield or return are given in the following sections.

Income yield

Income yield can be calculated through the use of a relatively simple equation, where the annual rent is expressed as a percentage of the value of the asset.

Income from shares

(Dividend) yield = dividend received per share ÷ value of the share

$$= \$0.10 \div \$2.00$$

$$= 5.0\%$$

Income from property

(Rental) yield = rent per year ÷ value of the house

$$= \$20\,020 \div \$400\,000$$

$$= 5.0\%$$

Return

Return can also be calculated through the use of a relatively simple equation: the increase in the value of the asset divided by the purchase price of the asset to produce a percentage.

Capital growth from shares

Return = increase in value of share ÷ original purchase price of the share

$$= \$0.20 \div \$2.00$$

$$= 10.0\%$$

Capital growth from property

Return = increase in value of property ÷ original purchase price of property

$$= \$40\,000 \div \$400\,000$$

$$= 10.0\%$$

★ ★ ★ ★ ★ ★ ★ **PROPERTY** ★ ★ ★ ★ ★ ★ ★

Most people invest in residential property but investors who are seeking a higher rental yield will also consider investing in commercial property.

The two types of residential property are

- houses
- flats, units or apartments.

There are three common forms of commercial property investment:

- retail
- office
- industrial.

Residential property

Residential property investors are sometimes attracted to properties on the fringes of the metropolitan area due to their higher yields. This kind of investment is often at the expense of capital growth, as it is properties that are located close to the city or the sea that tend to grow the most in capital value.

Commercial property

Location is critical to commercial property. It is imperative that retail property is located where most people are driving or walking past. If you own a service station, you should be on the corner of a main road. If you own a boutique women's clothing store, you should be on the high street, a section of road that has many shops and a high level of traffic. Office buildings tend to be grouped together according to the type of business. Legal offices will tend to be near each other and in close proximity to city or town courts. Office buildings that house the headquarters of the major banks tend to be in prestigious CBD locations. Industrial property should be located on wide main roads or corners where trucks and vans have easy access to the site.

Rental return from property

It is very difficult to determine a percentage rental yield for each of the five common forms of property investment (industrial; office; retail; flats, apartments and units; and houses), as there are many variables to consider. For example, the economic cycle has a large influence on returns on property. The condition of the property also has an impact, but the most significant impact will come from its location.

However, property investments can be ranked in order according to their rental return. Ranked in order from highest to lowest rental return, they are:

1 industrial

2 office

3 retail

4 flats, apartments or units

5 houses.

Now, before you all rush out to buy industrial property because of its relatively high rental returns, you need to consider one very important thing which was discussed in Round 7: risk. One of the reasons that the three types of commercial property have higher rental returns than both types of residential property is that commercial property has a higher risk. The risk comes from a potentially higher vacancy rate.

If you lose a tenant from your residential unit or house, it is relatively easy to find another tenant. Many people are looking for rental accommodation at any given moment, and they are generally willing to pay the rent being asked. It shouldn't take any longer than one or two weeks to find a new tenant for your residential property. The same cannot be said for commercial property.

Imagine you owned an industrial property that was purpose-built for a manufacturer that made car windscreens. When the new car market is booming, so is the company. This in turn means that it should easily be able to make rental payments and, if the good times continue, you could also probably increase the rent at some stage. However, the good times don't last forever! If new car sales are dropping, or fully imported cars become very popular, there is no need for this local manufacturer to make as many car windscreens. In time, the business will suffer and the company will struggle to meet its costs, including rental payments. If business goes very bad and the company needs to leave the property, how long do you think it will take you or your leasing agent to find another windscreen manufacturer? Weeks, months, years? It is not uncommon to find industrial property vacant for very long periods of time. Imagine going without rent for a year or more!

We know that a higher rental return is often associated with a higher risk. The other reason that commercial property rental returns are higher than those from residential property is that commercial property capital growth is generally lower than that of residential property.

Capital growth from property

Imagine that you have $500 000 to spend and you have two choices: invest in residential or commercial property. Here are some simple calculations to help you make your decision.

Purchase house

The calculation of yield for a residential property is as follows.

Value of house = $500 000

Gross rent = $25 000 per year (5% yield)

Purchase commercial property

The calculation of yield for a commercial property is as follows.

Value of property = $500 000

Gross rent (excluding GST) = $40 000 (8% yield)

Just based on these calculations, why would anyone invest in residential property when you can get a much higher rental yield from commercial property?

We have already noted that, since the Second World War, property prices have increased at a rate of approximately 8.5 per cent per year. This is not all property: just residential property. The capital growth of commercial property is fundamentally based on the rental income. If you can increase the rental income, you can increase the value of the property.

If we use an annual house price growth figure of 7 per cent to forecast the price of the house in 10 years' time, it will double in value:

Value of house today = $500 000

Value of house in 10 years' time = $1 000 000

If the rent of the commercial property can't be markedly increased due to low demand for that particular type of property, or because no upgrading of the property takes place, the growth in value over 10 years will be minimal, for example approximately 3 per cent per year.

Value of commercial property today = $500 000

Value of commercial property in 10 years' time = $700 000

If you bought the commercial property, you would be tens of thousands of dollars ahead in rental income. However, you would have missed out on hundreds of thousands of dollars due to the limited capital growth.

★ ★ ★ ★ ★ ★ ★ ★ SHARES ★ ★ ★ ★ ★ ★ ★ ★

The Australian sharemarket has more than 2100 companies listed on the stock exchange from which a share investor can choose to invest in. Each has its own level of risk and potential return, and this is determined by many factors, including:

- market capitalisation and liquidity
- business sector or industry
- business influences.

Market capitalisation

Size matters—or so they say! It's certainly the case when it comes to shares. We measure the size of a company by its market capitalisation (or market cap): the number of shares on issue multiplied by the share price. The higher the market cap, the safer the shares are considered to be relative to shares with a lower market cap. Liquidity (or the average number of shares available to buy or sell at any given time) is also important, as it will determine whether there is a buyer or seller willing to transact with you at your price.

The role of stock indexes

Standard & Poors, a global investment research company, develops and maintains share price indexes for the Australian Securities Exchange (ASX) and other global sharemarkets so as to track the average price movements of groups of shares. These indexes are based on market capitalisation, as well as a measure of liquidity.

The weight assigned to each company in the index is proportional to that company's capitalisation, with larger companies being assigned a greater portfolio weighting and therefore having a greater impact on index values.

On the Australian sharemarket, these indexes are reviewed every three months to ensure that the indexes are always tracking the top companies. The major market cap indexes by market capitalisation on the ASX are:

- S&P/ASX 20 index
- S&P/ASX 50 index
- S&P/ASX 100 index
- S&P/ASX 200 index

- S&P/ASX 300 index

- All Ordinaries index (the top 500 companies in Australia by market cap)

- S&P/ASX Small Ordinaries index (companies included in the S&P/ASX 300 index, but not in the S&P/ASX 100 index; this index provides a benchmark for small cap investments).

Business sector or industry

The business sector or industry that a company operates in will also influence the risk and return expectations of investors. For example, a health and biotech company such as CSL Ltd (CSL) operates in an industry demanding a huge amount of investment in research and development (R&D). CSL therefore typically pays shareholders a relatively small dividend each year (in yield terms). Investors who buy this share, however, expect to obtain significant capital growth in their investment over time. Other companies, such as the Commonwealth Bank (CBA), will provide higher yields to investors, because they have lower expected levels of capital growth than, say, CSL.

Once again, Standard & Poors provides and calculates indexes that we can use to segment and group companies into their respective industries. These GICS (global industry classification standard) indexes came into existence in 2002—and brought Australia into line with the rest of the world, allowing comparisons of companies against each other, their global peers and also against other sectors.

The GICS sector indexes are compiled from shares within the top 200 or top 300 constituent indexes by market capitalisation:

- S&P/ASX All Ordinaries Gold index

- S&P/ASX 200 A-REIT index

- S&P/ASX 200 Consumer Discretionary index

- S&P/ASX 200 Consumer Staples index

- S&P/ASX 200 Energy index
- S&P/ASX 200 Financial index
- S&P/ASX 200 Financials excluding A-REITs index
- S&P/ASX 200 Health Care index
- S&P/ASX 200 Industrials index
- S&P/ASX 200 Information Technology index
- ASX LIC index
- S&P/ASX 200 Materials index
- S&P/ASX 300 Metals and Mining index
- S&P/ASX 200 Resources
- S&P/ASX 200 Telecommunications Services index
- S&P/ASX 200 Utilities index.

Business influences

The economy and the business environment are two very important drivers of a company's profitability. For example, companies that sell products overseas are likely to be influenced by rises and falls in the value of the Australian dollar, as are companies that report their profit results in overseas currencies.

The price of commodities will also be a key driver of a company's potential profitability, and therefore of the return to investors.

Interest rates and other economic data, such as consumer confidence, unemployment and government policy, are likely to affect different sectors differently.

It is important to be aware of these influences and the likely effect they will have on the company's profit results, and therefore its share price.

 ## Peter's property insights

Different types of property offer the investor a range of yields and returns. Generally speaking, residential property offers a relatively low yield, but very good capital growth potential. Commercial property, on the other hand, can give a higher yield, but it has been shown historically that the capital growth potential is limited.

Zac's share insights

The return on a share investment will depend on what type of share you are investing in. Growth stocks typically perform well when the economy is doing well, and income (or defensive) stocks perform well when the markets are consolidating. Long-term investment success relies on knowing when to be invested in growth investments, and when to switch to defensive investments.

 ## Conclusion

Both property and shares are great assets for investors, as they provide very good returns over the long term. It has been shown that historically shares provide a greater overall return than property, but this comes at a greater risk. The timing of your share investment is also more critical than it is for an investment in property, simply because if you happen to invest in shares just before a major correction, your portfolio needs to recover lost ground before posting new growth, whereas property has historically been more consistent and less volatile in its returns over the longer term.

Round 9

COSTS OF INVESTING

Owning property and shares comes at a cost. There is a cost in purchasing the asset, holding it and then an additional cost when you sell it. The total outlay can vary greatly. In this chapter, we outline the common costs and give you an indication of the amounts involved.

★ ★ ★ ★ ★ ★ ★ **PROPERTY** ★ ★ ★ ★ ★ ★ ★

Property costs

Costs in owning property will vary, depending on many factors, such as which state the property is located in, the purchase price paid, the size of the mortgage, interest rate, annual rental income and the sale price of the property. Following is a summary of the main costs incurred as a property investor. The major difference in the nature of the costs is the location of the property, as some states and territories will have more or less costs and possibly different names for the costs listed here.

Buying property

The following costs can be incurred when you buy a property:

- *Stamp duty*. This government fee is the most expensive of all purchasing costs. It is approximately 5 per cent of the purchase price.

- *Land Titles Office (LTO) registration fee*. This fee is payable when purchasing (not selling) a property.

- *Government searches*. A conveyancer or lawyer will need to search official documents to ensure that you are actually buying what you think you are buying.

- *Bank fees.* These apply if you are borrowing money to buy the property. The fees should include application, valuation and establishment fees.

- *Lender's mortgage insurance (LMI).* If you are borrowing a significant amount of money, generally more than 80 per cent of the value of the property, you will have to pay LMI. This is an insurance premium paid by the borrower on behalf of the lender; it protects the lender if the borrower defaults on the loan.

- *Adjustment for council rates.* If the existing owner, or vendor, has already paid council rates for the full year and you buy the property halfway through the year, you will owe the vendor 50 per cent of the council rates. You pay this at settlement.

- *Adjustment for water rates.* This is similar to the adjustment for council rates.

- *Conveyancing fees.* This fee paid to the conveyancer or lawyer for their work.

- *Body corporate levy.* This cost applies if you are buying flats, units or apartments. For example, if the existing owner has already paid the levy for January, February and March and you settle on the property on 31 January, the existing owner is entitled to be reimbursed for the February and March levies they have already paid.

- *Goods and services tax (GST).* This may be applicable in some circumstances, especially if you are buying commercial property. If applicable, it is an additional 10 per cent of the purchase price.

The actual costs can vary greatly. To give you some idea of what you might be paying in costs to buy a house (see table 9.1), we have provided indicative amounts based on the following assumptions.

- house = $500 000

- mortgage = $400 000

- loan interest = 6.0 per cent

- annual rent = $25 000

Table 9.1: approximate costs for buying a property

Nature of cost	Amount
Stamp duty	$25 000
LTO registration fee	$2 000
Government searches	$500
Bank fees	$1 000
Adjustment for council rates	$500
Adjustment for water rates	$500
Conveyancing fees	$500
Body corporate levy	For units, flats and apartments only
GST and LMI	Where applicable
Total	$30 000

Holding property

The following costs can be incurred when you own property:

- *Loan interest.* Applicable if you have borrowed money to purchase the property.

- *Property management fee.* Applicable if you have engaged a property manager to manage your property. Management can include fees such as a rent collection fee, monthly account keeping fee, administration fee, two weeks' rent for finding a new tenant, and one week's rent for re-signing existing tenant. The fee all up totals approximately 12 per cent of the gross rent.

- *Repairs.* As the owner and landlord, you are responsible for repairing items (assuming the tenant is not at fault) on the property. These can include the hot-water system, leaky plumbing and faulty electrical work. In the case of flats, units and apartments, if the repair or maintenance is on common property, such as in the stairwell, the body corporate pays for this out of the levies paid by all owners.

- *Maintenance.* Includes painting, major gardening and landscaping, clearing gutters.

- *Council rates.* Payable by the owner of the property.

- *Water rates.* Payable by the owner of the property, but some costs can be passed on to the tenant.

- *Insurance.* The tenant should have their own contents insurance, but you need to have at least building and public liability insurance.

- *Land tax.* This is based on the value of the land, not the value of the whole property. This is a state government tax.

- *Body corporate levy.* This applies if you are buying flats, units or apartments that are part of a group. This money goes towards expenses such as building maintenance, building insurance and maintenance of common areas, such as driveways, stairwells and lifts. Levies can vary from hundreds of dollars per year to thousands of dollars when properties include amenities such as lifts, swimming pools, spas, saunas, and gyms.

- *Goods and services tax (GST).* In many cases, rent from commercial property includes a GST component. The landlord will need to pay the tax office one-eleventh of the rent received.

Table 9.2 shows the indicative costs for holding a property (house), based on the same assumptions as for table 9.1 (see p. 103).

Table 9.2: approximate costs for holding a property

Nature of cost	Amount (per year)
Loan interest	$24 000
Property management fees	$3 000
Repairs	$1 500
Maintenance	$1 000
Council rates	$1 000

Nature of cost	Amount (per year)
Water rates	$300
Insurance	$1 000
Land tax	$200
Body Corporate Levy	For units, flats and apartments only
GST	Where applicable
Total	**$32 000**

As you can see, owning property can be a very expensive business!

Selling property

The following are costs that can be incurred upon the sale of property:

- *Real estate agent fees.* Most agents will charge between 2 per cent and 3 per cent commission for selling a property. Some states set limits on what commission can be charged.

- *Advertising.* This is a cost in addition to the agent's fees. It includes such things as internet and newspaper advertising, signs and brochures.

- *Discharge mortgage registration fee.* If you have a mortgage on the property, a government fee may need to be paid to discharge the mortgage from the property.

- *Government searches.* These expenses will be the same as those incurred for buying a property (see p. 101).

- *Adjustment for council rates.* If you have already paid for a full year's council rates and you sell the property halfway through the year, you are entitled to a reimbursement from the purchaser of 50 per cent of your council rates.

- *Adjustment for water rates.* This is similar to the adjustment for council rates.

- *Conveyancing fees.* These expenses will be the same as those incurred for buying a property (see p. 102).

- *Body corporate levy.* An adjustment is made if you as the owner have already paid this levy in advance.

- *Goods and services tax (GST).* This may be applicable in some circumstances, especially in the sale of commercial property. If applicable, this will total one-eleventh of the total paid by the purchaser.

Table 9.3 shows the indicative costs for selling a property (house), based on the same assumptions as for table 9.1 (see p. 103).

Table 9.3: approximate costs for selling a property

Nature of cost	Amount
Real estate agent fees	$15 000
Advertising	$2 500
Discharge mortgage registration fee	$500
Government search fees	$500
Adjustment for council rates	$500
Adjustment for water rates	$500
Conveyancing fees	$500
Body corporate levy	For units, flats and apartments only
GST	Where applicable
Total	**$20 000**

★ ★ ★ ★ ★ ★ ★ ★ SHARES ★ ★ ★ ★ ★ ★ ★ ★

Share costs

The costs of buying, selling or holding shares are much less than they are for buying, selling or holding a property. This is largely due to increasing competition amongst brokers to attract clients, as well as technological advances in electronic trading and settlement systems that have improved the speed at which transactions are processed and have also reduced the overheads, resulting in savings for investors.

Typical costs of share ownership are likely to be as follows.

Transaction costs

Transaction costs are incurred when you buy and sell through a broker. Most transactions will take place on the secondary market, and these are facilitated by a stockbroker. You will pay a brokerage fee (or commission) when they place a trade to buy or sell a share for you. This may be based on a flat fee, or a percentage of the transaction, or a combination of these.

How much you will pay as a transaction fee when you buy or sell will depend on how you place your order:

- *Discount brokers with online trading.* Place the trade yourself online using a trading platform provided by a discount broker. Brokerage on trades using these platforms can start from as little as $9.95 per transaction.

- *Discount brokers with execution-only trading.* Contact your broker and have them place the trade for you in accordance with your instructions. Brokerage for these types of trades can start from as little as $39.95 per transaction.

- *Full-service brokers.* If you require your broker to provide you with advice and to place the trade on your behalf, then you can expect to pay a higher rate of brokerage. Brokerage rates are negotiable in most cases, according to how many trades you place per month, the size of the transactions and your relationship with the broker. They usually charge a minimum of $100.

Please note: GST is additional to the fees that are charged by your broker.

The broker's commissions are added to the cost of the shares you are buying or, in the case of a sale, they are subtracted from the proceeds you are due to receive.

When you buy shares through the primary market—for example, through a capital raising such as an initial public offering (IPO) or placement, you will generally not pay any transaction fees or GST.

Occasionally companies may announce a buy-back program where they are willing to acquire some or all of their own shares back from shareholders. In this case, a shareholder can sell their shares through the company's share buy-back program without paying a brokerage fee.

Holding costs

Unlike owning a property, you are not subject to holding costs while you own shares that you have purchased outright. This is certainly the case for holding your shares with an online broker.

Many full-service brokers or financial advisers, however, may charge a management, advisory or an administration fee to provide ongoing advice and manage your portfolio on your behalf or to provide administration services such as tax reporting. The cost of this depends on how much advice and management of your investments you require. Your adviser should be able to show you how they calculate this cost.

Shares can also be purchased through a margin loan facility. This usually does not cost anything to set up, although some lenders may charge a fee if you are using a company or trust structure for your investment, as they will have to perform document searches to set up the account.

Where shares are purchased through a margin loan facility, however, you will be required to pay interest to the lender on the amount of money you have borrowed.

Administration costs

An investment in property or shares requires you to maintain meticulous records of your investment activities. This is essential for taxation purposes, but also for your own benefit so that you can track the returns on your investments.

There are numerous ways of tracking your investments, from simple spreadsheets that you can create yourself, to accounting software such as Quicken, MYOB or Xero, which require you to input the data yourself, through to dedicated administration services provided by third party providers, such as PRAEMIUM, which will collate all your transactions automatically and reconcile them on your behalf.

Beyond this, there is also the cost of preparing your annual tax return through an accountant. How much your accountant charges will depend on how much work they have to do and the complexity of your investment structures, so it is likely to be cheaper if you provide your accountant with reliable investment tracking information in a format that they can use.

 Peter's property insights

There are many costs involved when you are a property investor, especially when buying property. The buying costs can add up to about 6 per cent of the purchase price, and the selling costs total about 4 per cent of the sale price. If you have borrowed money to purchase the property, you are probably negatively geared, as is shown in table 9.2 (see p. 104): $25 000 annual income and $32 000 in annual costs. That's a loss of $7000 per year. Thankfully these costs and losses can be used to offset some of your tax.

There is no doubt that shares win hands down when it comes to the costs involved in buying, holding and selling. This is one of the major disadvantages of purchasing property, but this needs to be considered alongside some of the advantages of property investment, namely leveraging, lower volatility and tax benefits, all of which are covered in this book.

Zac's share insights

The cost of buying, selling and owning shares is a lot less than for property. This means that you don't have to wait as long to recover your costs: your break-even price is a lot closer to the purchase price in percentage terms than it is for a property.

While the low transaction costs for buying and selling shares can be alluring, you should always remember that transaction costs can add up, especially if you are trading frequently rather than buying and holding. You also need to be aware of your break-even cost.

 ## Conclusion

Be aware of all costs involved in owning property and shares. If you are cost sensitive, some of these costs can be minimised or even eliminated if you are willing to do some of the work yourself—for property investment you could do the property management yourself. For shares, you could use a discount broker to handle the share transactions to keep costs low. But beware: property managers and brokers are engaged by clients because they assume that they are professional—that is, that they know more than the client and can do a better job than them.

Round 10

MARKET PARTICIPANTS AND FACILITATORS

A variety of professionals can help with buying, holding and selling property and shares. This chapter provides a list of these professionals and an outline of how they might be of service.

You will deal with different professionals whether buying, holding or selling property. Some you will have a long-term relationship with, such as your accountant or property manager, but you may only deal with some people once, such as the real estate agent that sells you the property. Let's look first at the professionals you can encounter when purchasing property.

★ ★ ★ ★ ★ ★ ★ **PROPERTY** ★ ★ ★ ★ ★ ★ ★

Buying property

You may need to consult or work with some or all of the following professionals when you buy a property.

Accountant

The accountant is critical in buying, holding and selling property. Before you sign a contract, you should consult with your accountant and discuss the investment structure that best suits you and your financial goals. They might advise you to buy the property in your own personal name or in joint names, or through a company, family trust or self managed superannuation fund, for instance. An accountant is qualified to give this advice as they understand your financial situation and your investment goals.

Banker

Your banker can organise the finance you need to purchase the property. They will require some documentation from you, including a statement of position, which will outline what you currently own and what you owe: in other words, your assets and liabilities. They will also require proof of your income and possibly a record of your expenditure. Your banker will of course only suggest loans or packages that the bank has on offer, unlike a mortgage broker.

Building inspector

If you are concerned about the integrity of the building structure, you should engage a building inspector to check this. To the untrained eye, a building may look fine, but a specialist such as a building inspector can detect building faults like cracks, water damage, dry rot and salt damp. The building inspector can also give you an indication of the cost to repair these faults. They should leave you with a written report detailing faults and outlining the costs of repairs, which you might be able to use as a bargaining tool in your negotiations to purchase the property at a discounted price.

Buyer's agent

As the name suggests, a buyer's agent works for the purchaser. Tasks that a buyer's agent can undertake include searching for properties according to criteria set by the purchaser, inspecting the properties and asking the selling agent probing questions in order to gather as much information as possible, undertaking an analysis of each of the selected properties to determine which property best fits the client's criteria, and discussing their findings with their client. If the client agrees that they wish to purchase the property, the buyer's agent can then negotiate the purchase of the property or bid at the auction.

Conveyancer

A conveyance is a paralegal professional trained and qualified to deal with some of the legal issues of property, in particular buying and selling. They operate in some states only. In states where there are no conveyancers, a lawyer can attend to this legal paperwork. A conveyancer's duties are numerous: they include preparation of the contract, organising searches of official government documents, making adjustments to rates and taxes, preparation of the transfer and settlement statement, liaising with the bank if you are borrowing money, arranging for the stamping of documents and subsequent stamp duty payment, registration of documents with the land titles office, and attending the settlement so as to exchange documents.

Lawyer

Lawyers are legal professionals trained and qualified to perform many duties, including the conveyancing tasks involved in buying and selling property (listed under Conveyancer previously). They can also set up legal entities such as trusts and companies if you and your accountant believe a property is best held in one of these entities.

Mortgage broker

Mortgage brokers conduct similar tasks to the banker, but their advantage is that they are not obliged to use the loans or packages from only one lending institution. If you use a mortgage broker, they can search hundreds of loans that are offered by many lenders. A banker will only suggest loans offered by their own bank. Brokers work for you and they can organise your application and determine which loan(s) are best for you, based on a number of criteria, including purpose for buying property, intended holding period, interest rate, conditions of loan, and fees. A mortgage broker is paid by the lending institution from which the money is borrowed, not by the client who takes out the loan.

Pest inspector

A pest inspection is commonly undertaken by prospective purchasers to determine the presence of pests, in particular termites (also known as white ants). Termites can cause significant damage, especially in buildings that contain timber, such as floorboards and wooden structural frames. This damage is often not visible to the naked or untrained eye, as it is underneath the surface of the floorboards or behind walls.

Qualified property investment adviser

At the time of writing, no legislation regulates property investment advice. Unlike buying shares or other financial products where professionals are required to be trained, educated, licensed and regulated, the same cannot be said for property investment advisers. However, an industry group known as the Property Investment Professionals of Australia (PIPA) has initiated a Qualified Property Investment Adviser (QPIA) qualification. This should provide consumers with peace of mind, as a QPIA is required to meet a minimum level of education in property, investment and advice, and is also required to undertake regular professional development. The unregulated property investment advice environment has unfortunately given rise to many scams (see Round 19 for a discussion of scams).

Quantity surveyor

A quantity surveyor is a qualified professional who can determine the cost of a building and the level of depreciation since its construction. They can provide the property investor with a depreciation schedule that details the attributes of the property and the written-down value of its components, such as the building, fixtures and fittings. This depreciation schedule should be provided to your accountant so that they claim on these depreciable items and increase any tax benefits available to the investor.

Valuer

A property valuer is a professional who can provide a formal valuation on a property. A valuer may be engaged by the lending institution if you are borrowing a large proportion of the purchase price. A valuer can also be hired by the purchaser to ensure that the asking price of a property is similar to its market value. A valuation is different to an appraisal, which is conducted by a real estate salesperson or agent. A valuation provides the definitive value of the property. It is based on recent comparable sales in the area. It is conducted by a qualified valuer for a fee. An appraisal is an estimation of the sale price of a property. Appraisals are conducted by real estate salespeople and agents, generally at no charge. (See the glossary for more information.)

Holding property

You may need to consult or work with some or all of the following professionals when you own a property. This will depend on whether you are lodging your own tax returns, managing your own property and are handy with a power tool!

Accountant

An accountant can prepare your annual tax return and maximise the tax benefits you can claim in order to minimise the tax payable by a property investor.

Property manager

A property manager is engaged to manage the property, including the day-to-day tasks. Duties undertaken by a property manager include advertising the property for rent, conducting open inspections, assessing applications from prospective tenants, assisting in the selection of a new tenant and placing the new tenant in the property. Routine tasks include the collection of rent, conducting regular inspections, dealing with issues such as repairs and maintenance, and keeping an account of rental income and expenditure. They also may need to deal with difficult tenants who are in breach of their lease and have to be evicted.

Handyperson

As in any home or building, repairs and maintenance need to be done from time to time. A dependable handyperson is worth their weight in gold! Knowing that someone can attend to breakdowns or issues in a timely manner and at a reasonable cost provides peace of mind to the investor. If you have engaged a property manager to oversee your property, they will probably have a handyperson that they use on a regular basis for all the rental properties on their list.

Selling property

You may need to refer to or consult with the following professionals. This will depend on whether you choose to sell your property yourself and do your own bookwork and tax returns.

Accountant

When selling an investment property, your accountant can calculate the capital gain or loss and also determine whether you are eligible for the capital gains tax (CGT) discount (there's more about CGT in Round 16).

Auctioneer

Many highly sought-after properties are sold through auction. The person that conducts the auction is known as the auctioneer. They can be the same person that is selling the property, or a specialist auctioneer engaged to conduct the auction while the real estate salesperson or agent assists on the day.

Real estate salesperson

This should be a trained salesperson. Currently, the training requirements vary from state to state but all sales people should be licensed. The real estate salesperson works for the vendor (seller) and tries to obtain the best possible sale price for them. The salesperson can advise on the most appropriate selling method, listing price or price range, and a marketing campaign. They will conduct inspections of the property, follow up on enquiries and present offers to the vendor for their consideration. They are not allowed to work without the supervision of a real estate agent. The commission a salesperson earns needs to be shared with the real estate agent, also known as the principal.

Real estate agent

This is the owner of the agency. A real estate agent has a higher level of training and education than a salesperson and is able to work for themselves, without supervision. They often have salespeople working for them and will share in the salesperson's commission in order to pay for costs such as administration staff, rent for the office and utilities. They will perform the same tasks as a real estate salesperson so as to sell the property for the highest price.

★ ★ ★ ★ ★ ★ ★ ★ **SHARES** ★ ★ ★ ★ ★ ★ ★ ★

Sharemarket participants and facilitators

Australia has one of the largest and fastest growing investment and funds management sectors in the world. Its growth is driven by the government-mandated superannuation contribution scheme, under which every salary- or wage-earner in Australia has 9 per cent of their gross salary directed into a superannuation fund. From 1 July 2013, this will increase each year (see table 10.1).

These funds are invested (directly or indirectly) in a range of assets, including cash, fixed interest, property or shares, in accordance with the fund's mandate.

Table 10.1: superannuation guarantee rates, 2013–14 to 2019–20

Year	Rate (%)
2013–14	9.25
2014–15	9.50
2015–16	10.00
2016–17	10.50
2017–18	11.00
2018–19	11.50
2019–20	12.00

The sharemarket in Australia is not a physical market. It is a market by virtue of the fact that it brings together buyers and sellers in a regulated medium of exchange. All buying and selling transactions are matched by a sophisticated computer system.

There are numerous market participants in the sharemarket and each has their own reason for participation.

Retail investors

Commonly referred to as 'mum and dad' investors, retail investors are ordinary individuals who invest directly (in their own names) or indirectly (through their superannuation funds) in the sharemarket. Approximately 6.7 million people (41 per cent of the adult Australian population) own shares, 36 per cent of which is through direct ownership. Investors have a long-term objective, holding their investments from a few years to a few decades.

Retail traders

These are individuals who buy and sell shares to profit from the short-term price moves in the market. They own their shares for only a short time, ranging from a few minutes to a few weeks.

Stockbrokers

Stockbrokers are licensed Australian Securities Exchange (ASX) market participants who execute purchase and sale transactions on behalf of investors in return for a service fee (brokerage). The term broker is now more commonly used to describe the firm you are dealing through, whereas previously it was used to describe the person you dealt with. About 80 broking firms are authorised to trade on the ASX. As an investor, you can choose to make your own decisions and just use the stockbroking firm to execute your orders. In this instance, you would use a non-advisory broking service (a discount or execution-only broker). The other option is to take advice from a professional adviser who works for an advisory stockbroking firm (full-service broker) and have them place the order for you.

Margin lenders

A margin loan is a loan that is set up to enable you to borrow money to invest in shares and managed funds. With a deposit of between 25 and 70 per cent of the cost of buying the shares (depending on the type of share you wish to invest in), you borrow the rest from a margin lender and pay the lender an interest rate, typically at a rate about 2 to 3 per cent more than the standard variable home loan rate. Most banks offer margin lending facilities, with the biggest lenders being Leveraged Equities, BT and Colonial Geared Investments.

Financial planners and other intermediary advisers

Financial planners and other intermediary advisers manage their clients' investment portfolios on their behalf and provide advice on how to best structure your investments. Intermediary advisers are advisers who use the services of a stockbroker to transact on behalf of their clients.

Institutional investors

This is the generic term given to investment management companies that manage assets on behalf of investors, including superannuation fund managers and managed investment funds. There are more than 130 of these firms in Australia. A significant institutional investor is the Future Fund, an Australian government fund that began investing in mid-2007 to provide for the future superannuation payments of public servants.

Boutiques and hedge funds

These are investment firms established by an experienced individual or group of individuals to focus on a particular investment strategy or niche, and typically charge performance fees. Hedge funds in particular can make investments that allow them to profit from the market rising or falling.

Listed investment companies (LICs)

These are companies listed on the stock exchange that exist to invest in other listed companies on behalf of their shareholders. The largest of these LICs includes Argo Investments and Australian Foundation Investments. Profits come from their skill in investing in other companies. They give an investor exposure to the sharemarket without the investor having to make decisions on what companies to buy.

Exchange traded funds (ETFs)

ETFs are investment funds that are traded on stock exchanges just like listed shares. ETFs are becoming popular investment alternatives to managed funds. ETFs buy shares in proportion to their weighting on the sharemarket, as measured by, for example, a stock or bond index, or a commodity, such as gold or oil. The fund buys and sells the underlying assets, such as stocks, commodities or bonds, so that the ETF trades close to the net asset value (being the market value of the underlying investments, less the liabilities). ETFs do not rely on a fund manager to make investment decisions: the ETF will buy and sell the underlying assets during the day in order to maintain its net asset value in proportion to the underlying index it is tracking.

Research providers

Many investors rely on a combination of their own ideas based on research they do themselves and also on their adviser's recommendations. Share research is available from stockbroking firms, which often have their own in-house research departments; and from external independent research companies, such as Morningstar, Lonsec, Canstar, Rainmaker, SuperRatings and Van Eyk Research.

Platform administrators

These are retail superannuation or investment funds that hold investments on behalf of their investors. A retail fund is one that an investor can choose to invest in directly with a nominal amount of money (for example, $1000), as compared with a wholesale fund, which requires a significantly higher minimum investment (for example, $100 000). Investing through a platform can make these wholesale funds more accessible to retail investors. The major platform administrators are dominated by domestic financial institutions such as BT, Macquarie, MLC, AMP, ANZ and Colonial Group.

Custodians

These institutions hold assets on behalf of investors such as super funds and managed funds. A custodian has title to the fund assets, but investment management remains with the trustees. This structure is intended to provide administrative efficiencies, bringing together the investment portfolios of a number of funds by collecting income, reporting on asset values and so on. The major custodian firms in Australia include National Custodian, JPMorgan, BNP Paribas, Citigroup and State Street.

Share registries

These registries manage and maintain a listed company's share register on the company's behalf and also provide a range of related services, such as coordinating share dividend payments. There are five main registry companies in Australia: Advanced Share Registry Services, Boardroom, Security Transfer Registrars, Link Market Services, and Computershare Services. Only a handful of listed companies still maintain their own share register.

CHESS (Clearing House Electronic Subregister System)

CHESS is an electronic book-entry register of the holdings of listed shares. It is managed by ASX Settlement and Transfer Corporation (ASTC), part of the ASX. CHESS facilitates the transfer and settlement of market transactions between CHESS participants (including stockbrokers on behalf of their clients, and large institutional investors on their own behalf), and speeds up the registration of the transfer of securities. When you open a new account with a stockbroker, you will have the choice of becoming CHESS-sponsored through your stockbroker. Essentially this means that all your shareholdings with that broker will be brought together under one Shareholder Identification Number (HIN), making it easy to identify and keep up to date with your shareholdings.

If you choose not to be CHESS-sponsored, each of your share purchases will be held under a unique Shareholder Reference Number (SRN) that you will have to provide to your stockbroker when you wish to sell your shares.

Peter's property insights

Some investors choose to do their own tax, manage their own rental property and even sell their property without the use of a salesperson or agent. Whom you decide to use will depend on how much time you have, your level of expertise and how much money you are willing to pay for these services. Some professionals will cost you hundreds of dollars; others will cost you thousands. When you consider that you are buying property that costs hundreds of thousands (or millions) of dollars, these fees may be relatively insignificant in the big picture, but these professionals can assist you in saving money initially and hopefully by making more money for you than if you tried to do it yourself.

Zac's share insights

You can choose to make your own decisions and place your own transactions, or use a professional to do it for you. The value of using a suitably experienced and qualified professional cannot be underestimated. I have seen many people make the wrong investment decisions themselves, just to save a few dollars. It has ended up costing them significantly more. Unlike buying or selling a property, when you buy or sell shares on the sharemarket you are not always transacting with just one buyer or seller. For example, if you are buying 1000 shares in Commonwealth Bank at $62.00, those 1000 shares could be sold to you by many different sellers who are prepared to sell their shares at $62.00.

 ## Conclusion

Market participants and facilitators should be considered as a team of people you can consult to buy, hold or sell property and shares. Not all investors will consult all the facilitators listed here, but what must be remembered is that most of them are trained and educated professionals abiding by a code of conduct and, in many cases, they are regulated by an authority (such as the ASX) or government. They exist to help you make informed decisions and assist you on your investment journey. (See Round 19 for more information on choosing trustworthy professionals and avoiding scams.)

Always ensure that you understand exactly what they are advising you to do, understand what it is you are buying, the risks involved, and ensure that they have considered an exit strategy for the investment—the point at which you will sell your investment.

Round 11

MANAGED INVESTMENTS

Owning assets such as property and shares can be time consuming. Some investors lead busy lives and don't have the time to manage their portfolios, and others prefer to leave the management of their assets to professionals.

If an investor prefers to have their assets managed by a professional, they are able to do so — at a cost. A share investor can buy shares through managed funds, managed investment schemes and listed investment companies, for example. If a property investor prefers a hands-off approach, they commonly invest in property trusts or property syndicates.

★ ★ ★ ★ ★ ★ ★ PROPERTY ★ ★ ★ ★ ★ ★ ★

Let's first have a look at property trusts and then move on to property syndicates.

Property trusts

A listed property trust (also known as a real estate investment trust, or REIT), buys property (generally commercial property) and then manages it on behalf of the investors. REITs exist all over the world. I won't try to discuss all of the different types of REITs around the globe, as there are far too many of them. I will just focus on Australian REITs.

An Australian real estate investment trust (A-REIT), is listed on the Australian Securities Exchange (ASX). You can buy units in the REIT through the ASX. Units are very similar to shares, except that you buy units in a unit trust and shares in a company. Either way, you own a proportionate part of the trust or company. You can buy and sell your units in the trust, just as easily as you can buy and sell shares in an ASX-listed company.

Some trusts focus on a particular sector of commercial property, such as retail, industrial or office, whereas others are diversified and invest in a mixture of property types. For example, the Westfield Retail Trust is one of the best-known A-REITs. Its focus is primarily on retail property, particularly shopping centres.

Real estate investment trusts are in some ways better than owning property yourself (also called direct property investment). Some of the advantages to buying into A-REITs include:

- *Quick and easy access to your capital.* It can take weeks and even months to sell a directly owned property investment; you can sell your units in an A-REIT in a matter of minutes. You can also sell part of your investment in an A-REIT, whereas with direct property you have to sell the whole asset, even if you only want part of your cash.

- *Low cost of entry.* A-REITs provide you with the opportunity to buy a share of a large commercial property portfolio for a relatively small amount of money. Compare that with direct property, where you need hundreds of thousands of dollars to invest. If you purchased, say, $1000 worth of units in the Westfield Retail Trust, it would entitle you to a small portion of the profit from the Westfield shopping centres and any other activities this A-REIT might be involved in.

- *Low cost of entry and exit.* You need to add an extra 6 per cent of the purchase price when buying property to cover costs such as government and banking fees, and another 4 per cent of the selling price to pay fees for the real estate agent, advertising, and so on (see Round 9). Compare this with the 1 per cent buying costs and 1 per cent selling costs if you invest in an A-REIT through a broker. Buying can be even cheaper if you do it yourself online!

- *Easier to diversify and spread your risk.* Purchasing property directly usually requires a large sum of money to put towards just one property. With A-REITs you can easily diversify your funds, and consequently your risk. For example, you don't have to put all your money into the Westfield Retail Trust. You could put just 25 per cent into Westfield, another 25 per cent of your money towards a property trust that focuses on industrial property, a further 25 per cent in an office property trust, and another 25 per cent into a trust that invests in airports (the percentages and sectors I have used are just examples—a multitude of REITs are available to invest in and you can allocate your funds to suit your own needs).

- *Exposure to a high-yielding sector.* Commercial property can provide investors with higher yields than residential property. The opportunity to achieve a higher relative return on your money is very appealing to investors. Of course, the higher return comes with a higher risk. The risk with A-REITs is that their value can drop as quickly as share prices, leaving investors with a lower level of capital than they originally invested. However, diversification across different properties or sectors can mitigate some risk.

- *Appeal for retirees.* A-REITs are particularly appealing to retirees, as the trusts are required by law to distribute all their profits. This compares favourably with investment in a listed company, such as News Corporation, which might decide to distribute only half of its profits to investors and use the other half to expand the company. This is great for retirees, who tend to be more concerned with income than capital growth.

Property syndicates

Property syndicates operate quite differently to A-REITs. A property syndicate can take a number of forms but it is basically a group of people who pool their money, develop property, lease it and then sell it.

Let's use an example to clarify the difference between syndicates and trusts, using a fictitious property syndicate, the Oreo Property Syndicate.

The Oreo Property Syndicate is made up of 10 investors, who have each put in $250 000 to buy some land, build a small shopping centre, lease it out and sell it after five years. At the end of the five-year lease period the investors will hopefully get all their money back, plus their share of the profits.

From this brief example, some differences with A-REITS are obvious:

- You needed $250 000 to invest in the property syndicate, whereas you could buy into an A-REIT for as little as $1000.

- In the property syndicate you might have to wait more than five years to make any profit. In A-REITs, you can buy and sell units within minutes.

- In the Oreo Property Syndicate, you have to deal with nine other investors. With an A-REIT, the management group takes care of the day-to-day activities and the administration.

- To be listed on the stock exchange, all companies must pass rigid tests and abide by strict regulations. This is not necessarily the case with all property syndicates, as they are by nature unlisted.

If you want to invest in property syndicates or property trusts, you need to get some independent professional advice before you invest your hard-earned money.

★ ★ ★ ★ ★ ★ ★ ★ **SHARES** ★ ★ ★ ★ ★ ★ ★ ★

Managed investments

Managed investments is the name given to financial products in which an investor's assets are managed by someone else. There are broadly three categories of managed investments: managed funds, exchange traded funds (EFTs) and listed investment trusts.

Managed funds

Managed funds have been the more common way that financial planners have recommended their clients access investment markets. For many investors, managed funds are a convenient way to invest, because they don't involve the time-consuming management required by hands-on investing.

A managed fund is essentially an investment structure, where your money is pooled with that of many other individual investors and is managed by a professional fund manager. These funds are then invested in different asset classes, such as shares, property or bonds, in accordance with the mandate of the fund. You can choose the type of fund you wish to invest in, and this will largely be influenced by your investor risk profile and also your financial goals.

When you invest in a managed fund you're allocated a number of units in the unit trust, making you a unitholder. Each unit represents an equal amount of the market value of the fund.

During the year the managed fund may earn income in the form of dividends or interest, and may benefit from growth in the value of the fund's investments. It may also make profits on any investments it sells.

Different investment styles adopted by a managed fund include:

- *A passive investment style.* The fund manager does not attempt to predict which investments will do well, and so simply follows an index such as the ASX 200, purchasing shares in proportion to their weighting in the index.

- *An active investment style.* The fund manager aims to consistently outperform the market by attempting to predict which companies, industries or countries will out perform indexes or other benchmarks, and investing in those areas.

The various types of managed investments can help you diversify your portfolio to achieve different investment sector allocations.

Managed investments can be grouped according to four main criteria:

- *The fund's tax structure.* Whether it is a superannuation fund (including rollover funds), or a trust (most managed funds are unit trusts), insurance bond, friendly society bond, term allocated pension, or allocated pension or annuity.

- *The fund's investment asset mandate.* Whether the fund invests in income (cash or fixed interest) or whether it is an equity fund (that invests in shares or property), or a multisector fund (one that does not fit into the other categories of income or equity).

- *The fund's geographical investment mandate.* What countries the fund invests in: such as Australia, the United States, Japan, the European Community, South East Asia, or the emerging BRIC countries (Brazil, Russia, India and China).

- *The fund's investor type.* Whether it is a retail, wholesale or corporate fund.

Managed funds do have some benefits:

- *You can start investing with a small amount.* Investors who have access to a small amount of money to invest can initially use managed funds to gain exposure to the investment markets.

- *Diversification.* You can choose the type of fund you wish to invest in and spread your risk over several asset classes, or different types of funds. You can also diversify your portfolio through buying into funds that invest in different companies, industries, sectors and countries.

- *Professional management.* Your investment funds are managed professionally, by fund managers who have years of experience and who have specialist qualifications and knowledge of a particular style of investment or sector.

- *Protection.* Managed investments are regulated by the Australian Prudential Regulation Authority (APRA) and the Australian Securities and Investments Commission (ASIC). But this doesn't mean you cannot lose money if the fund manager makes bad investment decisions!

- *Access to a broader range of products.* Your fund has access to sophisticated investment products, such as options and futures (discussed further in Round 22).

The disadvantages of managed funds can, however, outweigh the benefits:

- *Management fees (also called management expense ratios, or MERs).* These costs are a percentage of the amount of money invested; they can be high and even exceed the returns of the fund.

- *Fund manager risk.* If the fund relies on the expertise of one or more individuals, and they leave the fund, the new incumbent(s) may not have the same level of experience and expertise as the previous manager(s).

- *Lack of transparency.* You don't always know what assets the fund holds.

- *You don't own the underlying assets.* This means you are not entitled to traditional shareholder benefits, such as franking credits, or voting rights.

- *Liquidity can be a problem.* Your funds are not always readily available and, as some investors discovered during the GFC, if there is a run on the fund by investors, the fund may put a hold on withdrawals, meaning you may not be able to obtain your money when you want it if the fund has to sell down assets to finance investor withdrawals.

Exchange traded funds (ETFs)

An exchange traded fund (ETF) is an investment fund that is traded on the stock exchange. Just like a managed fund, an ETF can invest in virtually any asset according to its mandate, such as shares, property, fixed interest products, commodities, foreign currency, or even along themes, such as emerging markets or geographic locations. Most ETFs, however, will track an index, such as a share index.

ETFs have only recently started to gain favour with investors and advisers in Australia, and the ETF's share-like features, low cost, transparency and liquidity make ETFs attractive to investors. As more ETFs have been introduced to the Australian sharemarket over the last few years, there has been a notable transition out of managed funds and into ETFs by many investors.

The major ETF providers in Australia are State Street, iShares, BetaShares and Vanguard.

An ETF combines the valuation feature of a managed fund or unit trust (priced based on the net asset valuations of their underlying holdings), which can be bought or sold at the end of each trading day for its net asset value, with the ease of trading a share.

As a result an ETF trades during the trading day at prices that may be more or less than its net asset value.

Listed investment companies and trusts

Listed investment companies (LICs) and listed investment trusts (LITs) give investors an opportunity to invest in a diversified portfolio of investments, such as Australian shares, international shares, private equity and even specialist sectors, such as resources.

The primary difference between the two is that LICs are closed-end structures: this means they don't regularly issue new shares as investors join or leave the fund, so investors have to buy and sell shareholdings in the underlying LIC on the sharemarket, and therefore don't influence the capital invested by the fund. LICs manage the investment portfolio and produce regular income to investors as fully franked dividends.

A LIT, however, operates as a listed unit trust. It can have an open-ended structure, so that as investors buy or sell units in the LIT, the units on issue can vary. The counterparty to the investment transaction is the trust itself.

There may be differences in the way LIT and LIC dividends and distributions are taxed. LITs, being trusts, are obliged to pay out all their surplus income in the form of distributions—and also carry through to investors the franking levels on the underlying shares. LICs, being companies, can choose to retain some surplus income, and their distributions are paid out as dividends.

There are four categories of LICs and LITs based on the assets they invest in:

- Australian shares, investing principally in shares listed on ASX
- international shares, investing principally in shares listed on international stock exchanges
- private equity, investing in Australian or international unlisted private companies
- specialist, investing in special assets or investment sectors, such as wineries, technology companies, resources, and telecommunications.

The investment strategy and operational characteristics can differ from one entity to the next, as can their investment approach—ranging from very conservative to aggressive. The investment manager may either be internal (employed by the company) or external, where a separate entity manages the portfolio under contract to the company.

When it comes to selecting a LIC or a LIT, an investor needs to assess the fund managers' attributes, investment style and underlying investment portfolio to see whether it matches their own investment objectives.

Peter's property insights

Owning property is a great way to create wealth. However, you don't have to invest in property directly. You can purchase units in a property trust, or you could choose to become part of a property syndicate and share in the profits (or losses!). Each option has its advantages and disadvantages.

Zac's share insights

For time-poor investors, a managed investment can be the ideal way of investing. Managed funds and listed investment companies (LICs) are used by people who want to outsource the investment decisions to someone else in accordance with the fund's mandate. But as a result of relatively high fees and poor performance (particularly through the GFC), as well as a general lack of transparency as to the fund holdings, these products are now slowly being overtaken by exchange traded funds (ETFs). As more ETFs are introduced to the Australian market, investors can more easily gain exposure to a sector, the market, a specific investment theme (such as emerging markets, commodities or currencies), or even hedge their entire portfolio with a single transaction.

 ## Conclusion

Managed investments are an option taken up by many property and share investors for a variety of reasons. They may not have the time to manage their assets; they may feel they don't have the expertise to directly invest in these assets; or they just don't want to be hassled with the day-to-day effort of owning property or shares. Many of the advantages of managed investments over direct ownership of property or shares have been outlined in this chapter. However, you also need to realise there can be some disadvantages. One of the main disadvantages is that you lose some control over your assets.

Managed investments are not for everyone but they just might suit your investment style.

★ ★

Round 12

TRADING Vs INVESTING

In much of the financial literature, a distinction is drawn between investing and trading. The main difference is that an investment time frame is over a long period (years) whereas trading can occur within seconds in the case of the sharemarket, and within just a few weeks or months in the case of property. Both trading and investing are valid ways of making money, but generally speaking, trading is inherently riskier. One of the reasons that (short-term) trading is riskier than (long-term) investing is that the trader doesn't have time on their side to make up for any mistakes they might make as an investor would have.

★ ★ ★ ★ ★ ★ ★ **PROPERTY** ★ ★ ★ ★ ★ ★ ★

Investing in property

When most people invest in property, it generally means that they buy property and hold it for a number of years. There is no doubt that this can be the best way to make money in property, as there are fewer and lower transaction fees and no capital gains tax liabilities, unlike trading in property.

The most common reason people will buy and hold property is to achieve the goal of retiring richer. Following is an illustration of how buying and holding property can assist in creating a wealthier retirement.

Real value

If you bought a $480500 property, borrowed the whole amount and took out a 20-year principal and interest loan, you would own a freehold property in 20 years' time.

But how much will this property be worth in 20 years' time? If we take a historical point of view and base our figures on property doubling in value every 10 years, this property will be worth $1.92 million in 20 years' time. Unfortunately, due to inflation, having $1.92 million in 20 years' time is not the same as having $1.92 million today.

The more important question is 'How much will this property be worth in today's money?'—that is, take out the inflationary component. *In today's money*, a $480500 property today will be worth $700000 in 20 years' time.

The reason this $480500 property grows in 'real' terms (in economic speak, 'real' means excluding inflation) is that, historically, property increases on average at 2 per cent above the inflation rate. As mentioned in Round 2, one of the reasons investors buy property is because it is a great hedge against inflation.

How much will I need in retirement?

If your goal is to retire comfortably, you first need to ask yourself 'How much will I need in retirement?'

Many financial planners and retirement experts suggest you should have a lump sum equal to 14 times your salary to retire on.

Let's assume that your current income is $50000 per year.

This means that you should be aiming for a retirement nest-egg of $700000.

Example

This example is based on using direct property ownership to achieve a $700 000 lump sum to fund retirement.

Assumptions

In order to keep the example simple, I have made some assumptions:

- The mortgage will be paid off at the end of the loan period.

- The property is bought in a self managed superannuation fund to minimise or eliminate capital gains tax.

- At the end of the 20-year period, you sell the property, place the proceeds in a high-interest term deposit within your self managed superannuation fund and live off the proceeds.

Capital growth

Table 12.1 is an illustration of this example.

Table 12.1: increase in value of a $480 500 property over 20 years, growing at 2 per cent per year above the inflation rate (all values in today's dollars)

Years to retirement	Value of property ($)
1	700 000
2	686 274
3	672 818
4	659 625
5	646 691
6	634 011
7	621 579

Years to retirement	Value of property ($)
8	609 391
9	597 442
10	585 728
11	574 243
12	562 983
13	551 944
14	541 122
15	530 511
16	520 109
17	509 911
18	499 912
19	490 110
20	480 500

Table 12.1 shows that if you bought a property worth $480 500 20 years before you planned to give up working, it would be worth $700 000 (in today's money) upon your retirement. This would allow you to live a comfortable lifestyle if you placed the proceeds in a high-interest term deposit and you were happy to retire on the equivalent of $50 000 per year.

This example shows how investing in property can help the investor achieve the long-term goal of retiring richer. As will be shown next, trading in property can provide short-term profits.

Trading property

Trading in property is most commonly done through renovating and developing. These two activities can provide the investor with a supplementary income, the option of working part time or, if they are very successful, the option of giving up their day job and making money through renovating or developing property full time.

The following example illustrates how renovating and developing can help achieve some shorter term goals.

Property renovation

The most common approach to trading property as a way to supplement income is renovating. This involves buying a property that requires updating or upgrading, fixing it up and then selling.

Example

This example shows how you could make money from renovating a $400 000 property.

Assumptions

- Purchase a property worth $400 000.

- Purchase costs are 6 per cent of the purchase price ($24 000).

- Spend no more than 10 per cent of the purchase price on renovations ($40 000).

- Hold the property for five months while renovations are underway.

- Borrow all the money at an interest rate of 6.0 per cent per year.

- Total selling costs are approximately 4 per cent of the final selling price.

- Receive gross profit of 15 per cent on all costs.
- Current income is $80 000 per year.

Feasibility

Table 12.2 demonstrates the feasibility of the renovation; the figures are based on the assumptions we have, noted and this results in a gross profit of $75 000.

Table 12.2: basic feasibility study for a renovation

Cost	Amount ($)
Purchase price	400 000
Purchase costs (6 per cent of purchase price)	24 000
Renovating costs (no more than 10 per cent of purchase price)	40 000
Holding costs (6 per cent interest for 5 months)	10 000
Total selling costs (about 4 per cent of selling price)	21 000
Total costs	**495 000**
Profit 15 per cent (gross)	**75 000**
Final sale price	**570 000**

In the example shown in table 12.2, a $75 000 gross profit was made over a period of five months. However, tax will have to be paid on this profit. If you earn $80 000 in your day job, you may need to pay approximately $28 000 in tax, which will leave you with $47 000. However, an after-tax profit of $47 000 in just five months is still pretty good!

Property development

The riskiest but possibly most rewarding way to make money in the short term is through property development. Property development is basically finding land suitable for development, building property and then selling it.

Example

This example demonstrates how you could make money through property development.

Assumptions

- Purchase land worth $400 000.

- Purchase costs are 6 per cent of the purchase price.

- You need to demolish a small, old home on the block.

- Subdivide the allotment into two smaller parcels so that each new dwelling is on its own title.

- Costs are $1500 per square metre to build (including landscaping, fencing, house fixtures and fittings), and each dwelling is 150 square metres in size.

- The development time frame is 12 months (including council approvals and time to settle on the new properties).

- Development finance is slightly more expensive than a typical home loan: say 7 per cent per year.

- Selling costs are discounted as the agent will sell both properties and they are located next door to each other.

- Receive a gross profit of 20 per cent on all costs.

- Current income is $80 000 per year.

- GST is applicable, as you are creating new property.

Feasibility

Table 12.3 shows the feasibility of the development plan; it uses the assumptions we have outlined and it results in a gross profit of $200 000.

Table 12.3: basic feasibility study for a property development

Cost	Amount ($)
Land purchase	400 000
Purchase costs (6 per cent of purchase price)	24 000
Demolition costs (remove one old small home)	20 000
Subdivision costs	20 000
Building costs ($1500 m^2, 2 x 150 m^2 homes)	450 000
Holding costs (7 per cent interest for 12 months)	50 000
Selling costs (3 per cent of final sale price)	36 000
Total development costs	1 000 000
Profit 20 per cent (gross)	200 000
Final sale price	1 200 000 (600 000 each)

A total of $200 000 gross profit was made on this project, which took 12 months from time of purchase of land to settlement on both new dwellings. As a profit has been made, tax will be paid and in this property development, GST is also applicable. Once you have paid your GST liability and tax on the profits, you could be left with just under $100 000.

★ ★ ★ ★ ★ ★ ★ ★ SHARES ★ ★ ★ ★ ★ ★ ★ ★

Investment in shares

We have stated repeatedly in this book that successful investing requires you to know *what* to buy, *when* to buy, and also *when* to sell.

Most people understand investing in the sharemarket to be buying shares for longer term capital growth or income, or both. An investment in a fundamentally good share should, over time, provide the potential for significant capital growth.

What causes a share price to increase in value over the long term is based on the fundamentals and prospects of the company. This can be driven by many things specific to the company and the sector, its products and its management, but ultimately it is the perception or expectation amongst investors of that company's potential to provide shareholders with greater profits in the future that will motivate them to buy shares in that company.

As an investor you have to decide *why* you are investing in the first place — are you investing for capital growth or for income, or both? Income funds your lifestyle whereas growth creates wealth for you. No investment will provide unlimited capital growth forever, and a company's fortunes can change as its business, its environment or its management changes. Therefore you should have an exit strategy for every investment you hold.

Remember that it is only when you sell your investment that you actually realise the capital gains on your investment, and only then can you utilise them.

Very often investors become emotionally attached to their investments and do not contemplate selling their shares. They tend to hold their share investments during market uptrends and downtrends, giving up valuable unrealised capital gains in return for a cash-flow stream of dividends. This buy-and-hold approach to investment is commonly how most investors approach share investment—as passive investors.

Active investors, however, have an objective of remaining invested in a share while the underlying sharemarket trend is up, and will sell their share investments when they have identified that the market trend has changed. They also look for opportunities to repurchase their shares when they feel that the market trend is reversing again. They do this in order to try to realise the maximum capital gain that they can make on their investment. A drawback of this active management approach is that you can get out too soon, leaving potential capital gains behind; there is also the cost of commissions on transactions, which can erode the profits you make.

Figures 12.1 and 12.2 (overleaf) compare an active and a passive investment approach on an investment in ANZ. Figure 12.1 shows the prices at which an active investor bought and sold their shares; figure 12.2 shows the price at which a passive investor purchased their shares, and also how they held onto their shares during the GFC. Tables 12.4 (overleaf) and 12.5 (see p. 145) outline the costs and profit of the two approaches.

Figure 12.1: example of an active investment strategy in ANZ shares

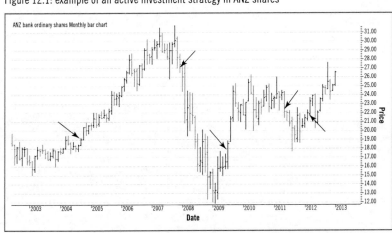

Source: Hubb Investor charting software, www.hubb.com.

Figure 12.2: example of a passive investment strategy in ANZ shares

Source: Hubb Investor charting software, www.hubb.com.

Table 12.4: example of returns on an active investment strategy in ANZ shares, 2004 to 2013

Active investment			Capital gain	Dividends	Total return
30-Sep-04	Buy	19.02			
31-Dec-07	Sell	27.46	8.44	4.72	13.16
31-Jul-09	Buy	18.53			
31-May-11	Sell	22.13	3.60	2.46	6.06
21-Feb-12	Buy	21.95			
29-Jan-13	Sell	26.51	4.56	1.45	6.01
		Total	16.60	8.63	**25.23**

Tables 12.4 and 12.5 show that an active investor would have outperformed a buy-and-hold investor using a passive investment strategy over the same period, had they made the investment decision to purchase ANZ shares on the same date, 30 September 2004, and both decided to sell their shareholdings on 29 January 2013.

Table 12.5: example of returns on a passive investment strategy in ANZ shares, 2004 to 2013

Passive investment			Capital gain	Dividends	Total return
30-Sep-04	Buy	19.02			
29-Jan-13	Sell	26.51	7.49	11.21	18.70
		Total	7.49	11.21	**18.70**

An active investor aims to outperform the passive investor's buy-and-hold strategy by realising valuable capital gains as the market changes trend, whereas a passive investor has the objective of maintaining an income stream through their dividend payments. The passive investor is willing to ride out the market trends up and down due to their underlying opinion that the company will continue to provide shareholder value in the future.

Ultimately, the decision of when to sell a share investment will be driven by whether you choose to manage your share investments actively or passively—and that will depend on many factors, including how much time you have to manage your investments, how much confidence you have to analyse and act on market trend changes, the amount of commissions you will be charged to buy and sell, and of course the taxation consequences of making capital gains and losses. This is a personal decision that only you can make, based on your own investment needs and goals, or in consultation with your financial adviser.

Trading shares

In contrast to longer term investing, professional, and even amateur, traders choose to take a much shorter term view on a company's share price. Their objective is to profit from short-term overreactions in price movement, and they are willing to take a large number of smaller profits trading in and out of shorter term price trends.

Traders are usually unconcerned with a company's fundamental information, focusing instead more heavily on price and volume trends. They usually will analyse a company's share price and volume charts looking for short-term trends or potential reversals in prices, price momentum and volume.

Trading in shares can be of many types—usually defined by the duration of the trade intra-day traders (or day-traders), who will rarely hold a share overnight, through to position traders, who may hold a position in a share for days or weeks before exiting the trade.

Differences between share investing and share trading

The main differences between share investing and share trading are as follows.

- Investors rely on fundamental analysis factors that affect the long-term view of a company (company financials, company research and valuations, the prospects of the company, and so on), while traders make decisions based on taking advantage of shorter term price movements.

- Investors are interested in slow, steady portfolio growth, and also in benefitting from dividends, whereas a trader isn't necessarily interested in dividends—just short-term price moves.

- Investors will typically hold a portfolio of 10 to 20 different shares over a long-term time frame, whereas traders will usually hold fewer shares and buy and sell them frequently.

- Investors usually see lower prices of quality shares as an opportunity to acquire fundamentally good shares at a cheap price for the longer term, while traders see lower prices as an opportunity to make money from a declining market by (short) selling shares at a high price with the intention of buying them back at a lower price later. This concept is called short selling (discussed further in Round 22).

- Investors seek higher gains from fewer transactions (and pay fewer commissions), whereas traders seek smaller gains from more transactions (and are likely to pay more brokerage).

- Investors seek to create wealth and a passive income stream from their share investments, whereas traders are more concerned with generating regular or additional income.

Peter's property insights

Due to the relatively high transaction costs involved, trading in property can be very costly. If you also add the burden of a GST liability, which might be applicable in a property development, net profit can be less than half of the total gross profit. However, trading in property can provide a supplementary income or even give people the option of cutting back work hours or give up their day job.

Zac's share insights

Trading shares certainly seems a lot sexier than longer term investing. While on paper it has a greater potential for reward than investing for the long term, the reality is that this potential for greater reward comes with greater risk. Despite the attraction to take a trade with lower entry and exit fees (commissions) or take a trade using a discount broker, to be a successful trader requires significant education and experience, and unlike what you would expect, a trader requires a larger amount of money available to them with which to trade. Many people who set out to trade shares fail, largely because they are undercapitalised, or because they are unprepared for the emotional effects (stress) of how they will react to the short-term moves in the market.

Investing may seem boring on the surface, but ultimately it can be a smarter and less stressful way of building wealth over time.

 ## Conclusion

We encourage people to invest their money for the longer term; trading is not for everyone. You must understand the risks involved and that profits will be eroded through transaction costs (especially in property) and taxes. However, if your goal is to make money in the short term, trading in property and shares can be very profitable.

★ ★ ★ ★ ★ ★ ★ ★ ★ ★ ★ ★ ★ ★ ★ ★ ★ ★ ★ ★

Round 13

FINANCING YOUR INVESTMENT

Borrowing money to buy assets allows you to buy more property and shares than you could otherwise afford. For example, if you had $40 000 in cash and earned 3 per cent per year in interest in a term deposit, you would earn $1200 in one year ($40 000 × 3 per cent). However, if you used this $40 000 towards the purchase of a $400 000 property and the property increased in value by 3 per cent in one year, the value of your asset will have increased by $12 000 ($400 000 × 3 per cent). This is ten times the profit you would have made if all you did was place your $40 000 in a term deposit. Imagine if the property increased by 10 per cent in one year. You would be $40 000 richer just by leveraging, or using borrowed money, to buy assets!

However, borrowed money can also work against the investor. If you borrowed money to buy the $400 000 property and it dropped in value by 10 per cent, you would lose $40 000. As a result of this drop in value, the property you own is now worth only $360 000. This means you have lost your $40 000.

The same can be said for leveraging to buy shares, except the gains (and losses) can be greater, as the price of shares fluctuate much more than property.

The use of borrowed money gives you leverage—magnifying your potential gains, but also bringing with it greater risk as it magnifies the potential loss. However, without leveraging your money, it is almost impossible to achieve your investment goals.

★ ★ ★ ★ ★ ★ ★ **PROPERTY** ★ ★ ★ ★ ★ ★ ★

Property loans

Following is an overview of the common types of loans and their advantages and disadvantages. Two beneficial features of loans are also discussed.

Types of loan

If you want to borrow money to buy property, you have many lenders to choose from, and a number of different loan options. All of the loans detailed here offer principal and interest, or interest-only repayment options.

Principal and interest (P & I) loan

Every mortgage repayment on this loan includes an interest component plus some of the original capital (principal) you borrowed. If you took out a 30-year principal and interest (P & I) loan, you would have paid off the mortgage at the end of the 30 years and the property would be yours. This is the most common form of loan. It can be either on a fixed or variable interest rate, and it is the loan most borrowers feel comfortable with. However, many investors will opt for interest-only loans, as the repayments are lower (no principal payments required), which helps improve their cash flow.

- *For.* Your loan will be paid off at the end of the term.

- *Against.* Your weekly, fortnightly, or monthly repayments are higher than if you had an interest-only loan.

Interest-only (IO) loan

With this type of loan you don't make any repayments of the principal. If you borrowed $300 000 to buy a $400 000 house and had an interest-only loan for a total of 30 years, at the end of this period you would still owe the bank $300 000. These are popular with investors because they know their property will be worth much more in 30 years' time ($3.2 million if the property value doubles every 10 years). Paying off $300 000 is only a comparatively small portion of the value of the property in 30 years' time. As investors are able to claim their interest payments as a tax deduction, there is no urgency for them to pay off the loan.

- *For.* Lower repayments increase cash flow.

- *Against.* You still owe money at the end of the loan term.

Basic or no-frills loan

This loan offers a very competitive interest rate with few or no ongoing costs, but it doesn't have the flexibility and features of other home loans. Its interest rate is variable and so it goes up and down with the market. This also means your mortgage repayments will vary as interest rates move.

- *For.* It offers some of the lowest interest rates available.

- *Against.* It lacks the choices and functionality of many of the other loans, which, depending on your loan size, could actually cost you money in the long run.

Standard variable rate loan

This is the most popular form of loan offered by lenders and taken up by borrowers. As the name suggests, the interest rate will vary, as it is set by the lender. It is similar to a basic or no-frills home loan but it has more features and flexibility, such as the ability to make extra payments, or redraw your funds. As a result, the interest rate is slightly higher than that of a basic home loan.

- *For.* If interest rates go down, so does your repayment.

- *Against.* If interest rates go up, so do your repayments.

Fixed rate loan

This is a home loan with a fixed interest rate for a period of between one and 15 years. At the end of the fixed rate period, you can choose to fix your interest rate again, change to a variable rate loan or opt for a split loan (which is covered next). These loans become popular with borrowers if they foresee interest rates increasing.

- *For.* You know exactly what your repayments will be for the fixed period. You will not be forced into making higher mortgage repayments if interest rates increase.

- *Against.* If interest rates fall, you are stuck with paying the higher fixed rate. If you wish to get out of this loan before the fixed period has expired, it can be costly. These loans have less flexibility than variable rate loans, as most lenders will restrict the amount of additional payments you can make in the event of your wanting to pay off your loan earlier or faster.

Split loan

A split rate loan allows you to fix the interest rate on a portion of your mortgage and leave the remainder at a variable interest rate. This type of loan is popular with investors who want to hedge their bets and benefit whether interest rates go up or down.

- *For.* This loan allows you to have an each way bet if you're not sure in which direction interest rates are heading.

- *Against.* You can't take full advantage of a fixed or variable rate loan and you will only partially benefit if the variable rates fall.

Line of credit (LOC) loan

This is also called an equity loan. It allows the property owner to borrow against their equity (the portion of the property they own or have paid off). A line of credit loan permits the borrower to withdraw money from their loan up to a pre-arranged limit. For example, a property owner who owns a $500 000 property, but has a mortgage of $100 000, still has equity of $400 000. They could take out a LOC for, say, $250 000, and withdraw all the money at once or portions of this money from time to time. It is similar to an overdraft facility and interest accrues on the balance.

- *For.* Money can be withdrawn when needed without having to make an application to the lender each time. Also a useful alternative to a margin loan if you wish to borrow money to buy shares.

- *Against.* This should only be utilised by the most disciplined of budgeters. As no repayment is required, interest can build up very quickly and you can reach your borrowing limit in no time! Interest rates tend to be higher than a standard variable rate loan and these loans often attract high annual fees.

Introductory or honeymoon loans

These loans are generally available to brand new borrowers. Their advantage can take one of two forms. First, the loan may offer you a discount of, say, 0.5 per cent off the institution's standard variable rate for a honeymoon period, which can be anywhere from six months to three years. If interest rates move up or down, so does the interest rate on your loan, but it stays 0.5 per cent below the market rate during the honeymoon. Alternatively, you might be offered a discounted fixed rate for a period of time so no matter what happens to interest rates during your honeymoon period, your repayments remain the same during the honeymoon.

- *For.* This can assist with making the repayments in the early stages of the mortgage.

- *Against.* There are often extra conditions on these loans, such as high early-repayment penalties. When the introductory loan period expires, you are obliged to either pay a higher standard interest rate or pay a fee to have your loan renegotiated.

Professional packages

When professional packages were first introduced they were available only to those in professional occupations, who were on relatively high incomes and were willing to borrow large amounts of money. Nowadays these loans are available to almost anyone who is willing to borrow more than $100 000. For an annual fee, a professional package bundles a number of features, which can include a discounted interest rate, credit card(s) with no yearly fee, and the ability to take out multiple loans without the need to pay multiple establishment, application or valuation fees.

- *For.* There are valuable interest rate discounts for the repeat borrower so this loan can be of great value to investors who plan to buy a number of properties.

- *Against.* The annual fee can sometimes be more than the savings, depending on the amount you're borrowing. The lender will often ask to oversee all of your existing finances, such as all loans, credit cards, savings accounts and insurance.

Low documentation — no documentation loans

These low-doc or no-doc loans were very popular in the period before the GFC, and almost disappeared soon after. They have now made a comeback into the mortgage market. These loans require minimum documentation and are suited to the self-employed or small-business owner who may not have all the financial documentation that the bank normally requires before approving a loan.

- *For.* There is less hassle to arrange a loan, as you require less paperwork.

- *Against.* The lender will require a larger deposit than normal, and the interest rates and fees are higher; the lender is taking on greater risk as they are not 100 per cent sure of your long-term financial position.

Features of loans

Many of the loans we have discussed have features and flexibility that are particularly useful to the borrower, as they allow borrowers to pay off their loan more quickly, increase their cash flow or gain access to their money in times of need. Two of the most popular features, mortgage offset account and redraw facility, are outlined here.

Mortgage offset account

A mortgage offset account is a savings account that is linked to your mortgage account, and it can help reduce the interest you need to pay. Your savings, income and any other money you earn can reduce the interest payable on the home loan.

Example

Here's an example to show how a mortgage offset account can help you pay off your mortgage more quickly.

Assumptions

- Your net income is $52 000 per year.

- You have a $400 000 loan at 6 per cent per year on your home.

- Your savings account has a balance of $20 000, earning interest at a rate of 3 per cent per year.

Calculations

If you kept the loan and savings accounts separate, in a year you would need to pay $24 000 ($400 000 × 6 per cent) interest on the home loan, and you would earn $600 ($20 000 × 3 per cent) in interest on your savings. You would have to pay tax on the interest earned from your savings, which means you would be left with $400 after tax. If you put this $400 towards your home loan interest payments, you would have paid $23 600 in loan interest from your own pocket.

(continued)

Example (cont'd)

If you linked the savings and loan account into a mortgage offset account, you would be much better off. Your loan interest would not be calculated on $400 000, but the lender would include the $20 000 savings as off-setting the outstanding loan balance and charge you interest on only $380 000 ($400 000 − $20 000). Your total loan interest bill for the year would be $22 800 ($380 000 × 6 per cent per year). If you total this loan interest reduction over the life of the loan, you can cut tens of thousands of dollars off your total interest bill, or reduce the life of the loan, or both.

An offset account works even better if your salary is directly paid into it. If you were paid $1000 per week and this was deposited directly into your offset account, this $1000 would offset the outstanding loan balance while it was in the account and reduce your loan interest bill. As you periodically take money out from your salary to pay bills and more weekly income is deposited, the remaining balance is used to offset your outstanding loan balance.

Redraw facility

A redraw facility allows you to access additional payments you have made on your mortgage that were over and above the minimum repayments.

If you were paying an extra $100 per week in one year, you would make additional repayments of $5200 ($100 × 52 weeks). If you have a redraw facility on your mortgage, you could withdraw this money when you needed it. Alternatively, you could put a lump sum of money into your mortgage in the knowledge that you could access your own money when you required it. Whether the money comes from regular extra payments or from paying in a lump sum, the extra money in the loan account offsets the outstanding loan balance and reduces your total interest bill. Some banks charge for this redraw so make sure you know in advance how much this fee is.

Margin loans

Another financing option for share investment is available to investors who want to gear into a share investment portfolio: margin lending.

A margin loan is a loan that is provided to you by a lender specifically for the purpose of investing in shares and managed funds. A margin loan provides you with a means to invest more than you could using your own money, allowing you to increase your potential returns.

Using a margin loan is very similar to purchasing an investment property, in that you are required to provide the lender with a deposit in cash or existing shares, and they will lend you the rest. The amount required as a deposit will depend on the type of share or managed fund you are investing in. Typically, a blue-chip share will require a deposit of between 25 per cent and 30 per cent, while a speculative share may require a deposit of up to 70 per cent or more (provided the lender will give you funds to purchase it)! This is known as the LVR (loan-to-valuation ratio), and the lender will require you to ensure that the loan value of your portfolio as a percentage of the market value does not rise beyond specific levels. If it does, you will have a margin call and be required to reduce the LVR (and therefore the loan) by providing additional collateral (cash or shares), or by selling some of your existing shares.

In exchange for lending you the money to purchase the shares, the margin lender will charge you a higher rate of interest than you would obtain if you had a line of credit using the equity in your home. Interest rates are typically 2 to 3 per cent higher than the standard variable rate for a home loan.

Margin loans can be used by investors who:

- have a medium to long-term outlook for their investments
- have relatively high levels of disposable income
- are willing to accept higher levels of risk for opportunity to achieve higher levels of return
- have the capacity to meet a margin call—if it is triggered
- understand that margin lending magnifies their potential losses as well as potential gains
- are planning to use the tax benefits of interest payments on the loan to reduce their tax bill.

There are numerous benefits of margin loans:

- It is an interest-only loan.
- There is typically no term for the loan.
- Your investment capacity is increased. The use of gearing gives you leverage, and this provides you the means with which to establish and grow an investment portfolio with only a relatively small amount of your own money.
- You have the opportunity to diversify your investments. Diversification can reduce the investment risk of a portfolio, making returns less volatile. With more funds available to invest, an investor can spread their investments across a variety of different asset classes and within each asset class.
- You can get higher returns. Using leverage can magnify your potential returns by virtue of the fact that your buying power is much higher than it would be if you did not use leverage. (However, leverage is a double-edged sword, as it can also magnify your losses.)

- There are tax benefits. By financing your investment, you can use the expenses of financing as a deduction against your taxable income. Therefore, the interest that you pay on a margin loan is tax deductible.

Margin loans also have disadvantages, however:

- There is a higher potential for losses. Margin lending magnifies the effect of a loss, as you are exposed to a larger investment than your investment capital.

- Your investment portfolio could suffer a margin call. This is when there is a large or sudden drop in the market value of your investments that brings the LVR to a level above the limit agreed when the loan was taken out. You may then be forced to add more collateral (either cash or shares) to the portfolio to reduce your loan and bring the LVR down, or worse yet, you may have to sell your shares at the worst possible time.

 ## Peter's property insights

Most people can't afford to buy property unless they borrow money. Thankfully, a wide variety of loans are available to the property purchaser. I encourage you to speak to your bank *and* a mortgage broker to determine which loan best fits your needs. I particularly like interest-only loans on investment properties, with an offset facility, but there may be other options that better suit your goals.

Zac's share insights

There is certainly a case to support borrowing money to invest. However, this should be managed prudently, and according to your risk profile. Just like any business, though, you should ensure that your costs (such as financing costs) are as low as possible. Usually, margin loans attract higher interest rates than you could otherwise obtain using a line of credit on your home loan. In my opinion, a better alternative than a margin loan (when you wish to use gearing in a share investment portfolio) is to use the equity in your home and redraw funds from that, which you can use for share investment. This is because of the fact that there are no restrictions on what you can buy and, importantly, there is a reduced potential to trigger a margin call against your investment if your shares suddenly decrease in value.

 ## Conclusion

Borrowing money to buy assets is a great way to increase your wealth. However, if economic times are tough and property or share markets drop, borrowed money can be a burden.

As you can see, financing a property investment is much easier and less expensive than borrowing money with only a share portfolio as the security. If you do wish to borrow money to buy shares and you have some equity in property, you might want to consider a line of credit loan, but you should first consult with your accountant and financial planner. The use of a line of credit loan to purchase shares will allow you to take advantage of property and its greater security, and put the money towards an asset with a potentially higher return—that is, shares.

Round 14

INVESTMENT STRUCTURES

Many people purchase investment assets in their own name, or joint names, though other ownership structures may be more suitable. The legal ownership of your investments can have a significant impact on your investment results, because there are significant taxation and legal consequences depending on who the beneficial owner of the investment is, and how they are treated from a legal and taxation perspective. It is worth ensuring you get it right from the start! We strongly suggest you consult a financial adviser or accountant who understands your existing financial situation and what you want to achieve from your investments. There is no right or wrong structure for everyone, only a right or wrong for your own financial situation, goals and future needs.

What to consider

Your choice of investment structure will largely depend on which is the most advantageous outcome for you, and therefore these are some of the issues that will influence your decision:

- What are your asset protection requirements?
- What level of control do you require?
- What financing will you use to purchase the investment?
- How much time and expense are you prepared to spend on administration?
- Is succession or estate planning important to you in relation to that investment?
- What is the ultimate tax rate payable on the investment?

- How important is it for you to be able to distribute income or gains from the investment to different people?

- What is the level of tax deductibility that you require for expenses incurred by the investment?

- What effect will the investment have on your social security or pension benefits?

- Does the structure allow you to maximise your superannuation contributions?

- What level of flexibility do you require to make use of tax losses and carry forward losses?

Types of structure

There are essentially four major investment structures:

- individual name or sole trader

- partnership

- company

- trust.

See table 14.1 for the characteristics of the four investment structures. Each has its own advantages and disadvantages.

Table 14.1: characteristics of the four major investment structures

Feature	Individual	Partnership	Company	Unit trust	Discretionary trust	Superannuation fund
				Trust		
Administered by	Individual	Partners	Directors	Trustee	Trustee	Trustee
Responsible to	N/A	Partners	Shareholders	Unit-holders	Appointer	Members
Cost to establish and run	Low	Fairly low	Higher	Higher	Higher	Higher
Protection of assets from outside risk/ claims	No	No	Only if owned by a discretionary trust	Only if owned by a discretionary trust	Yes	Yes
Maximum tax rate	Top marginal rate + Medicare levy	Top marginal rate + Medicare levy or 30% if partner is a company	30%	Top marginal rate or 30% if unit-holder is a company	Top marginal rate or 30% if beneficiary is a company	15% if complying fund 45% if non-complying
Flexibility	Poor	Fairly poor	Fair	Good	Very Good	Fairly Poor
Potential for splitting income	No	Between partners	Between shareholders	Between unit-holders (fixed)	Between beneficiaries	No
Streaming of income	No	Limited	No	Dependent on trust deed	Yes, subject to trust deed	No
Taxable capital gains	Paid by individual	Paid by partners	Paid by company	Paid by unit-holder	Paid by beneficiary	Paid by trustee
Access to CGT discount	Yes	Yes (if partner is not a company)	No	Yes	Yes	Yes (lower discount)
Can losses be distributed?	Yes	Yes	No	No	No	No
Admission of new parties	New structure is required	Usually permitted	Usually permitted	Usually permitted	May be difficult for non-family members	Usually permitted with restrictions. Up to 4 members only
Changing ownership	N/A	Partnership interest	Shares	Units	By appointer	N/A

Source: Australian Investors Association.

Individual name or sole trader

This is the simplest form of holding an investment, and also the most common. Investments are owned in an individual's name. Where two or more individuals want to hold ownership together, you can establish ownership in joint names—this has the same effect of ownership as an individual name.

The advantages of this structure are:

- It is convenient and efficient to set up ownership in an individual name.

- It is easy to administer since income, and capital gains and losses, must be included in an individual's personal tax returns.

- It is the least expensive ownership structure, as no costly legal structures have to be established or maintained.

- It is the most tax effective structure, if the investment is negatively geared.

- You can take advantage of capital gains tax (CGT) provisions available to individuals such as discounted CGT for assets held for more than 12 months.

- Revenue and capital losses may be carried forward indefinitely to be offset against future profit.

The disadvantages of this structure are:

- There is no flexibility for the distribution of income.

- There is no asset protection at all, so the assets are at risk if you suffer a claim from a creditor. Asset protection should be of particular importance to you if you are in an occupation with a high risk of legal action (for instance, if you are a doctor, lawyer or finance professional).

- There is also the potential to incur a greater tax liability over time, since individual tax rates are higher than the marginal tax rates of other structures.

Partnership

A partnership is where two or more individuals or other legal entities agree to form a business relationship and form a structure in which they own the asset together. The difference between a partnership and an ownership in joint names is that a partnership is considered to be a separate legal entity for tax purposes only. Each partner is, however, taxed for their share of the income or loss of the partnership at their individual tax rates. Holding a property as joint tenants is usually not considered to be a partnership.

The advantages of this structure are:

- Set up costs are fairly low.

- Profits and losses are taxed in the hands of the individuals, not the partnership.

- Individual partners can take advantage of the 50 per cent CGT discount, as capital gains are also taxed at an individual level.

- A deduction for interest incurred on money borrowed is also available to the partners.

- Ideally suited if the purchase of a property or investment is to be negatively geared as the deductions are claimed by the partners at an individual level.

The disadvantages of this structure are:

- Partners are jointly and severally liable for each other's debts, which means one partner could personally be liable for all the debts of the partnership!

- There is unlimited liability to the partners for all partnership debts.

- No more than 20 people can form a partnership.

- There is no flexibility for the retention or distribution of profits within the partnership—all profits and losses must be distributed to each partner specifically in proportion to their ownership.

- A partnership ceases when one partner dies.

- A partnership will require its own tax file number, and a tax return needs to be lodged on its behalf.

- It is costlier to own assets through a partnerships than in your own name, due to the additional administrative costs.

There are other more specific types of partnerships, such as corporate limited partnerships, professional partnerships and joint ventures that can be considered, which will offer variations to the advantages and disadvantages we have mentioned here. To find out about these, and what structure is right for you, you should consult a financial adviser or accountant who understands your situation and is able to provide you with the right advice.

Company

A company is a legal entity in which the owners are given shares in accordance with how much they have invested in the entity. It is a separate legal entity to its shareholders. A company structure is more commonly used for conducting a business, rather than for investment ownership. In saying that, however, due to the advantages that a company structure provides, many investors use a company to act as trustee for an investment that is held in a trust structure, which we will be discussing later in this chapter.

A company requires at least one shareholder and one director, who can be one and the same.

The advantages of this structure are:

- Shareholders are protected if the business is sued or fails: an individual's liability is limited to the amount that is unpaid on their shareholdings.

- A company has a perpetual existence: it does not cease to exist if a director or shareholder dies or leaves the company.

- A company can retain profits within the business: it does not have to distribute profits to shareholders.

- The company tax rate of 30 per cent makes it attractive for holding income-earning assets, and it can therefore be advantageous for high income earners, who pay tax at higher marginal rates.

The disadvantages of this structure are:

- As a director, you may be personally liable for debts of the company, if the company cannot repay them.

- Losses can only be offset against future gains, but they cannot be distributed to shareholders.

- Companies cannot use the 50 per cent CGT discount provisions on the sale of assets. Therefore it is not the ideal structure to hold assets that you expect will appreciate considerably.

- Setup and ongoing administration costs are high due to the need to maintain separate tax returns, accounts and ASIC fees.

- There is limited flexibility for paying dividends.

Trust

A trust structure is one of the more powerful and flexible investment structures for holding investments. A trust is a separate entity for tax purposes, and it is essentially a structure in which a person or entity (the trustee) holds and deals with assets entrusted to it by its beneficiaries, in a manner that is for the benefit of the beneficiaries. The trust deed sets out the obligations imposed on the trustee and the relationship between the trustee, the beneficiaries and the trust property. The trustee has a responsibility and legal duty of care to the beneficiaries to ensure that its decisions over the trust property are made in the interests of the beneficiaries. The trustee may personally be responsible for the debts of the trust.

A trust can distribute income and capital gains in accordance with the trust deed, but it cannot distribute losses. Losses can be carried forward to be offset against future income. A trust can also retain income, and if that income is taxable, then tax is payable at the top marginal rate.

A trustee can also be a beneficiary of the trust, but not the only beneficiary. Each beneficiary (except for minors and others who are under a legal disability) is taxed on their entitlement to the net income of the trust, including capital gains.

An investor can limit the liability of the trustee by having a company as a trustee for the trust. A typical arrangement is where the trust will purchase the assets and a trustee company controlled by the owner acts as the trustee of that trust.

A trust may be the ideal vehicle for owning investments if you expect to make significant capital gains, because the gain can be distributed to individuals who can apply the 50 per cent CGT discount concession.

As trust losses cannot be distributed to an individual, it is not ideal to structure a negatively geared investment through a trust, unless you have other trust income that can offset the investment loss.

The advantages of this structure are:

- A trust cannot retain profits, and also is not liable for tax in its own name. Therefore profits are distributed to the beneficiaries, who are taxed for the profit they receive from the trust at their marginal tax rates.

- A trust provides the ability to vary the amount distributed to each beneficiary from year to year.

- Capital gains can also be separately split and distributed to income. This means that capital gains can be distributed to lower-taxed beneficiaries.

- Assets of the beneficiaries are safe from claims by creditors of the trust.

- A new trustee can be appointed easily.

The disadvantages of this structure are:

- Trusts can be expensive to set up and maintain, especially if there is a company trustee.

- The trustee has legal ownership over the trust assets, even though they are held in trust for the beneficiaries.

- The trustee's power is limited to what the trust deed allows.

- Franking credits that are attached to dividends are not refunded if no tax income is declared by the trust for tax purposes.

- If the trust makes a loss, that tax loss cannot be distributed to the beneficiaries in the way that profits are. Tax losses are retained in the trust, and are offset against future profits until the losses are extinguished.

Types of trust

There are five types of trust. They are:

- *Discretionary (or family) trusts.* These are amongst the more common types of trusts. This is where a trustee can distribute income and capital gains to beneficiaries at their discretion (usually this is done according to the most tax-effective outcome for each beneficiary). Creditors cannot access the assets in the trust, as no individual owns them. In order to distribute franking credits, a family trust election may be required. Franking credits cannot be distributed to beneficiaries unless the trust has net income. A company, just like an individual, can be a beneficiary of a trust.

- *Unit trusts.* In this kind of trust, a trustee administers the assets of the trust on behalf of the unit-holders. A unit trust is similar to a company because units are held in the trust, much like shares are held in a company. Unit trusts are commonly used when unrelated parties decide to operate a business together, and where units in the trust are held by another structure, such as a family or discretionary trust.

- *Hybrid trusts.* These trusts are a composite of a discretionary trust and a unit trust, and they can be very powerful investment structures. They are primarily used if you are seeking to gear into property and want to borrow money to purchase units in the trust. The trust purchases the property, using it as security until the loan is repaid, and then the trust repurchases the units.

- *Self managed superannuation funds (SMSFs).* These are a special type of trust that exist with the sole purpose of funding the beneficiary's retirement. It is an investment structure that can own property or shares directly, and you can use the money within your superannuation to make these investments (see Round 15 for more information on SMSFs).

- *Testamentary trusts.* This type of trust is formed upon the death of a person who has specified the trust's creation in their will.

 ## Peter's property insights

Property investors most commonly hold property in their own name, joint names or a family trust. It is becoming more common in recent times is to acquire investment property through a self managed superannuation fund (SMSF) because of the tax benefits and protection that it provides.

Zac's share insights

The decision on what structure to use for your share investments will be driven by whether you will be trading or investing, and also by whether you will be using gearing or not. This needs to be overlaid with the importance you place on asset protection, as well as how your tax situation will impact the gains you are likely to make. This is where good financial advice from an accountant, financial planner or lawyer who understands your goals and situation is invaluable!

Conclusion

There are many factors to consider when choosing the most appropriate investment structure to hold your assets. Your decision may have significant implications for the amount of tax you will be liable for, as well as the appropriate level of protection in case a claim is made against you personally. For some individuals, asset protection may be an important consideration. For others, it could be making sure that your investment assets and the continuity of the investments is unaffected by the death of its owner.

Ultimately the right decision will depend on your individual goals and situation, and that is something that you need to discuss with a financial adviser, accountant or lawyer.

Round 15

SELF MANAGED SUPERANNUATION FUNDS

In Australia, there is a legal requirement for employers to pay a proportion of their employees' salary into each employee's choice of retirement fund, or superannuation fund. This is known as the superannuation guarantee. Investors can choose from several types of superannuation funds to invest in, but for ultimate control, and the flexibility to invest directly in almost any asset class, a self managed superannuation fund (SMSF) is the most viable option.

SMSFs are becoming increasingly popular in Australia, and offer particular advantages for investing in both property and shares. More and more Australians are taking advantage of the opportunities that SMSFs provide, which is flexibility and control, and, as you will see later in this round, SMSFs offer some very attractive tax benefits to investors, particularly when they have retired.

According to tax office statistics released in September 2012, there were nearly 481 000 SMSFs in existence, most of which invested in listed shares and cash (see table 15.1).

Table 15.1: range of investments held by SMSFs, 2012

Type of investment	Number of SMSFs invested	Percentage of total
Listed shares	141 529	30.9
Cash and term deposits	134 836	29.4
Non-residential real property	53 082	11.6

Type of investment	Number of SMSFs invested	Percentage of total
Unlisted trusts	41270	9.0
Other managed investments	21460	4.7
Listed trusts	19041	4.2
Residential real property	16251	3.5
Other assets	13288	2.9
Unlisted shares	5039	1.1
Debt securities	3271	0.7
Loans	2943	0.6
Other overseas assets	1880	0.4
Derivatives and instalment warrants	1565	0.3
Overseas shares	1477	0.3
Artwork, collectibles, metal or jewels	758	0.2
Overseas managed investments	358	0.1
Insurance policy	178	0.0
Overseas residential real property	134	0.0
Overseas non-residential real property	90	0.0
Total Australian and overseas assets ($m)	458451	100

Source: ATO, Self managed super fund statistical report, September 2012, p 6.

What is an SMSF?

An SMSF is a superannuation fund that has one to four members (beneficiaries) and is established as a special type of trust structure, where the members have total responsibility for the management of the fund. The law requires that the assets of the fund be held 'in trust' for the benefit of the members of the fund. To establish an SMSF you need to appoint the trustees and draft the fund's trust deed. Each member of the fund must also be a trustee, but the Superannuation Industry Supervision (SIS) Act allows for no more than five members to be part of an SMSF. If there is only one member, then the SMSF is required to have a corporate trustee.

Super funds are regulated by trust law and the SIS Act, and these acts provide the legislative requirements relating to the proper conduct of the trustees and the content of the fund's trust deed, which determines how the fund is run. This arrangement is similar to the way the Corporations Act guides the operations and conduct of all companies, directors and shareholders in Australia.

While an SMSF offers investors some advantages over holding their superannuation in other kinds of super funds (such as retail, corporate or industry funds), there are restrictions on the type of assets SMSFs can hold, the method of investing and from whom assets can be acquired, that do not occur in other, less regulated structures such as partnerships, discretionary and fixed trusts, sole traders and companies.

What does an SMSF do?

Section 62 of the SIS Act prescribes that SMSFs have a sole purpose. This sole purpose prescribes exactly what an SMSF must do. It must 'be maintained for the sole purpose of providing its members with retirement benefits or providing its members' beneficiaries or dependants with benefits in the event that the member dies before retirement'.

This is an important distinction, as individuals, trusts and companies are able to determine, and vary, the investment purpose for which they were established at any time. Purchasing assets in a company or individual name may provide more flexibility, however, than purchasing through an SMSF. Every investor will therefore need to look at their specific circumstances and needs to make a decision about what structure is most suitable for them.

The primary reason an SMSF exists is to provide its members with financial benefits during their retirement.

An SMSF can invest in many types of assets, but we will focus only on property and share investments through an SMSF.

What can an SMSF receive?

For an SMSF to have cash to invest in shares or real estate, it first must receive it. Cash can enter an SMSF in two ways:

- contributions by its members
- eligible termination payment (ETP) rollovers.

A range of contributions that can be made to an SMSF (as for any super fund), all of which fall into two main categories. These are:

- mandated employer contributions on behalf of a member (superannuation guarantee payments or payments required by an employment award)
- non-mandated contributions, such as additional personal contributions.

Non-mandated contributions are voluntary contributions made by a member of the fund or by someone else and include:

- personal contributions made by employees
- personal contributions made by self-employed or unsupported individuals
- contributions made by employers in addition to the superannuation guarantee (SG) and award obligations, such as salary sacrifice arrangements.

Types of investments available

Complying with the SIS Act investment rules is one of the most important obligations of the trustees of an SMSF. The rules are designed to protect members from undue risk and to ensure that the assets of the fund are being held to provide a retirement benefit for the members. SMSFs are generally not set up for short-term benefits. The trustees of an SMSF are free to make investment decisions in line with their duties and responsibilities to members and in accordance with their investment strategy, which has to be prepared in writing when the fund is set up.

Generally, any investment that an individual, trust, partnership or company is permitted to invest in, an SMSF is also permitted to invest in, provided the trust deed and investment strategy do not preclude it. These investment classes are as follows:

- cash
- fixed interest deposits
- listed and unlisted shares
- listed and unlisted unit trusts
- managed funds
- real estate
- foreign investments
- other assets, such as collectibles and artwork
- certain derivative products, such as options and instalment warrants.

The only qualification to this general condition is contained in section 66 of the SIS Act, which requires that all SMSF investments to be made on 'an arm's length basis'. Put simply, an SMSF is restricted from acquiring certain assets from related parties (in other words, a member or an associate of a member of the fund, such as a relative, spouse or child). For example, if your sister owns a residential property, you are not allowed to buy it from her and put it in your SMSF. The only exception to this rule is business real property, which is defined in the SIS Act as 'any freehold or leasehold interest in real property that is used wholly and exclusively in one or more businesses'. This means that your SMSF can own a premises that your business rents from your SMSF. Your business must pay rent at market rates directly into your SMSF, and you need to have a legally binding lease agreement in place as a result.

For business owners who run their businesses from a commercial property that they own, it is a very prudent strategy to consider transferring the property into their SMSF, subject to contributions caps that will be discussed later.

★ ★ ★ ★ ★ ★ ★ PROPERTY ★ ★ ★ ★ ★ ★ ★

Investing in property

SMSFs are the only type of superannuation funds that are permitted to directly hold property.

An SMSF can acquire and hold both residential and commercial real estate for investment purposes, as long as the acquisition of such property occurs on an arm's length basis, as described earlier, except for business real property.

Business real property is defined in the SIS Act as: 'any freehold or leasehold interest in real property that is used wholly and exclusively in one or more businesses'.

A strategy used by some business owners is to have their business premises owned by their SMSF. Basically the owner will be paying rent to their own SMSF! There are strict rules in relation to this arrangement, so if you are interested in using this strategy, you should first seek qualified advice.

SMSFs cannot run a business or trade in trading stock, so most, if not all, investments held by SMSFs will be 'held on capital account', which means that any gains or losses incurred when you sell will be either capital gains or capital losses.

Once property has been acquired by an SMSF, it can rent that property to earn income, just as any individual, trust or company can.

Tax benefits

Prior to the retirement of a member of an SMSF, their earnings will incur a flat tax rate of 15 per cent for income tax purposes, and have access to a 33.3 per cent discount on gross capital gains for assets held for more than 12 months before sale. (When assets are held in, say, your personal name, your income is taxed at your marginal tax rate and the capital gains tax, or CGT, discount is 50 per cent.) Upon retirement of the member of the SMSF, the fund's earnings will be tax free. As we have discussed, the sole purpose of an SMSF is to provide benefits to members in retirement. Once a member reaches retirement age, also known as preservation age, the SMSF can enter into an income stream–paying mode, more commonly referred to as 'pension phase'. Once the income-producing assets of the fund are within the pension phase, all pension-phase asset income is taxed at a rate of zero per cent, which includes all realised capital gains. In other words, no income or capital gains tax is payable! This is one of the greatest tax advantages of using an SMSF to buy growth assets such as property and shares.

An SMSF might hold property for, say, 15 years, with an underlying capital gain of $1 000 000. When an SMSF member commences pension phase within the fund, the fund can sell the asset and it will be completely CGT-free. To put it another way, in an SMSF you could make a $1 000 000 profit and not have to pay any tax!

In comparison, if you bought the property in a company name, held it for 15 years and made a $1 000 000 profit, the company would have to pay 30 per cent of the capital gain in CGT. That's a saving of $300 000, just because the property was owned by an SMSF rather than a company.

Factors to be considered

In most cases the decision to acquire property in an SMSF revolves around the following factors:

- availability of equity or cash in the SMSF
- restricted loan-to-value ratios (LVR) due to bank lending requirements to SMSFs
- reduced benefits of negative gearing (through non-recourse loans) due to low flat rate of taxation
- complexity and increased costs of buying within an SMSF, imposed by the SIS Act and bank requirements.

Borrowing in an SMSF

Generally SMSFs cannot borrow money from lenders to acquire assets or to fund operations, except to acquire property under the strict conditions outlined in section 67 of the SIS Act. The arrangement requires a separate 'property custodian' or 'bare' trust to be established to receive the property and manage the borrowings, to limit the lender's recourse to the asset involved in the arrangement. This 'limited recourse borrowing arrangement' (LRBA) requires the asset to be held beneficially for the SMSF members, while legal ownership remains with the bare trust. Limited recourse means that the lender is limited to selling off only the security that is held to recoup any losses (for instance, if the trust defaults on the loan). They cannot sell any of the investors' (trust's or SMSF's) other assets. This is a complex area of trust and SMSF law. It adds increased cost to establish an LRBA, compared with the relatively simple investment loan arrangement for an individual. A qualified accountant or financial planner will be able to provide you with detailed information if you would like to buy property through your SMSF.

Under a limited recourse borrowing arrangement, where an SMSF has borrowed up to the current maximum lending ratio, say 80 per cent, we could assume that the property would be negatively geared for income tax purposes. Given the rental loss could be offset against other income, the SMSF would receive a tax benefit of 15 per cent per year. This is opposed to a company deducting the loss and receiving a tax benefit of 30 per cent per year against current income, or an individual that can claim the tax benefit at their marginal tax rate. Over the life of the loan's negative gearing period, this differential between an SMSF and a company's or individual's marginal tax rate could prove to be substantial. However, if the property is positively geared, the benefit lies with the SMSF because of lower tax rates on superannuation funds.

The choice of structure to hold an investment is crucial. In this case, the present cost of the reduced tax benefit from the negative gearing loss annually has to be compared against the value of the future ability of the SMSF to sell the property CGT-free in pension mode.

★ ★ ★ ★ ★ ★ ★ ★ **SHARES** ★ ★ ★ ★ ★ ★ ★ ★

Investing in shares

SMSFs are generally permitted to invest in shares the same way as an individual, partnership, trust or company. Shares can be classified into two categories:

- publicly listed shares
- unlisted shares.

Publicly listed shares are any securities traded and listed on the Australian Securities Exchange (ASX). SMSFs can acquire shares freely on the open market and are also permitted by section 66 of the SIS Act to acquire listed shares from related parties at market value.

Unlisted shares are shares in public or private companies not listed on the ASX. SMSFs are able to acquire such investments on an arm's length basis (that is, not from a related party) and can continue to hold such assets so long as the company remains unrelated to the SMSF trustees/members.

The concept of related parties is important when you are deciding what structure you should use to hold the shares. If an individual's aim is to acquire additional shares and eventually control the company over what it initially acquired, then this aim will not be able to be achieved by acquiring it in an SMSF structure, as the SIS Act would prevent a majority shareholding from occurring.

SMSFs have access to a CGT concession on the sale of listed and unlisted shares held for 12 months or more. This concession is similar to the 50 per cent CGT concession extended to individuals. SMSFs are able to reduce discounted gains by one-third, thus reducing the effective tax rate on capital gains on shares held for more than 12 months to 10 per cent.

SMSF trustees need to be conscious of share acquisition dates, as holding a share beyond the 12-month period can create a considerable CGT saving, compared with disposing of a share parcel in the 11th month of its holding.

Shares sold by an SMSF whose members are in 100 per cent pension mode also attract a tax rate of zero per cent. This is a very important differentiator between non-SMSF versus SMSF structures, as once a member reaches preservation age and commences a pension the SMSF tax benefits are immense and immediate.

Administering an SMSF

A lot of investors mistakenly believe that it is expensive and onerous to administer their own SMSF. While there is no doubt that it can be costly to maintain an SMSF, the reality is that the cost is not likely to be much more than operating a normal trust—except that the SIS Act requires each member to ensure that they monitor how much money has been contributed into the SMSF in any year, how it has been invested, and, if you are eligible, how much is withdrawn. While the ultimate responsibility for compliance falls on the trustee(s) of the SMSF, you can enlist the assistance of experts such as financial planners and accountants and lawyers to ensure your SMSF is administered and invested correctly.

Costs of running an SMSF

Costs associated with setting up and administering an SMSF include the following.

- the ongoing costs of running the SMSF, such as administration, reporting to the Australian Taxation Office (including annual audits) and lodgement

- the adviser's fee if you are planning to use the services of a financial adviser.

Set-up costs for an SMSF can be from a few hundred dollars for a basic SMSF up to about $3500 if you are also establishing a company as a trustee and a bare trust through which you will finance a property investment.

The annual administration costs for running an SMSF should also be considered: this could be between 0.5 per cent and 1.5 per cent of the average fund balance.

Peter's property insights

Buying property through an SMSF can be very beneficial, however there are a number of considerations. One of the important considerations is tax. The 15 per cent tax rate for SMSFs is great if you are earning income (positive gearing). If you own a negatively geared property, it is more tax effective to structure that in your individual name outside of the SMSF in order to take advantage of deductions that can be claimed at the higher individual marginal tax rates. The constrained rules and compliance issues of SMSFs also need to be considered. Owning business premises in your own SMSF and leasing it back can be a great advantage to the business owner.

Zac's share insights

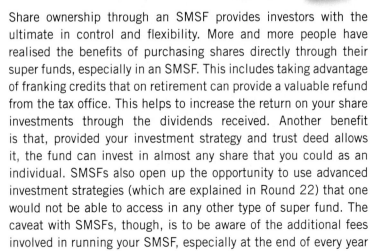

Share ownership through an SMSF provides investors with the ultimate in control and flexibility. More and more people have realised the benefits of purchasing shares directly through their super funds, especially in an SMSF. This includes taking advantage of franking credits that on retirement can provide a valuable refund from the tax office. This helps to increase the return on your share investments through the dividends received. Another benefit is that, provided your investment strategy and trust deed allows it, the fund can invest in almost any share that you could as an individual. SMSFs also open up the opportunity to use advanced investment strategies (which are explained in Round 22) that one would not be able to access in any other type of super fund. The caveat with SMSFs, though, is to be aware of the additional fees involved in running your SMSF, especially at the end of every year (reporting and audit costs, for instance) to remain compliant. These costs need to be worth the benefits, and that is something that you can determine using the assistance of a qualified and experienced adviser.

Conclusion

Owning property and shares in an SMSF can be a great way to help secure your retirement. However, it is critical that you realise SMSFs are set up for just that: retirement. They are not meant to be used for making short-term profits that are spent before you retire. Owning assets in an SMSF is a complex area and we strongly recommend you obtain advice from your accountant and financial planner before you decide to set up your own SMSF.

Round 16

TAX AND INVESTMENTS

Tax is an important consideration for investors, as there are many instances where the tax benefits from such things as franking credits and depreciation can greatly assist with cash flow.

★ ★ ★ ★ ★ ★ ★ **PROPERTY** ★ ★ ★ ★ ★ ★ ★

Property and tax

Buy a property; find the tenant. Take advantage of tax benefits to help pay off the mortgage. When you retire, sell the property, pay out any remainder of the loan, and keep the capital growth to fund your happily ever after. Is it really that simple?

Before purchasing a property

Before purchasing a property it is important to ensure that the correct entity owns the property (see Round 14). The structure you choose will directly affect the amount of tax you pay on your investment.

Principally, the entities that may own property are individuals, either as joint tenants or tenants in common; partnership; superannuation fund; trust or company. It is critical that you make the decision about the entity in which you will buy the property *before* you buy.

Everyone's situation is different, and the structure you choose should not be made solely on tax advantages.

During ownership

You will need to be aware of the treatment of the various outgoings associated with property ownership in order to get the maximum tax benefit from your property over the period of ownership. Some expenses are claimable in full in the financial year in which the expense was incurred; some costs have to be spread over five years; and some depreciable expenses, such as the cost of construction, are spread over 40 years. Some costs are not claimable until the property is sold.

Expenses during ownership

Initial expenses, such as the purchase price of the property, stamp duty and conveyancing fees, all form part of the cost base for your property and are not deductible expenses at the time you purchase the property. However, these costs will be used to determine the capital gain of the disposal of the property so you should keep careful records.

Borrowing costs, typically the expenses incurred when taking out a loan or refinancing, if they are greater than $100, cannot all be claimed in full in the year they are incurred and are deducted over five years. If you pay out the loan before the five years is up, then any remaining unclaimed borrowing expenses can be claimed in full. Periodic bank fees and interest are not borrowing expenses; these expenses can be claimed in the year they are incurred.

Ongoing costs, such as interest, bank fees, council rates, water rates, agent fees, land tax, advertising, repairs and maintenance (but *not* initial repairs or improvements or new plant and equipment) are all deductible in the year in which they are incurred.

Depreciation of items of plant and equipment and the cost of the building may be able to be depreciated, meaning that the cost is claimed over a number of years. You can claim this even if you didn't build the property.

When purchasing a property, it may be a good idea to get a quantity surveyor to prepare a depreciation schedule to ensure you are getting maximum deductions each year. Depreciable items include floor coverings, hot-water system, light fittings, oven, cook top, dishwasher, internal window blinds, exhaust fans—and the list goes on!

Selling expenses are the costs related to selling the property. These are capital costs and they will be used in determining any capital gains or losses on the disposal of the property. They may include expenses such as advertising, agent fees and conveyancing costs.

Negative gearing describes an investment in which the deductible expenses, including interest, relating to the investment exceed the assessable income in any year, resulting in a loss that can then be used to offset other income earned by a taxpayer, reducing their overall tax bill. Negative gearing on its own is not good: it means your rental property is making a loss. However, it may be beneficial if:

- you pay tax, and this tax can be reduced by the negative gearing
- in the long term the property is positively geared
- the capital growth in the asset exceeds any losses over the ownership period.

Selling the property

Proceeds from the sale or transfer of property are a capital gains event and are subject to capital gains tax (CGT). Broadly speaking, capital gains or losses are the difference between the proceeds from the sale and cost of purchase plus selling expenses. If an individual, partnership of individuals or a trust that distributes to individuals or a super fund owns the property for more than 12 months before the sale then they will be eligible to reduce the capital gain by the capital gains discount of 50 per cent (33.3 per cent for superannuation funds) and then pay tax at their marginal rates on the remainder.

The timing of capital gains is based on contract date, not settlement dates of buying and selling. Here is an example.

Example

You signed a contract to buy a property on 27 June 2014 and the vendor countersigned this contract on the same day. You both agree that settlement for this property is to be 28 July 2014. Your plan is to rent the property for several months, then renovate and sell at a profit. As planned, you rent it out for a while, renovate and sign a sales contract on 2 July 2015 with settlement on 24 July 2015.

Your capital gains tax liability is based on the fact you *signed* to buy it on 27 June 2014 and *signed* to sell it again on 2 July. This is quite important, because if you made a profit, you could be eligible for the CGT discount of 50 per cent (depending on which entity owned the property), as you held the property for just over 12 months.

The timing of the capital gains event is not based on the settlement dates of 28 July 2014 and 24 July 2015. If it were based on this, the investor would *not* be eligible for the CGT discount, as the settlements were just under 12 months apart.

Record keeping

As a general rule, you should keep all records relating to your rental income and expenses for five years from the date you lodge your income tax return. Items that will be included in calculating any capital gain need to be kept for five years after the income tax return in which any gain or loss was reported. This may include keeping details of any depreciation claimed, which may result in an adjustment of the cost base of the asset when calculating capital gains.

You don't know exactly what the future holds for you and your rental property before you buy it, so decisions need to be made on the information available. Important considerations will be:

- Is the property going to be negatively geared?
- Is there a reasonable prospect of capital growth?
- How long do you plan to own the property?
- Is there a significant litigation risk for any of the potential owners?
- Is land tax likely to be an issue?

- Is cash flow a major consideration?

- What are the income levels of the individuals buying the property, and is this likely to change in the short term?

- Do you want to be able to use the property at some stage for private use, such as a holiday home, or move into at a later date, or did you live in it before you rented it out?

Before making important and expensive decisions regarding rental properties, it is important to seek professional advice from an accountant who understands property. Visit www.propertyvsshares.com.au and download a copy of our rental income and expenses worksheet to help you calculate your rental income or loss.

★ ★ ★ ★ ★ ★ ★ ★ **SHARES** ★ ★ ★ ★ ★ ★ ★ ★

Shares and tax

Share investment requires you to maintain good records for two reasons: to ensure you are fully informed about how your money is invested, and how each of your share investments is performing; and, especially, for tax purposes. There are many nuances when it comes to tax, so we will provide a general discussion of the tax issues to consider in share investment. It's a good idea to consult a qualified accountant or financial adviser *before* you make investment decisions, as they are likely to impact the effectiveness of your share investment.

Matters to consider for the tax implications of share investment include:

- What structure are your investments held in?
    - ~ An individual investor is taxed at their marginal tax rate.
    - ~ An investment through a company structure will attract tax at company tax rates, currently 30 per cent.
    - ~ An investment through a trust structure will attract tax at your individual marginal rate, because a trust has to distribute profits to its beneficiaries. However, losses are contained within the trust and can be offset only against future profits.

- Are you a share investor or a share trader?

  ~ The distinction between an investor and a trader can be subjective. As a rule, the tax office will consider you to be a trader if you are regularly buying and selling shares and not holding on to them for a long time; according to the type of shares or derivatives you are trading (for example, CFDs or options); and if you are carrying on a business, or are set up to be running what appears to be a business of trading shares.

  ~ Share investors are subject to CGT and the provisions to pay tax on only half of the capital gain (at your marginal rate) *if* you have held the share for more than a year before selling it.

  ~ Share traders are *not* eligible for the 50 per cent CGT concession. Traders' sales are treated as income when they occur, not capital gains, and so are taxed along with your other income at your marginal rate. All purchases by traders are treated as an expense at the time they are made. Therefore traders are required to account for trading stock and cost of sales, much as if they were selling tangible products.

The tax implications at each stage of a share investment, from the perspective of a share investor, are outlined here.

Acquiring shares

There are several ways of acquiring shares: mostly people buy shares through a broker. When you buy shares through your broker, you will receive a purchase contract note. At the end of the month during which you have made the purchase, you will also be sent a letter from the clearing house (CHESS) to confirm that you hold the number of shares you have purchased. You will also probaly receive paperwork from the share registry shortly after the purchase that will ask you to provide the share registry with your tax file number (TFN) and details of the bank account you want your dividends to be paid into. Providing your TFN is very important, because you may otherwise be taxed on dividends at the highest marginal tax rate, and you will be required to claim back the difference from the tax office.

You may also obtain shares in other ways, for example through inheriting them, or receiving them as a gift, through an employee share scheme, through a conversion of notes to shares, through mutualisation schemes, through a bonus share scheme, through a dividend reinvestment plan, or through mergers, takeovers and demergers. There will be differences in the tax treatment of each when you sell shares that are acquired through any of these means, largely because of strict rules affecting the calculation of the cost base of those shares. This will impact the calculation of how much tax is due and payable on the sale.

The way you acquire shares can affect your tax liability and also your ability to claim tax deductions (and franking credits):

- If you did not personally buy the shares you should find out and record the cost base or market value of your shares at the time you received them.

- You cannot claim a deduction immediately for the costs associated with the purchase of your shares, such as brokerage fees and stamp duty. These costs form part of the cost base (costs of ownership) for CGT purposes.

- If you receive shares because you hold a policy in an insurance company that demutualises, you may be subject to CGT, either at the time of the demutualisation, when you actually receive the shares, or when you sell your shares.

Holding shares

While you own your shares, the following events may have an impact your annual income tax calculation and also on the deductions you can make:

- dividends that you receive

- dividend reinvestment plans

- bonus share schemes

- call payments on bonus share schemes

- receiving non-assessable payments
- mergers, takeovers and demergers.

As a rule, you need to remember the following:

- You must declare all dividend income that you are paid, and that includes dividends that you use to purchase more shares through a dividend reinvestment plan. If franking credits are attached to the dividend payment, they can be used to reduce your tax payable.

- You can claim ongoing tax deductions for expenses associated with owning the shares, such as adviser or investment management fees, subscriptions to specialist investment journals and also the cost of interest on money that you have borrowed to buy the shares.

- When you receive bonus shares, the CGT cost base (costs of ownership) of both your original and bonus shares will be changed and you need to take care to record the changes and when they occurred.

- If you receive a payment from a private company in which you are a shareholder, it may be treated as if it was a taxable dividend paid to you. Depending on the payment, franking credits may be attached.

Disposing of shares

You can dispose of your shares in the following ways:

- selling them
- giving them away
- by transfer, as the result of a breakdown in your marriage or domestic partnership
- through company liquidation
- through share buy-backs
- through mergers, takeovers and demergers.

When you sell your shares, your broker will send you a sell contract note to confirm the transaction. At the end of the month during which you have sold your shares, the clearing house (CHESS) will send you a statement to confirm the number of shares you have sold.

The disposal of shares in any of the ways discussed here may trigger a CGT event: that is, a capital gain or capital loss event. You will need to be aware of the following:

- The amount of the capital gain or loss: this is the difference between your cost base (which is the original, or deemed, purchase cost of those shares) and your capital proceeds (what you receive when you sell your shares). The ATO provides calculators on its website at www.ato.gov.au that are useful to help you work out your capital gain or capital loss.

- If you have owned your shares for more than 12 months, you can use the CGT discount provision and you will only be required to pay tax on 50 per cent of the capital gain (at your marginal tax rate).

- If you transfer your shares into someone else's name, including into your super fund, this also triggers a CGT event, and you may have to pay capital gains tax.

Remember, for tax purposes a capital loss can only be offset against a capital gain, meaning you pay tax on the difference only.

Franking credits

Franking credits are the result of the dividend imputation system that was introduced in Australia in 1987. When a company pays a dividend to shareholders, this dividend can be paid out of pre-tax income or post-tax income.

If dividends are paid from post-tax income, it means the company has already paid tax at the 30 per cent company tax rate. These dividends are paid to investors along with franking credits — for the share owner, these are like a rebate for the 30 per cent of tax on those dividends that the company has already paid. This means that share investors in effect only pay tax on the difference between the company tax rate and their marginal tax rate on the dividends they receive because they use the franking credits to reduce the amount of tax they have to pay.

Since 2000, franking credits have been fully refundable, meaning that if you didn't have to pay tax at all that year (for example, retirees who obtain a tax-free income stream from their superannuation fund), you can claim the franking credits back from the tax office.

Here's an example of how you can benefit from franking credits.

You have received $700 in dividends that are 100 per cent franked and are paying tax at the highest marginal rate of 45 per cent. Table 16.1 shows how your tax is calculated.

Table 16.1: calculation of tax on dividends, taking franking credits into account

Item	Amount
Dividend received	$ 700
Grossed up dividend (@ 30%)	$1000
Gross tax payable @ 45%	$ 450
Less franking credits	−$ 300
Tax payable	$ 150

The grossed up dividend is the amount of the dividend, plus the 30 per cent tax paid by the company (dividends $700 + franking credits $300 = $1000).

The 45-day rule

To prevent investors from simply buying shares, getting the franking credits and selling the shares, the tax office introduced the 45-day rule: a shareholder must hold shares for at least 45 days (not counting the days of purchase or sale) before they can claim any franking credits over $5000.

Peter's property insights

It is critical that you find an accountant who understands property, before you start buying. Most investors (and some accountants!) don't know the full extent of what can and can't be claimed. Having a thorough understanding of this, especially depreciation of plant and equipment and the capital works deduction, can vastly increase your tax refund and improve cash flow.

Zac's share insights

Just as with property investment, you need to keep meticulous records for your share investments. Remember to keep proof of all your share transactions from the beginning, when you acquire the shares through purchase or some other means, to ensure you can claim everything you're entitled to. Not only will it help you lodge your tax returns, maximise your deductions and potentially help minimise your tax liability, but good record-keeping will allow you to keep track of how your shares are performing.

 ## Conclusion

Tax is a critical consideration for all investors. The tax implications of who owns the asset, what deductions can be made and whether you are eligible for the CGT discount can all greatly impact on investors' after-tax income. Remember that as a general rule, the Australian tax system allows investors to claim as a deduction any expense that they incur in the generating of income. So keeping a record of all your expenses, with receipts, is essential and sensible.

Round 17

LEGAL ISSUES

There can be a minefield of legal matters to consider when dealing with property and shares. Legal documents that pertain to property can be particularly difficult to read, comprehend and act upon. Thankfully, for most of us contemplating the sale and purchase of real property in modern times, the complexities of the legal system are addressed by the solicitors or conveyancers that we engage to conduct the transaction.

This chapter provides an overview of some of the most important legal issues in investing in shares and property, so you will have an idea of what is involved.

★ ★ ★ ★ ★ ★ ★ PROPERTY ★ ★ ★ ★ ★ ★ ★

People talk of owning land, but in reality when we buy property we are really just acquiring an interest in land referred to as an 'estate in land'.

The estate is recognised by a certificate of title, which records your interest as the registered proprietor, as well as that of the bank or other institution as mortgagee, if you are borrowing money and using the property as security. The most common title acquired in buying land is known as freehold. Other types of titles include strata and community titles, which occur mainly in relation to units, flats and apartments.

The contract—transferring title

Conveying land from one person to another requires the transfer of title. This is done with the execution of a contract.

In Australia all land (property) sales must be by a contract in writing. Making a *verbal* offer or acceptance is not binding on either the seller or the buyer.

The contract records the names and addresses of the parties, the property being sold and any inclusions or exclusions, the price, the deposit payable, the date upon which settlement is to take place, and any special conditions.

While standard form contracts exist for all kinds of title, if changes are made to clauses or special conditions, you should seek advice from your conveyancer or lawyer before you sign.

Certain prescribed particulars of land

All states prescribe that sellers must disclose to purchasers certain particulars about the property. Most commonly these particulars include details of mortgages, rights of way over the land, zoning, and any building additions or extensions (which should have received the appropriate approvals).

These particulars are contained in a standard form, which is signed by the seller (or agent) and given to the purchaser.

This form reveals to the purchaser a considerable amount of information about the property and deserves close examination by you and your conveyancer or lawyer.

Cooling-off rights

Most Australian states and territories give a purchaser a certain amount of time after executing the contract to change their mind; this is called the 'cooling-off period'. In South Australia a prospective purchaser has two clear business days to cool off. In Victoria it is three days, in the Northern Territory it is four business days and in New South Wales, ACT and Queensland it is five days. In Western Australia and Tasmania there is no cooling-off period.

Before you buy property, you should find out what your cooling-off rights are. The cooling-off rights are determined by the state or territory in which the property is located, not the state or territory you live in.

If a purchaser signs and later decides they want to cancel the contract within the prescribed time period, they need to follow a set of procedures outlined in the contract documents.

If you buy at auction or under a company name, you have no cooling-off rights.

The purchaser

The party buying the land is known as the purchaser. That may be one or more people, a company or a trust.

The title to the property can be recorded as joint tenants, where if one dies the other automatically becomes the sole owner. This is generally the way people in a domestic partnership buy their home. Alternatively, you can buy as tenants in common: upon the death of one, their interest in the property passes according to their will. This is the way many friends and unrelated parties buy investment property.

Fixtures and fittings

Generally fixtures and fittings are included in the sale. These include such items as built-in wardrobes, plants in the garden and permanent outdoor structures, such as a shed. However, it is sometimes unclear what is a fixture or fitting.

Dishwashers are a common source of confusion in property transactions. In addition, sellers often want to take built-in large screen televisions and surround sound stereo systems with them, and the resultant damage caused to walls can be expensive to repair.

It is critical to determine precisely what is included and excluded in the contract. If required, you can ask for changes to the contract to include or exclude certain items.

The purchase price, the deposit and the balance

It is usual for the purchase price to be split into a deposit, which is payable on or shortly after the date of the contract, and the balance, which is payable at settlement.

Deposits can vary from as little as 1 per cent to 10 per cent or more of the purchase price.

If you are buying at an auction it is assumed that you are buying under auction conditions, which in most cases means you need to pay a 10 per cent deposit at the fall of the hammer and the remainder at settlement, which is usually 30 days. If you want these auction conditions changed, you need to negotiate this *before* the auction.

Settlement

The date when the balance of the purchase price is exchanged for the title is called settlement. Settlement usually takes place 30, 45, 60 or even 90 days after the signing of the contract, but the time frame can be negotiated between the purchaser and the seller.

Settlement involves the parties' conveyancers or solicitors meeting face to face with lenders and other interested parties to exchange legal papers and cheques. At the time of writing, e-conveyancing is slowly being introduced around the country and conveyancing procedures will change markedly when most transactions will occur over the internet.

Settlement is also the date that keys are exchanged and the seller hands over the property.

If settlement is delayed the inconvenience to the seller and the purchaser can be extensive, especially when removalist trucks are waiting in the street to move in.

Long delays in settlement can constitute a breach of the contract by the person who is not able to settle on time (the defaulting party). This often involves payment of penalty interest, and worse still, gives the non-defaulting party the right to terminate the contract and recover or retain the deposit, or sue for losses suffered, or both.

Special conditions

Contracts often contain special conditions that need to be satisfied before the contract binds the parties unconditionally. In other words, the contract will come into effect if and when the special conditions listed in the contract are satisfied. The most common special conditions include subject to finance, subject to a pest or building inspection and subject to the sale of an existing property.

The special condition as to finance plays a significant role in land transactions because a purchaser who is borrowing money from a bank wants to be assured of a loan before they are compelled to buy.

A seller wants to ensure that the purchaser makes their best attempt to secure finance on the terms agreed. After all, the seller wants the deal to proceed and wants to remove the opportunity for a purchaser to pull out by declaring that they couldn't get the loan.

A purchaser, on the other hand, wants to ensure that they have flexibility in the choice of bank, the loan terms and the interest rate, and doesn't want to be locked into accepting whatever is offered.

Therefore a carefully worded finance clause is essential for both parties.

After settlement

If everything goes smoothly, then usually after settlement the seller and purchaser get on with their lives and have no reason to deal with each other again. However, sometimes there are problems.

The most common issues that arise concern the condition of the property, items that don't work, dying gardens, insufficient keys, and the removal of fixtures and fittings that were part of the deal.

In addition, many sellers leave things behind that were supposed to be taken away. Old cars, pavers, pot plants and timber are just some of the unwanted items that are commonly left at the property. The cost to the purchaser to remove these items and the legal issues relating to abandoned goods can make for a very stressful affair.

House and land packages

Purchasing an existing property is not the only way to get into the property market. Developers, both large and small, offer house and land packages or off-the-plan purchases of apartments or units. This is where the purchaser agrees to buy both the land and the completed building.

You should get legal advice for these contracts, because they effectively combine land contracts and building contracts in the same deal.

★ ★ ★ ★ ★ ★ ★ ★ SHARES ★ ★ ★ ★ ★ ★ ★ ★

Australia has one of the highest percentage of sharemarket investors of any country in the world. Owning shares can be a lot simpler and cheaper than holding property.

Ownership

There are two types of share ownership:

1 *Direct ownership.* In this case you buy shares in your own name, or in the name of a structure that you control, through a broker. You are the beneficial owner of the investment.

2 *Indirect ownership.* Here you buy shares through a managed investment (managed funds) or through a listed investment company or trust, or through arrangements where your shareholding is not beneficially held by you, for example where shares are held by a person or company as trustee for another.

As a shareholder of fully paid ordinary shares, you a legal shareholder, or part-owner, of the company. You do not owe any further liability to the company beyond what you have originally invested. In the unfortunate situation of a company going broke, you cannot lose more than you have invested in the company. If you hold your shares indirectly, then you do not have these rights or ownership in the underlying share.

Shareholder rights and obligations

A company shareholder is entitled to the following benefits:

- You have a right to vote at the annual and special general meetings held by the company. This vote relates to nominating directors and also as to shareholder resolutions.

- You have the right to receive dividends, if they are declared, in accordance with the type of shares you hold.

- You have the right to purchase new shares as and when they are issued by the company.

- You may be eligible to receive bonus shares if they are declared by the company.

- If the company has a shareholder benefit program, you can use this to purchase products or services provided by the company at discounted pricing.

However, as an indirect investor where shares are not beneficially held by you, you do not have these rights: the institutions that holds the investment has these rights instead.

The settlement process

When you buy or sell shares, you have an obligation to exchange the title or legal ownership of those shares for money. The exchange is called settlement—just as it is for property. Unlike for property, you do not need to use a conveyancer or lawyer: the entire settlement process is handled by your broker through the ASX's clearing house electronic settlement system (CHESS).

In summary, the settlement process works as follows:

- A buyer and seller are matched and trade on the exchange. As a buyer or seller of shares, you will receive a buy or sell contract note from your broker.

- The buyer agrees to provide funds to the seller, who agrees to supply the shares in return for the funds.

- Settlement of this transaction occurs after three days (T+3), when the title is transferred from the seller to the buyer. Figure 17.1 shows the process.

Figure 17.1: the settlement process for shares

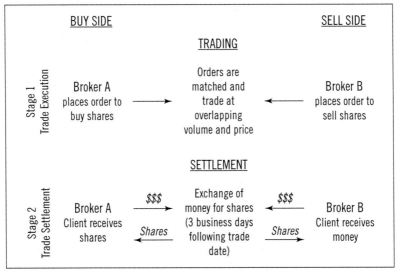

Source: Based on Figure 1: Trading and Settlement services, on the ASX website: www.asx.com.au/products/chess_settlement.htm

On settlement, the shares you have purchased are transferred to you in exchange for your paying the consideration to the seller.

Settlement is guaranteed to both the buyer and the seller. As a buyer, if you fail to pay, your broker will cover the transaction and then may charge you interest and fail fees for not settling on time.

An investor has a choice to have their shareholdings registered and held in one of two ways:

- as issuer sponsored (through a shareholder reference number—SRN)

- as CHESS sponsored (through a holder identification number—HIN).

Every ASX listed company manages its own issuer-sponsored subregister for the registration of shares in their company alone. This form of registration is also referred to as being issuer sponsored. Alternatively, shares in any listed company can be registered in the CHESS subregister. This form of registration is held within the CHESS system and allows brokers to manage their sponsored client's shareholdings. This form of registration is also referred to as being broker sponsored. It is also the most efficient system for you as an investor, as all your holdings with a broker are held under one identification number.

The characteristics of the two systems are shown in table 17.1.

Table 17.1: comparison of the two types of share registrations

Shares CHESS sponsored	Shares issuer sponsored
Legal title is electronically registered and is similar to a bank account.	Legal title is electronically registered and is similar to a bank account.
Your shares are sponsored or controlled by your broker.	Your shares are controlled by the particular share registry used by the listed company.
You receive one holder identification number (HIN) for all holdings sponsored by a single broker. For example, a shareholder with securities in 10 different companies will have one HIN if they are all sponsored in CHESS by one broker.	You may receive a security holder reference number (SRN) for each company's securities. For example, a shareholder owning securities in 10 different companies may have 10 different SRNs if the shares are issuer sponsored.
You only need to contact your sponsoring broker to change your name, address, notification of TFN and so on, for all the securities held by that broker.	To change your personal details you may need to contact the share registry for each of the company's securities they hold.
Your shares are already on CHESS so they are ready to trade.	Before you can trade your broker will need to move your shares from your issuer sponsored account onto CHESS.
CHESS issues monthly holding statements for each security where the holding balance has changed. These look the same for all the securities held.	Each share registry issues their own monthly issuer sponsored holding statements for each security held where the balance has changed.

Advisers and brokers

Any business that provides financial products or services in Australia is required to have an Australian financial services licence (AFSL). Therefore, before you buy or sell any shares through a broker, or take any investment advice from a financial advisory business or person, you should check with ASIC that the adviser and broker you are dealing with or does indeed hold a valid. AFSL that they hold the specific licence conditions to provide the services they offer and that the adviser is an authorised representative of that business. This can be done through the ASIC website at https://connectonline.asic.gov.au.

General versus personal advice

It is important to understand the type of financial advice that you receive from an adviser, and whether it is of a general nature, or whether it is specific to your financial situation.

- *General advice.* This is financial advice about a product that does *not* take into account whether it is appropriate for you, such as a general research report from a broker, or an investment newsletter that provides an opinion on an investment based only on the facts of the investment. You then have to make the decision yourself as to whether you wish to invest in it.

- *Personal advice.* This is financial advice that you receive from a financial planner who has undertaken a fact-finding exercise to understand your financial situation and has therefore considered whether a particular investment is suitable for you to invest in.

ASIC requires that all personal financial advice be provided to investors in a statement of advice (SoA) document that presents the investment advice in a concise manner and also the reasons why the advice is appropriate to you and your situation. Your adviser will also be required to keep a record of advice (RoA) for any subsequent changes to the advice they have provided you.

 ## Peter's property insights

Buying property involves a great deal of paperwork, much of it legal. While some people choose to do the buying, selling and managing of their properties on their own, I strongly discourage people trying to manage the legal documentation on their own. You should use a conveyancer or lawyer for these property transactions.

Zac's share insights

Investing in shares is a lot simpler and cheaper, legally, than buying or selling property. You do not need to enlist the services of a lawyer or conveyancer to coordinate the transaction. This, along with the fact that you can start investing in shares with just a small amount of money, makes share investment an easier and less intimidating option for most people who want to invest in growth assets. Your adviser will also be required to keep a record of advice (RoA) for any subsequent changes to the advice they have provided you.

 ## Conclusion

The legal issues relating to property and share investment can be the most complicated aspect of buying, holding and selling these assets. There is an old saying that it takes money to make money. The value of good advice (be it personal advice from a financial planner or legal advice from a lawyer or conveyancer) should not be underestimated: in addition to it being tax deductible, it will be money well spent.

Round 18

OVERSEAS INVESTMENTS

Buying property and shares overseas can be very different from buying locally. You will be affected by different markets, different rules and regulations, and different currencies. In this chapter we provide you with an overview of buying investments overseas and some of the implications of doing so.

★ ★ ★ ★ ★ ★ ★ PROPERTY ★ ★ ★ ★ ★ ★ ★

There are thousands of overseas real estate investment trusts (REITs) that you could invest in, but in this chapter we focus on direct property investment overseas. That is, buying real property in another country.

There are more than 200 countries in the world and theoretically you could buy property in most of them. However, most nations have rules about property ownership by foreigners. In Australia, for example, few restrictions are placed on foreigners who want to buy commercial property. There are more constraints when it comes to purchasing residential property. In Australia, foreigners are encouraged to add to the supply of residential property and therefore are allowed to buy new, off-the-plan property or vacant land for development. However, foreign non-residents or short-term visa holders cannot buy Australian established (secondhand) dwellings, unless it is for redevelopment.

The rules and regulations vary considerably across the world. Some countries forbid foreigners to directly buy property, though they may do it in partnership with a local or through an offshore company. Other countries strongly encourage foreign ownership. If you are seriously interested in buying overseas, I strongly recommend you visit the location you wish to buy in and conduct your own due diligence.

Owning property in a location a long way from where you live comes with its own challenges. Imagine you own an investment property several hundred kilometres from your home and you need a plumber to replace taps in the bathroom. If the property is managed by a competent property manager, that shouldn't be a problem. They should organise quotes, arrange access to the property for the repairs to be done and pay the bill on your behalf. This is quite simple in Australia, where we have strict rules and a code of ethics that most property professionals should abide by, but that cannot be said of all places around the world.

Let's imagine that you own a cute farmhouse in a village in the French countryside. It is charming, rustic and has a lovely view of the valley below. Sounds wonderful! Now suppose that the bathroom needs some new taps. Your property manager, who is a relative of a friend of a friend you met while you were in France on holidays, has organised a quote from the local plumber. The plumber says that the job will cost the equivalent of A$7000 and he wants full payment before he starts. You tell the property manager that this is outrageous and you want another quote. The property manager says that there are no other plumbers in the village and if you want other plumbers to quote, it will cost you much more as they have to travel from other areas. (Unbeknown to you, the plumber is your property manger's cousin and they are running a scam to rip off foreign owners.) What do you do now?

If this occurred in a small town in Australia, you have a number of options. When this occurs in a different country, thousands of kilometres away and you are unfamiliar with the language, let alone your property management rights, you have very limited options.

Buying property overseas can be fraught with difficulties for many reasons. They include:

- *Arranging finance.* Australian banks are reluctant to lend money to borrowers who want to buy property overseas.

- *Lax property laws.* Australia's property laws are very tight, with parties' rights and obligations made very clear. The same can't be said for many countries around the world.

- *Tax issues.* You may need to find an accountant overseas, as you are earning income overseas and you may need to pay tax in that country.

- *Different language and culture.* The landlord/tenant relationship varies considerably around the world.

- *Susceptibility to being ripped off as an absent landlord.* The temptation is there, as scammers know there is not much chance that you will fly over each time there is an issue.

- *Currency risk.* Your earnings from a property may be affected by changes in the value of the local currency.

Currency risk is very important. Not only do you need to do your due diligence before you purchase the property and try to keep an eye on it from afar, but you are also susceptible to movement in the currency.

The following example shows how your cash flow can be affected by fluctuating exchange rates.

Example

You have bought that cute farmhouse in France. The purchase price is €100 000 and the tenant pays €10 000 per year in rent. Cash expenses, such as property taxes, repairs and property management fees, average €3000 per year.

First, let's assume that when you bought the property, A$1 = €1. The effects of currency are shown in table 18.1.

Table 18.1: property investment if A$1 = €1

Cost	Amount in Euros (€)	Amount in Australian dollars ($)
Purchase price	100 000	100 000
Rent	10 000	10 000
Expenses	3 000	3 000

Table 18.1 shows that purchase price, rent and property expenses are dollar for dollar.

Now let's assume that the exchange rate has changed, and it is now A$1 = €0.50 (see table 18.2).

Table 18.2: property investment if A$1 = €0.50

Cost	Amount in euros (€)	Amount in Australian dollars ($)
Purchase price	100 000	200 000
Rent	10 000	20 000
Expenses	3 000	6 000

In the scenario shown in table 18.2, you have to pay double in Australian dollars to buy the property; your rent doubles in value, but so do your expenses.

In the final scenario, let's assume that the exchange rate adjusts the other way to A$0.50 = €1 (see table 18.3).

Table 18.3: property investment if A$0.50 = €1

Cost	Amount in Euros (€)	Amount in Australian dollars ($)
Purchase price	100 000	50 000
Rent	10 000	5 000
Expenses	3 000	1 500

Because of the fluctuation in the exchange rate, you need to pay only half the original price in Australian dollars, but the value of your rent halves, and so do your expenses.

The best scenario is that you buy when A$0.50 = €1 and sell when A$1 = €0.50! Unfortunately you have no control over exchange rates, but as you can see from the examples, it can greatly affect your cash flow and wealth.

★ ★ ★ ★ ★ ★ ★ ★ SHARES ★ ★ ★ ★ ★ ★ ★ ★

The Australian sharemarket comprises just 2 per cent of the value (market capitalisation) of the world's sharemarkets. Yes, Australia offers some of the biggest and best-managed companies to invest in, such as BHP Billiton and Commonwealth Bank, but what if you want to invest in shares in companies such Apple, Samsung, Microsoft, Google, General Motors, Johnson & Johnson or McDonald's?

Well you can. Investors who want to invest directly in overseas-listed shares can now do so much more easily and cheaply than ever before!

Online and full-service brokers

Thanks to the advances in technology and the internet over the last 10 years or so, share investors can now access almost any investment market in the world from the comfort of their home, using just a computer and a brokerage account. Almost all the major online brokers, including CommSec, E★TRADE and Macquarie as well as a myriad of overseas brokers now based in Australia, such as Interactive Brokers, are now offering investors and traders access to overseas markets from one account. More and more full-service brokers are now also offering access to direct investment in overseas shares through affiliated brokers in other countries.

Online brokers will usually be cheaper in terms of transaction costs, and possibly provide a faster trading service than full-service brokers will for overseas trading.

Managed funds

One problem with investing in overseas shares is that you may not have access to the right research. A solution for many investors is to invest through a managed fund that invests in the markets (and shares) you want to invest in. These funds spend hundreds of thousands, if not millions, of dollars on researching their designated markets, and presumably can provide better investment returns than if you were to invest directly into these shares yourself. Some funds also hedge their exposure to currency movements.

A big advantage of investing in this way is that you can invest with just a small amount of money, sometimes with as little as $5000.

The biggest drawback, however, is that you don't have transparency or direct control over the underlying investments, as well as the additional costs involved.

Exchange traded funds (ETFs)

We discussed exchange traded funds in Round 11 and explained that exchange traded funds (ETFs) are an efficient way of purchasing a basket of shares with one investment. ETFs present an ideal compromise for most investors who want exposure to overseas markets without investing in overseas markets directly themselves—and who don't want to pay fees to a managed fund.

More and more ETFs are being released on the Australian sharemarket every month, and you could easily gain exposure to virtually any market around the world with these, depending on your views, in the same way that you buy a share.

Exchange traded international securities (ETIS)

A new product that gives exposure to a limited number of international shares in Australian dollars is available to Australian investors and is traded on the ASX. These are exchange traded international securities (ETIS) and are offered by Royal Bank of Scotland (RBS) on the ASX, meaning there is some potential for counterparty risk.

These products have a 10-year term and pricing is linked directly to the underlying overseas share price, and so they are subject to exchange rate fluctuations (a fall in the rate means your investment will increase in value). RBS is responsible for providing buy and sell prices for each ETIS, thereby providing volume (liquidity) for trading.

So if you wanted to buy Google shares, for instance, you could instead just buy Google ETIS on the ASX. The number of shares you buy gives you the same exposure as buying Google on the NASDAQ exchange in New York.

A disadvantage of ETIS is that they don't provide the investor with voting rights, or rights to dividends or other distributions. ETIS investors instead will receive an income amount directly from RBS when dividends are paid, subject to a 15 per cent withholding tax that it deducts from the proceeds on your behalf and pays to the ATO. Of the remainder, 50 per cent is paid to the investor in Australian dollars, and the other 50 per cent is retained by RBS!

Benefits of overseas investment

The main advantages of overseas investment in shares are:

Diversification. By investing overseas, you can further diversify your investment portfolio to other markets. We have learned that diversification is part of a risk management strategy to minimise the risk on your investment portfolio.

Access to opportunities not available in Australia. With 98 per cent of the world's sharemarket market capitalisation overseas, there is likely to be much more opportunity to invest in sectors such as IT and biotechology, which are so much bigger overseas, and also in companies that are not listed in Australia, such as Apple Inc.

Liquidity. The Australian sharemarket is relatively small and, depending on the shares you own, it can sometimes prove difficult to buy or sell the quantity you want to transact at the price you want, because there simply may not be sufficient supply of shares at those prices.

High Australian dollar. The value of the Australian dollar has recently been relatively high against most overseas currencies, so you have had more buying power to invest in overseas shares. In a situation where you expect the Australian dollar to fall in value, you could also profit from the devaluation of the currency when you sell your investment and convert your overseas currency back to Australian dollars.

Risks of overseas investment

The main risk of overseas share investment is currency or exchange rate risk. When you invest overseas, your transactions are made in the relevant foreign currency. This means you have to buy or sell the local currency against the Australian dollar in order to settle the transaction, so if the currency moves against you, any gains you have made on your investment could be lost when you convert your overseas currency back to Australian dollars.

Questions to ask your broker

What markets can you access through your broker? Ideally you will have the ability to trade most markets from one account; alternatively, you may need to use different brokers for different markets.

- Who does your broker use at the other end of the transaction? If your stockbroker is not using ASX World Link, are their overseas trading orders being placed through an affiliated stockbroking firm in the overseas market, or is some third party involved? If it's the latter, it can be costly, as you are likely to pay multiple brokerages.

- How much do they charge for brokerage?

- Do they charge custody fees, or other fees and charges?

- Does the broker have minimum amounts for a transaction?

- How and when can you place your orders? Does the broker operate a night desk (when overseas markets will be trading) or can you place the orders yourself online?

- How do they settle transactions? Will you be required to settle in Australian dollars or the overseas currency?

- Where are your shares held, and how are they registered? Are you the beneficial owner?

- How is foreign currency interest accounted for and reported for Australian tax purposes?

- What research do they provide?

- Are you able to buy other types of investments too, such as ETFs or derivatives?

Peter's property insights

Buying property overseas can come at a high risk, but the rewards can also be high. Some of my students bought property overseas straight after the GFC, when property prices plummeted in many countries, and they have since seen marked capital growth as the overseas property market has picked up. The benefits of buying property overseas can include a relatively cheap entry price and high rental returns. Some of the pitfalls have been outlined in this chapter. If you are seriously considering buying overseas, you need a local lawyer who can also speak English, a bilingual property manager, buyer's advocate and possibly an accountant. Your due diligence should also include visiting the area and inspecting the properties you wish to buy.

Zac's share insights

Investors tend to forget that a lot of Australian-listed companies do have overseas affiliations or subsidiaries. Companies such as BHP and RIO, for example, are international companies that are listed on multiple exchanges overseas. In addition, it could be argued that because a lot of our locally based companies have business interests overseas, they do provide some exposure to overseas markets anyway. So an investment in a company such as these indirectly gives you access to overseas markets.

Another reason that you might invest in overseas shares is to diversify your portfolio or to gain exposure to an opportunity or sector that does not exist here in Australia. But because of the alternative, indirect, ways of investing in overseas markets that are available, such as using ETFs and managed funds, there may be little need for the average retail investor to look overseas.

 ## Conclusion

Overseas investing is fraught with danger if you don't have access to the right research, and it also brings currency risk that can erode part if not all of your gains. It is vital that you conduct due diligence before investing overseas in any asset, as different markets operate in different ways.

Round 19

SCHEMES AND SCAMS

Every year in Australia and around the world, thousands of naïve and innocent investors are tricked and defrauded out of their money by scammers. Unfortunately it is very difficult to totally eliminate unscrupulous operators from the property and finance areas, so you should you educate yourself so that you are more likely to be aware if someone claims to be running a scheme but is really running a cleverly disguised scam. Knowing how to distinguish a scam from a legitimate investment scheme will help save you money if you are ever to come across a scam, and also save you a lot of stress and embarrassment.

Legitimate investment schemes include those products and services that have been developed with benefiting the investor as a main priority. This is not the case with scams. Scams are set up for the sole purpose of benefiting the scammers. It can very difficult to differentiate between schemes and scams. Conducting your own due diligence, such as searching their respective websites, calling their number and making enquiries and checking property and share forums and blog sites will help assist you in determining what is a scheme and what is a scam.

Investment scams usually appear to be legitimate and it may be difficult to distinguish them from a genuine investment opportunity. There are, however, some ways to prepare yourself, by knowing what to look out for—because it is inevitable that you will come across a scam during your investment life.

Identifying a Scam

Be wary of emails, phone calls and letters from people or companies that you have never heard of or asked for, that offer you a wonderful investment opportunity. In fact, it may even be an offer from someone you trust who is also in the process of being scammed!

Scams have one thing in common: the money being 'invested' goes into the scammers' bank account, not towards any real investment. There are usually three types of scams:

- where the investment itself does not exist
- where the investment exists, but the money you give the scammer to invest is never invested
- an outright lie about the scammer, and the product, service or investment.

The warning signs of a scam

Here is a list of tell-tale signs that you may be dealing with a scammer:

- unsolicited communications, including cold calls, from companies or people you have not met
- an invitation to attend an 'education seminar', which is really a cleverly disguised hard-sell opportunity for the scammer
- an offer that promises *extraordinarily* high returns and tax benefits
- an offer that promises 'no-risk' or 'low-risk' investments for high returns
- the scammer contacts you many times
- the scammer tries to entice you to invest by telling you to make a quick decision or you will miss out
- you receive glossy brochures or the scammer provides you with details for a slick website.

How to avoid scams

Here are some tips for avoiding scams:

- Never give out any of your personal information to anyone you don't know or you haven't invited to talk to you. This is especially true for your bank details.

- If an offer seems too good to be true, it usually is.

- If you get an unsolicited communication that sounds suspect, do some due diligence on the people making the offer:

  - ~ Check the ASIC website (www.asic.gov.au) to confirm that the company is in fact a real company and that it holds an Australian financial services licence (AFSL).
  - ~ Check the ASIC website to confirm that the person talking to you actually is an authorised representative of that licensee.
  - ~ Call the company yourself and ask to speak to that person.
  - ~ Check the MoneySmart website at www.moneysmart.gov.au, the consumer website run by ASIC, to see whether there is a listing of that person or company as a scammer or company you should not deal with. Also, use an internet search to see if anyone else has had an experience with that person or company.
  - ~ Ask the person offering the investment these questions: What is their name and what company do they work for? Who owns the company? What the AFSL number of the company? What is their address?

- If you suspect that the offer is a scam, report the offer to ASIC or to the police and warn your family and friends.

- *Buyer beware!*

★ ★ ★ ★ ★ ★ ★ **PROPERTY** ★ ★ ★ ★ ★ ★ ★

Legitimate property schemes

There are numerous legitimate property investment schemes. Here we will described three: Defence Housing, the National Rental Affordability Scheme (NRAS) and Property Options for Pensioners and Investors (Popi).

Defence Housing

Defence Housing Australia (DHA) has been around since 1988. It was established to provide housing for members of the Australian Defence Force (ADF) and their families.

In the past, it had been very costly for the government to build and maintain houses for the defence forces. Money spent on housing means less money they can spend on military equipment and personnel. In more recent times, the ADF has moved from owning houses to leasing property for its personnel.

Under the DHA scheme, homes are built for defence personnel and are then offered for sale to investors. Investors are able to purchase properties on a long-term lease through DHA. Leases will often run for three, six or nine years and include an option for DHA to extend the lease.

Most properties are located close to military bases, and this can be a downside if you are seeking long-term capital growth, as military bases are often a long way from the CBD and facilities. However, this scheme can be ideal for investors who want a hassle-free investment, as DHA takes care of most of the property management issues and there are no vacancies to worry about during the term of the lease.

For more information, go to www.dha.gov.au.

National Rental Affordability Scheme (NRAS)

NRAS is a federal government initiative, in partnership with the states and territories. It commenced in 2008 and was established to address the shortage of affordable rental housing by offering incentives to property investors willing to rent to low- and moderate-income households at 20 per cent below the market rent. NRAS is not a public housing scheme; it is a tax incentive to encourage more private housing for lower income households.

At the moment the tax incentive offered is a tax-free payment of approximately $10 000. This payment will be made each year for 10 years, provided the investor continues to stay in the scheme. This cash payment is indexed to inflation and will increase as market rents increase. Here is an example of how it works.

Example

Here is a simple example of how NRAS works.

Calculation

Property value: $400 000
Market rent: $20 000 per year
Discounted rent: $16 000 (20% discount on $20 000)
Rent shortfall: $4000 ($20 000 − $16 000)
Tax-free incentive: $10 000
Gain: $6000

Companies involved in the administration of NRAS, such as property managers, have to be paid their fees and charges by the investor, so the total benefit to the property investor is less than the $6000 illustrated in the example, but in the end they should be better off, so far as cash flow is concerned, if they buy an NRAS property.

NRAS is great for investors who are seeking high cash flow, as the tax-free incentive goes a long way to paying rental expenses. If you also want to ensure good potential for capital growth, you should make certain that the property is well located and has a significant land component.

Be careful! There are some rogue operators who will try to sell the property to you at a price that is much higher than market value, or charge exorbitant fees, which results in the investor missing out on most of the $10 000 annual incentive.

For more information, go to www.fahcsia.gov.au.

Property Options for Pensioners and Investors (Popi)

Popi Australia was established in 2010. Its purpose is to bring pensioners and property investors together through a 'Popi'.

A Popi is an option agreement between a senior home-owner (whether they are an age pensioner or self-funded retiree) and an investor. Under a Popi, the pensioner gives the investor the option (right) to buy their home at a pre-agreed price upon the occurrence of certain specified 'trigger' events, in exchange for a monthly payment. These trigger events can include the pensioner wanting to sell their property or dying. The monthly payment (Popi payment) to the pensioner may continue for months or years, depending on when a trigger event takes place.

The following simplified example shows how a Popi could work.

> ## Example
>
> Here is a simple example of how Popi works.
> Property value (2014): $400 000
> Average Popi payment: $10 000 per year
> Property value (2024): $800 000
>
> Basically, a pensioner gives the property investor the option to buy their property for $400 000. If the trigger event doesn't occur until 2024, the property could be worth $800 000, but the property investor pays only $400 000 for it. Why? The property investor has made regular Popi payments over 10 years for the option (not the obligation) to buy the property at the pre-determined price.

There are number of different types of Popis. For example, an investor can receive 100 per cent of the capital growth if they make 100 per cent of the cash payment. Alternatively, an investor can make 50 per cent of the cash payments and share the capital growth with the pensioner, 50–50. The type of Popi offered is determined by the pensioner.

For the pensioner, the main advantage is that they receive extra income. It doesn't affect their age pension and is not considered taxable income. For the investor, they don't need to find money for a deposit or qualify for a bank loan. They really don't have a 'tenant', in the traditional sense of the word, who needs to be managed. The pensioner is still the owner of the property and looks after it accordingly.

Investors need to be aware that if they decide to terminate the option agreement before a trigger event occurs, any Popi payments made are kept by the pensioner.

For more information, go to www.popiaustralia.com.au.

Property scams

One of the reasons property attracts so many scammers is that the property investment advice industry is not regulated. You don't need a licence or a qualification to engage in advising on property investment, nor are there any continuing professional development requirements of anyone or any organisation that provides property investment advice. In my opinion, this is a totally unsatisfactory situation but, at the time of writing, the Property Investment Professionals of Australia (PIPA) is talking to the federal government about regulating the industry. There has been no action from the government to date, but the talks are continuing.

The two most recent property scams have involved selling vacant land on Queensland islands, and mezzanine finance. This is not to say that all land sales on Queensland islands and all mezzanine finance deals are illegal, immoral or unethical, but these are two recent activities that scammers were heavily involved in.

Land sales

In the 1980s and 1990s, some companies were involved in the sale of land on islands off the Queensland coast. These operators lured unwary potential buyers from interstate to Queensland by offering free flights, free rides to and from the site in a limousine or helicopter, and all meals and drinks. They flew investors up in the morning, took them to the island and then gave the hard sell and pressured people to sign a contract on the spot before they were flown home that evening.

The reason they targeted interstate buyers was that they did not have any local knowledge and could easily be duped into buying a small piece of a tropical island in the Sunshine State. The problem was that they were being shown coastal land at *low tide*. These unwary buyers were being coaxed into buying waterfront land but were unaware that, at high tide, there was no land: it was all covered by water!

Potential investors were attracted by the dream of owning a piece of paradise, but what they were getting themselves into was a watery nightmare.

Mezzanine finance

In the 1990s and early 2000s, mezzanine financing was very popular. Mezzanine finance is commonly used in large-scale property developments. It often works like this: the bank is willing to provide, say, 65 per cent of the total funds required to purchase land and construct a resort-style complex. The developer is able to contribute 10 per cent, but they still require 25 per cent to begin the project. This 25 per cent is known as mezzanine finance as it sits in the middle of the owner's and bank's finance.

On the face of it, there is nothing wrong with mezzanine finance. Lending money towards a development can be a very legitimate and profitable way to make money.

The problem occurred where companies were seeking finance from investors and not fully disclosing what the investors' money was to be used for. Most investors thought that they were investing in a development and would own a portion of it upon completion. Unfortunately they were wrong. The investors' money was being used to finance the construction of the buildings and they would eventually not own any of the property. In theory, they would earn a share of the development profits. However, these companies regularly went broke, leaving developments unfinished and the investors with empty pockets.

The investors were originally attracted by high returns, often 20 per cent or more. As we have stated in this book many times, a higher return is often associated with a higher risk. The investors were happy with the projected return, but were unaware of the huge risks involved, as not all the information was fully disclosed.

So, what will be the next scam? Currently popular are off-the-plan apartment sales. Again, I wish to state that not all off-the-plan property sales are a scam. In fact, most of them are legitimate businesses, but because high commissions can be paid, the area attracts rogues who are slick salespeople and just want a quick dollar. To avoid being duped by a rogue operator, you should do your own due diligence and don't be pressured into buying anything without this research.

★ ★ ★ ★ ★ ★ ★ ★ **SHARES** ★ ★ ★ ★ ★ ★ ★ ★

Shares scams

Just as it is for property, an investor may encounter several types of share scams. I will describe several of the more common ones and provide you with insights on how to identify a possible scam. A more detailed list can be found on ASIC's MoneySmart website (www.moneysmart.gov.au) and also on the ACCC's ScamWatch website (www.scamwatch.gov.au).

Pump-and-dump scams

In these scams the scammer will hold shares in small companies on the sharemarket and try to drive up the price of those shares, and then sell their holdings at a profit. They do this through sending out false tips and research to suggest that the company has great prospects, but it actually does not. When the share price increases because people are buying on rumours, they are selling into that strength. This is illegal, and ASIC is always on the lookout to find people that spread these rumours. The penalties can be significant. The lesson here is to be wary of stock tips, especially from non-professional sources. Always take a cynical approach with tips. Ask yourself: 'What could be the reason someone is touting a particular share? Could it be that they want others to buy it so the price goes up and they can get out?'

Offers to buy your shares off-market

In this case a scammer obtains a record of your shareholdings from a share registry, and then contacts you with an offer to buy your shares at a fixed price, often significantly below the real market value.

This type of scam has resulted in thousands of dollars being lost by unsuspecting investors (usually elderly investors) who did not know the market prices of the shares at the time of the offer, or know how to find them, in order to compare the offer price to the market price. The result was that they sold their shares at a discount to the scammer.

Pyramid (Ponzi) schemes

Many scams are in the form of Ponzi schemes: these are pyramid-type arrangements where the scammer pays investors from the proceeds of their original investment or from investments by further investors, rather than from profits from the underlying investment. Naïve investors have an impression that a legitimate investment opportunity exists, until there are no more investors entering the pyramid—at which point the scammer disappears.

A notorious case of a Ponzi scheme that rocked the global investment markets in December 2008 was that of Bernie Madoff's investment company, Bernie Madoff Securities LLC in New York. It became the longest running Ponzi scheme in history, until its collapse in 2008 due to the effects of the GFC. When investors tried to withdraw money from the firm they discovered there wasn't any!

Madoff's firm was founded in 1960 and there were many high-profile individuals, celebrities and high net-worth investors investing significant sums of money in his business. He claimed to invest in blue-chip shares and also traded options to protect the portfolios and extract additional income. The reality was that Madoff never invested the money at all, and the reported returns he provided to his existing clients was from the new money being invested by people who entered his funds.

Investors should have seen the warning signs: he issued little or no detailed documentation about the investments he was making; he didn't allow his clients online access to view their accounts; he was secretive about his investment strategy; and he had unusually consistent returns (around 10 per cent per year), with just five negative months in 15 years! Other red flags were that the auditor of the massive fund was a small one-person accounting firm, and there was a lack of transparency in trading—Madoff's company did not use external brokers to place trades: it processed them all itself.

Early access to your superannuation

Some companies offer systems—scams—to give you early access to your superannuation for a fee. These offers may appear to be made by legitimate financial advisers who will ask you to agree to a 'story' to tell your super fund in order to secure the early release of your money. Then they deceive your superannuation fund into paying out these benefits directly to them, and then they disappear, leaving you with nothing!

Remember: you cannot withdraw the preserved part of your super fund until you reach your preservation age or you meet conditions of release as set out in the SIS Act, including exceptions such as severe financial hardship or compassionate grounds.

If you do withdraw money from your super fund early for an illegal reason, you may be subject to legal action and heavy penalties (including tax penalties, because your super has been built in a concessional tax regime).

Fincorp Investment Ltd

Fincorp was established as a finance company that offered debentures (a type of fixed interest investment) to retail investors. The funds raised were lent out to businesses involved in development and construction of non-CBD land subdivision projects in Brisbane and Newcastle. This type of lending (to fund construction) is a very risky sector of the mortgage market compared with loans for existing housing. This is because if a borrower of a house defaults, the house can be resold and the loan extinguished; an incomplete project may not be able to be sold for as much as the loan amount.

Unfortunately, Fincorp used misleading advertising to claim that investing in debentures was as safe as investing in a bank, and it offered investors very high returns. Another warning should have been that it made loan approvals within one week!

In March 2007, the company collapsed and lost more than $200 million invested by over 8000 retail investors, most of them over 60 years of age.

Opes Prime Group

Opes Prime was an Australian brokerage that collapsed in March 2008. It provided margin lending facilities for the purchase of shares, including loans for speculative shares (shares that have low market capitalisation, have no or negative cash flow, and are priced below $1), whereas most margin lenders will generally not allow investors to use margin lending for shares that are outside the top 200. Opes held the shares as collateral until the loans were paid off.

What investors did not realise was that they had assigned beneficial ownership of their shares to Opes Prime when they took on the loans. These shares were then provided to ANZ Bank by Opes as security for the funds it borrowed to then provide loans to investors. However, Opes Prime also borrowed some of the stock itself from its investors and lent it to other investors, who used it to short sell (selling someone else's stock while planning to buy it back when the price falls). In addition, Opes favoured several clients that the company tried to assist by transferring funds and shares to increase their portfolio values. But when the effects of the GFC on the sharemarket caused a discrepancy from which Opes eventually could no longer hide, the company collapsed and clients lost both their money and their shares.

Storm Financial

Storm Financial was a financial advisory business with more than 13 000 clients across Australia. Its model was to advise clients to draw on the equity in their homes and investment properties, and then apply those funds to obtain margin loans for buying shares—in effect creating gearing on gearing, which would magnify the risk of loss substantially.

The loans were funded largely by the Commonwealth Bank. While the market rose, everyone seemed to make a lot of money, but the problems started in 2008 when the sharemarket suffered large losses due to the effects of the GFC, which drove down the price of almost all shares significantly. This triggered margin calls on many investors' portfolios, even those with low-geared investment portfolios. (You will recall from our earlier discussion on margin lending that to meet a margin call, you have to deposit additional cash, or shares, to reduce your loan value. If you don't, the lender has the right to sell your shares to reduce the loan.)

Storm's clients, who were doubly geared, suffered significant losses, and eventually reached a point at which they could no longer reduce their borrowings and meet margin calls. Commonwealth Bank forced Storm into administration in January 2009 as a result of this failure to finance margin calls on their clients' portfolios

Many of Storm's clients lost their homes as a result of this collapse. Several factors caused this, including the double gearing, and the collapse of the sharemarket, in addition to the fact that margin lending was not classified as a financial product by ASIC at the time, so it was not regulated. The unfortunate outcome of the Storm collapse was that it affected a lot of retirees who should not have been advised to use margin lending (due to the risks associated with borrowing to invest in volatile assets) at their stage of life.

Peter's property insights

Due to the large amounts of money involved in purchasing property, and the lack of regulation in property investment advice, real estate tends to attract more than its fair share of scammers and rogues. Ensure that you conduct your own research and due diligence, and get a second and third opinion from people that you trust, such as an accountant, lawyer or qualified property investment adviser.

Zac's share insights

It is an unfortunate fact of life that if there is an opportunity for someone to profit from deceiving another person, that it will be exploited. When it comes to your money and, in particular, your share investments, you really need to adopt a sceptical approach from the start. Question *everything*. Especially if there is something about the share investment opportunity that you do not understand, or that appears suspicious.

As a result of the GFC, a lot of significant changes have been made to the financial services industry, including changing the classification of margin lending so it is now classed as a financial product, putting the onus on advisers to be qualified to advise on these loans. But the law can only go so far: it is ultimately the responsibility of the individual to beware!

Be especially wary of promises of high returns with little or no risk. These are usually the first signs that you are about to be the victim of a scam. Be wary of unsolicited emails, letters or phone calls from people who appear to be interested in helping you with your share investments—particularly schemes and people that offer to buy your shares directly. Ensure that your share investments and your money are beneficially held by you, or in entities that you control, such as trusts or companies, at all times. Finally, always consult the ASIC website to check whether the people you are dealing with have the appropriate qualifications and licence to provide advice.

 ## Conclusion

Investment guru Warren Buffett is quoted as saying: 'It's only when the tide goes out that you know who is swimming naked'. This is a very relevant statement when it comes to investment schemes that are actually scams. When everyone is making money, it seems that everyone forgets to use common sense and question things that may seem to good to be true. It is only when things go bad, as they did during the GFC, that many of these schemes unravel and show their flaws. And that is usually when people look to blame someone else for their own naivety.

Scams, on the other hand, are prevalent any time and anywhere, and they can be very sophisticated and deceptive. It really is a case of buyer beware when it comes to making investment decisions.

Round 20
TOP QUESTIONS TO ASK

You will need to deal with many professionals when you are buying, managing and selling your property or shares. It is crucial that you ask the right questions of these professionals so that you understand their roles, how they can help you and what their help or advice will cost. In some circumstances, they won't give you all the information you need upfront, because they fear it might jeopardise their opportunity to make money, but most of the time they just don't know what you don't know, as they aren't mind readers! You should also have a good rapport with your advisers: find someone who speaks your language and doesn't use a lot of jargon, and whom you believe will act in your best interests. There's no point in dealing with someone who isn't transparent or that you don't like or feel comfortable with.

Following is an outline of the questions you should be asking.

★ ★ ★ ★ ★ ★ ★ **PROPERTY** ★ ★ ★ ★ ★ ★ ★

Buying property
The following are some of the key questions you should be asking in relation to the purchase of property.

Accountant—What experience do you have with setting up structures within which to buy property?

It is critical that you work out in whose or what name the property should be held *before* you finalise the purchase contract. The easiest option is to buy in your personal name, but this may not be the best option for your circumstances. Rounds 14 and 15 have more information about structures. Make sure you consult an accountant who understands property and will be able to give you guidance in this area.

Banker—What are the interest rate, and the upfront, ongoing and exit fees of the most appropriate loan for my circumstances?

It is relatively easy to determine the interest rate of a loan, but what can be more difficult to find out are some of the hidden fees. When I say hidden, I mean that they are somewhere in the contract but they are often specified in the small print or somewhere among the volume of pages that makes up the loan contract. Typical upfront fees include application, establishment and valuation fees. Many loans have regular ongoing fees that are generally charged monthly. Banks can also charge hefty exit fees if you pay off the loan too early or want to terminate a fixed rate loan before the end of the period.

There is no point in accepting a loan that seems to have a relatively low interest rate if the fees and charges are very high.

Building or pest inspector—Can you please provide me with a written report and an estimation of the repairs that are required on this property?

Generally two types of reports can be provided by a building or pest inspector: written or verbal. A verbal report is not worth the paper that it is not written on! A written report provides a permanent record of the inspection carried out. It can be very useful to show the selling agent to try to discount the asking price by factoring in repair costs. It could also be critical at some time in the future if a building fault is discovered that should have been apparent to the inspector at the time of the inspection.

Conveyancer or lawyer—Is there anything out of the ordinary in this contract?

Contracts that deal with land are legal documents and they can be difficult to read and understand. A conveyancer or property lawyer should be able to read through the contract and determine if your property or contract is typical or whether there is something that should be noted. For example, it might be heritage listed or there might be an easement (a section of land you cannot build upon) on an unusual part of the land.

Mortgage broker—Do you charge for your services?

Mortgage brokers should not charge you for their services. They are paid by the lender with whom you decide to take out the loan.

Mortgage broker—What is the best and most appropriate loan for my circumstances?

One of the great advantages of speaking with a mortgage broker is that they have access to the loans offered by many banks, whereas when you speak to someone at your own bank they can only offer you loans from their own institution. Your mortgage broker should have around 20 or more lenders on their panel from which they can select the right loan for you. This means that they will have hundreds of loans that you can choose from.

Real estate salesperson or agent—Why is the vendor selling the property?

If you can find out why a vendor is selling a property, this can greatly enhance your bargaining position. A vendor may *need* to sell for a number of reasons: they may have already bought another property; separation or divorce may cause a sale; or following a death, the estate just wants to sell off the property. Some vendors may *want* to sell, but don't need to sell. They may just be trying out the market and if they get the price they want, they will sell.

You must remember that the salesperson or agent is working for the vendor, so they shouldn't tell you, the prospective purchaser, anything that will disadvantage their client. They don't have to tell you why the vendor is selling.

Valuer—What is the market value of this property?

Just because an owner puts a price on a property, doesn't mean that it is worth that much. The price specified might be the price that they hope for or need to sell at to buy their next property. If you are unfamiliar with property or don't have any idea about the worth of a particular property, you should ask a valuer to value the property you are considering. If you are borrowing money to buy the property, the lender will probably have the property valued, but this may not be the *market* value of the property. The bank's valuation will probably be based on a worst-case scenario where it wants to know what it could sell the property for if you default on the loan and it has to sell in a hurry—in other words, a fire sale price.

Before you make an offer on the property, you should have a very good idea what its *market* value is.

Holding property

The following are questions you should be asking of your accountant and property manager if you own property.

Accountant—What items can I depreciate in order to boost my tax benefits?

There are many items in and around a property that can be depreciated and added on to your expenses to reduce the income tax you pay. Your accountant should advise you to have a depreciation schedule done by a quantity surveyor. Ideally a depreciation schedule should have been done when you bought the property. However, you can organise for a depreciation schedule to be done on your property at any time.

Property manager—What are your fees and what are the conditions of the property management agreement?

Property managers usually charge a general upfront property management fee and then additional fees, such as a new lease fee, renewal of lease fee, payment of utilities fee and inspection fee. When selecting a property manager to look after your property, don't just focus on the upfront property management fee, as all the other fees can actually add up to more than the upfront fee! A standard upfront fee can range from 6.6 per cent to 8.8 per cent of the gross rent but all the other management fees can total thousands of dollars a year.

Read the property management agreement carefully and pay particular attention to the termination clause. This clause details how much notice you need to give them if you want to change property manager or possibly manage it yourself. Sixty days notice is an industry norm, but if you can negotiate and terminate it earlier, it can work to your advantage.

Selling property

The following questions should be asked of your accountant and the professional selling your property when you are considering selling your property.

Real estate salesperson or agent—What is my property worth?

Before you select an agent to sell your property, you should invite three *local* agents to the property and ask them for an appraisal: this is their opinion of the worth of the home. Three different agents will probably give you three different prices. You think you should sign up the agent who provides you with the highest appraisal? Wrong!

Unfortunately a few rogue agents use a practice known as buying the listing. They know that if they provide you with a relatively high price, you will select them as your selling agent, and if and when the property is sold, they will collect the commission. The reality is that an over-priced property stays on the market for a much longer period of time and often sells for below its market value as prospective purchasers think that there must be something wrong with the property for it to be for sale for so long.

Do your own due diligence so that you have an idea what your property is worth by finding out what comparable properties have sold for so that you are not 'sucked in' by an artificially high appraisal.

Don't be attracted to the agent just because they offer the lowest sales commissions. A recommendation from a friend or colleague who has used an agent in your area is one of the best indications of which agent you should choose to sell your property.

Accountant—What is my capital gains tax (CGT) liability and am I eligible for the CGT discount?

An accountant experienced with property should accurately calculate your CGT liability based on what you paid for the property, the costs of improvements and the sale price. They should also be familiar with the CGT discount and know if you are eligible for it, based on the ownership structure and the length of time you have held the property.

★ ★ ★ ★ ★ ★ ★ ★ **SHARES** ★ ★ ★ ★ ★ ★ ★ ★

Buying shares

Successful share investing isn't as simple as opening an account and picking a stock. It is important to get quality advice before you open an account, as well as obtain quality investment advice on what to buy. Following are some relevant questions you need to ask.

Accountant or financial adviser—What investment structure should I use to hold my share investments?

As described for property, and in Round 14, the decision of what structure to use for your investments is one of the most important things to consider—*before* you make your first purchase. Having the right structure for your situation could make a substantial difference to the outcome of your investment endeavours because of things such as the tax implications of the investment profits. This is especially important if you plan to borrow to invest. A financial planner or accountant can be very useful to help advise you in this regard.

Financial planner or adviser—Do you work for the holder of an Australian financial services licence (AFSL), and what are your qualifications and experience?

When you decide to get advice from a financial planner or adviser, one of the first things to ask is whether the business they are working for has an AFSL, provided by ASIC. In addition, you should ask whether the adviser is an authorised representative of the company, and check these facts on the ASIC website.

Ask the adviser how much experience they have, and if they are comfortable with providing you with references of other client's experiences with them.

Financial planner or adviser—How much of my portfolio should I invest in shares?

In Round 7, we discussed the importance of diversification in your investment portfolio. This is achieved by having your money invested in different asset classes, according to your investment risk profile, your financial goals and also your tolerance for risk and volatility of returns. A financial planner can help you determine the appropriate amount of money to allocate to each of the asset classes.

Margin lender or bank, and financial planner or adviser—How much can I borrow?

If you are considering borrowing to invest in the sharemarket, then you should consider the most appropriate loan arrangement to use: redraw on equity in your home or investment property? An investment loan? A margin loan? Each will have its own advantages and disadvantages. Once again, a licensed financial planner or accountant can assist and provide advice on this.

Financial adviser or stockbroker—What shares to buy?

In Round 5, we provided many suggestions on where and how to do research on what shares to buy. This is also where a licensed and experienced financial adviser can assist and advise you on the most appropriate shares or managed investments to consider. Alternatively, you may wish to do your own research on what shares to invest in. In either case, you should consider the most appropriate shares for your goals and situation: growth shares, dividend shares or speculative shares.

Once you have decided what shares you wish to buy, you need to ask what *type* of shares you will buy, as they have different rights and obligations. Are the shares you wish to buy fully paid ordinary shares?

Are they preference shares? Are they instalments? The type of share you are buying is important as it could possibly place further financial obligations on you. As a rule, if a share has more than three letters in its code (such as CBA for Commonwealth Bank), then you should double-check what type of share it is and ensure you understand whether it carries financial obligations beyond your initial investment.

Financial adviser or stockbroker—What type of broker should I use?

The only way to purchase shares is through a share broker. The question to ask is whether you will use an online discount broker (and place the buy orders yourself) or whether you want to use a full-service sharebroker, who will provide investment advice and research, as well as placing your orders on your behalf. The answer to this question will depend on how much control you want to make your own decisions, how much advice you need and of course how much you are prepared to pay.

Holding shares

Once you have bought your shares, you have to ensure that your investment is managed properly. This involves administration (including tax reporting of income and expenses), and also managing your investment portfolio to ensure that the shares you hold are still worthy of your investment. This involves managing your investment risk.

Accountant—What information about my shares do I need to include in my yearly tax return?

The Australian tax system allows you to claim deductions for all expenses you incur in relation to your investments, including any interest expenses on funds you borrow to invest. You should therefore keep good records of your income (such as dividends received) and expenses associated with managing your portfolio.

Your accountant should take all of these into account in preparing your tax return, along with claiming franking credits received with your dividends (provided you have held the shares for more than

45 days), and this will reduce your income tax liability. You will only pay tax on the dividends you receive while you hold your shares.

Financial planner—How will my portfolio be managed? What advice will I receive? How much will it cost me?

If you are using a financial planner or adviser, you need to ask how they will manage your portfolio. How often will you hear from them? How much input will you have into the management of your portfolio? How often will they review your investment holdings? How will they manage risk? How much will it cost you? What level of performance and tax reporting will be provided to you and your accountant yearly?

Selling shares

There will come a time when you have to sell your shares. It's important to understand that selling your shares may have tax consequences for you.

Financial adviser or stockbroker—When should I sell my shares?

One of the most important decisions you will make regarding your share investments is when you will sell them. You need to decide what your selling decision will be based on. Will you use a technical reason, such as a trend change? Or will you use a consensus of research recommendations? Will you rely on the advice of your financial adviser or stockbroker to tell you when to sell your shares? Will you sell your entire holding of a particular share, or just part of it? If you are making a capital gain from the sale, can you offset it with a capital loss by selling something else? Or should you delay the sale to the next financial year so you don't have to pay capital gains tax in this financial year? You can see there are a lot of considerations, and these may require specialist advice.

Accountant—What is my CGT liability and am I eligible for the CGT discount?

When you lodge your annual tax return for the previous financial year, you will be required to provide the ATO with details of the sales of your shares in addition to any income you have made from your investments during the year (for example, from dividends). Depending on your situation, and the structure you have used for your investments, you may be liable to pay tax on your profits or, if you have made a loss, you may be entitled to use the loss to offset other income or capital gains. Your accountant can assist you with this. Ask your accountant whether you are going to be taxed as an investor (on the capital gain or loss) or as a trader (in which case gains will be treated as income and losses treated as an expense).

Peter's property insights

There is a classic saying in real estate: *caveat emptor*, or buyer beware. The purchaser of property takes on most of the risk, so you should conduct your due diligence and ask lots of questions. Remember, there is no such thing as a silly question when it comes to your hard-earned money: there are just silly people who don't ask questions.

Zac's share insights

Knowing what questions to ask when it comes to buying or selling shares is very important. There are so many things to consider, from what shares to buy, when to buy them, how much to buy, who to buy it through and when to sell them. Then of course there is the administration and tax reporting of your investments. It can become overwhelming for most people. This is why having the right support is critical, and that's where you should consider using the advice of a professional. Don't be afraid to ask questions, and enlist the help of professionals to ensure you are fully informed about all aspects of your share investments.

Conclusion

Successful investing relies on being informed. Whether you choose to be self-directed and make your own decisions, and conduct your own research and administer your investments yourself, or whether you choose to enlist professional assistance, there are specific questions that you need to ask and have the answers to before you make the decision to invest.

Round 21

CASE STUDIES

In this Round we outline a few hypothetical wealth-creation strategies for situations people are likely to encounter at various stages of their lives. This stage of life concept revolves around the fact that you are likely to have different financial priorities when you have just started working than when you are just about to retire (or have already retired).

For example, when you are younger and are just starting to build your investment portfolio, you have different goals, such as saving a deposit for a home. If you are retired, your goal is likely to be stability of income: you are more likely to rely on the continuity of your investment to fund your lifestyle, and therefore your investment choices will be different.

We can't discuss everybody's situation, but you should be able to modify the strategies we outline to suit your particular situation.

A good starting point for all is that if you wish to invest you first need to have some money. Where does this money come from? In the first instance, it will be money that you have saved from your income. We have assumed that you can manage your finances, and that you earn more than you spend so that you have money left over for savings. Ideally, you should be able to *save at least 10 per cent of your salary*. You may be able to save more, but this can vary depending on the stage of life, dependants and your financial commitments.

The following case studies are fictitious, but their purpose is to illustrate what is possible with some planning and vision. Most people become financially independent not because they won the lottery but because they were willing to take some risk and make some short-term sacrifices for future benefits.

Case study: starting a savings plan

Melissa has two more years before she completes her property degree. She lives at home with her parents and pays some board. Her fixed expenses consist only of her bus fares and mobile phone bill. Her university fees won't be paid until she starts work and earns enough money.

Details

Name: Melissa
Age: 20
Occupation: university student
Salary: casual part-time work in café, $20 000 per year
Risk profile: conservative

Goal

Melissa hasn't worked out what her investment goals are yet, but she does know that she wants to buy a house as soon as possible, as she can see house prices and rents just continue to increase. She is careful with her money and doesn't want to risk losing any.

Strategy

Melissa could save $200 per week and put this in a high interest bank account. In two years she will have accumulated over $20 000 towards a deposit for a home, and once she gets a full-time job she will be able to save even more, claim any first home bonuses, borrow money and purchase her first home by the time she is 23 years old. After this, she can consider saving to buy shares.

Case study: building savings and starting to invest

Sebastian has just started full-time work in the supermarket. He lives in a flat with a friend and pays $150 per week rent and another $50 per week for electricity, gas and phone expenses.

He also owns a car, which costs him a further $100 per week in petrol, insurance, registration and repairs.

Details

Name: Sebastian
Age: 20
Occupation: storeman in supermarket
Salary: $35 000 per year
Risk profile: high growth

Goal

Sebastian is keen to make money as quickly as possible, as he aspires to owning expensive cars, travelling and living in a mansion.

Strategy

Sebastian could put aside $150 per week into a managed fund or an exchange traded fund (ETF). This money is invested in Australian and overseas shares and, provided the sharemarkets around the globe continue to rise, he could make close to $20 000 in two years. He can then take advantage of any first homebuyer incentives that are available to him, borrow money and buy a property. As his property grows in value, he can use the equity to buy more property or shares, or both.

Case study: saving for a home

Sophie has been working for a few years but hasn't been able to save much money. She has been overseas numerous times and borrowed money to buy a luxury car. Her car repayments are $250 per week. She lives on her own and rents a two-bedroom apartment for $400 per week.

Details

Name: Sophie
Age: 30
Occupation: lawyer

Salary: $80 000 per year
Risk profile: balanced

Goal

Sophie is desperate to buy her own home, but her rent and car expenses take up a large portion of her take-home pay.

Strategy

Sophie could get a flatmate, which would halve her rent and utilities costs. Alternatively, she could move into a smaller or cheaper property. In the meantime, she could set up a separate savings account and save $300 per week and also pay off her car as soon as possible. Once the car is paid off, she can put aside the $300 per week towards her home deposit. Within two years, she will have saved over $30 000, enough money to use as a deposit to buy her first home. As her income and equity in the house grow, she can buy more shares, investment property or upgrade to a bigger and better home.

Case study: an early start to a comfortable retirement

Nicole has been working as an accountant since she finished her degree. She still lives at home with her parents. She pays board and owns a modest car. Board and car expenses total $350 per week. She already owns one investment property, which is negatively geared and costs her $100 per week.

Details

Name: Nicole
Age: 30
Occupation: accountant
Salary: $60 000 per year
Risk profile: conservative

Goal

Nicole's goal is to accumulate wealth as safely as possible, as she wishes to retire comfortably by the time she turns 60.

Strategy

Considering her low risk profile, Nicole will put most of her investments in property and only a small proportion in shares. Nicole could put $250 per week into a high interest savings account and put this towards the deposit for her next property. As the equity in her first investment property grows, she can also use this, along with a cash deposit, to buy more property. Sooner or later she will probably leave home so she can use one of the properties as her home. Nicole should also regularly contribute a small amount to a savings account to build a small share portfolio.

Case study: two goals, two strategies

Nathan and Anne are married and have two children. The children both go to a private primary school at a total annual cost of $15 000. Nathan and Anne own their home, which is worth $500 000, but they still owe $250 000. Their mortgage repayment is $400 per week. They have no other debts.

Details

Name: Nathan and Anne
Ages: 40
Occupation: teachers
Salary: combined income $140 000 per year
Risk profile: balanced

Goal

Nathan is keen to make money as soon as possible and wants to invest in shares, whereas Anne wants to buy more property to help secure their retirement.

Strategy

Based on the equity they already have in their home, and their combined income, Nathan and Anne can borrow some more money to buy one, or possibly two, investment properties, depending on location, price and rental income. This satisfies Anne's goal.

They should be able to save at least $200 per week and Nathan can use some of this to invest in a share portfolio so as to accelerate their wealth creation.

Case study: managing a divorce settlement in cash

Alexandria is a single mother with one child. She has recently been divorced and currently rents a two-bedroom unit at $300 per week. As part of the divorce proceeds, she received $150 000 cash.

Details

Name: Alexandria
Age: 40
Occupation: receptionist
Salary: $40 000 per year
Risk profile: conservative

Goal

Alexandria wants to use this money wisely to secure the future for her and her child. She has no debts.

Strategy

Alexandria has a sizeable deposit, which she could put towards buying a house so that she doesn't pay any more rent. The amount she can borrow will depend on a number of factors, but she should have enough to buy a home, instead of paying rent.

As she is the sole income earner with one dependant, it will be difficult for her to save much money; however, Alexandria should be eligible for some monetary assistance from the government which will assist in her cash flow. A savings target of $70 per week should be achievable.

Case study: preparing for retirement

Victor lives alone in a house that is worth $600 000 and is fully paid off. He has two children, but they are adults and don't live with him. He also has a share portfolio worth $100 000. It was worth much more but he lost most of it in a scam.

Details

Name: Victor
Age: 50
Occupation: mechanic
Salary: $55 000 per year
Risk profile: growth

Goal

Victor is keen to retire or semi-retire as soon as possible. He has been working as a mechanic since he left school, working 5½ days per week, and now just wants more time to play golf and go fishing.

Strategy

Victor hasn't lost his appetite for risk, despite losing money in the past. He wants to grow his money as quickly as possible. If Victor were to take a more conservative approach, he could use some of the equity in his home to buy an investment property or some shares. If Victor was willing to take an aggressive approach, he could buy property to renovate and develop, or learn how to trade shares and create the potential to make quick profits.

Case study: reducing work hours

Ross and Christy have operated a café for the last five years. They have three children, one of whom is 20 years of age and still living at home with them. They live in a home worth $700 000 and still owe $150 000. Their mortgage repayment is $250 per week. They each have a car, which is leased, and lease payments are made through the earnings of the business.

Details

Name: Ross and Christy
Ages: 50
Occupation: small business owners
Income: $100 000 per year
Risk profile: balanced

Goal

Ross and Christy both like working in the café, but they wish they didn't both have to be in there seven days a week. They would each like to take two days off per week. To do this, they need to supplement their income so they can pay for some casual staff.

Strategy

One obvious strategy is to grow their business or cut back on costs so that they can pay some casual wages. However, they prefer to invest wisely and increase their cash flow so that they can afford to pay themselves for time away from the café. One option is to make profits through renovating property and use the profits to pay for casual wages. Alternatively, they could invest in a high-growth share portfolio.

Case study: preparing for retirement

Pablo and Christine are both 62 years old, and they plan to retire in three years' time. Pablo is a salesman and Christine works part time at a law firm doing administrative work. They live in the home they have owned for the last 30 years; they have $550 000 (combined) in superannuation; $150 000 in fixed deposits outside of their super fund; and another $100 000 in shares outside of their super fund.

Details

Name: Pablo and Christine
Ages: 62
Occupation: Pablo is a department store manager and Christine is a bookkeeper. They plan to retire within three years.
Income: Pablo, $95 000 per year and Christine, $50 000 per year
Risk profile: conservative

Goal

Pablo and Christine would like to ensure that they can retire comfortably with an annual income of at least $70 000, and they want to minimise their tax now and prepare for their retirement.

Strategy

Pablo and Christine decide to set up a self managed super fund with themselves as individual trustees and both roll over their individual superannuation balances (totalling $550 000) into it.

They are each allowed to contribute $150 000 of after-tax or (non-concessional) contributions each per year into superannuation, so they decide to transfer their shares through an in-specie transfer (that is a transfer of shares without actually having to sell them and subsequently buy them back in the super fund) and their fixed term deposit (amounting to $250 000) into their fund. Their total super fund balance is now $800 000.

They both receive superannuation guarantee payments from their employers, which are now paid into their self managed super fund. But as they are both over 60, they can also use a transition to retirement pension strategy, whereby they can make additional salary sacrifice contributions to the accumulation part of their fund and start drawing a part pension at the same time. Their pension payments will be tax-free and can be used to supplement the income that they have lost through additional salary sacrificing. Pablo decides to salary sacrifice an additional $16 000 into his super fund. Christine salary sacrifices an additional $20 000 into her super fund—they can each contribute up to $25 000 each year (at time of writing) in concessional, or before-tax, contributions. This means they can contribute a combined $36 000 extra into their superannuation, each year for the next three years. This saves on the tax they pay outside their superannuation, while maximising their contributions to superannuation. This strategy allows them to prepare for their retirement by maximising their superannuation contributions and to minimise their tax liability.

Case study: achieving less volatility in retirement investments

Yuan and Lin have been retired for 10 years. They live a modest lifestyle, and rely on their share portfolio of $500 000 (largely consisting of low–dividend paying growth shares) that is held in a SMSF, an investment property valued at $400 000 and a fixed deposit of $100 000 (which is held outside of their SMSF) to provide them with income. They have experienced a lot of volatility in their income over the last three years, largely from their share portfolio, which is invested mostly in low–dividend paying growth stocks such as News Corporation and CSL Ltd.

Details

Name: Yuan and Lin Tse
Ages: 75
Occupation: retired
Income: $57 000 per year
Risk profile: conservative

Goal

To have less volatility in their annual income and maximise their income from their investments.

Strategy

Their financial planner advises Yuan and Lin that their investments are not adequately diversified to suit their conservative risk profile. A conservative investor profile in their age group should have most of their investments allocated to defensive assets, such as cash and fixed interest; in their current investments, the allocation to defensive assets is just 10 per cent.

As they are 75 years of age, and retired, they cannot contribute anymore into their SMSF. However, they restructure their growth share investments by selling these shares and replacing them with a portfolio of $100 000 of high-yielding defensive shares such as Telstra and Woolworths that pay fully franked dividends. They invest the balance of the money in their SMSF in a high-yielding fixed interest investment fund (such as a managed fund) that pays interest quarterly.

By reallocating their portfolio, they are able to reduce the volatility they have been experiencing, and stabilise their income, while also maximising the returns on their investments. In addition, they are able to benefit from a rebate of the franking credits associated with their dividends.

 Peter's property insights

In all the case studies, investing in property was recommended. Whether it was just buying a home to live in, renting an investment property or, for those with a higher appetite for risk, renovating or developing property, property plays an important role. The strategy you select will depend on a number of factors, but most importantly you need to consider your investment goals, time frame and risk profile.

Zac's share insights

Shares are the most volatile asset class. As a result, if you have a short-term need for the money you have invested, or you rely on income regularly, it may not be the right investment for you because of the potential for short-term volatility. The right investment mix for you, however, will be based on your goals, as well as your stage of life. If you are nearing retirement, you should consider changing your asset allocation to be more conservatively invested—in case unexpected volatility causes your portfolio to suffer losses that will be difficult to recover from if you have a reliance on the investment portfolio for income. A starting point for everyone is to consult a qualified and experienced financial adviser who can assist you to determine the right investment mix for you and help you reach your goals.

 ## Conclusion

Both property and shares can be used to meet any investment goal, no matter what your risk profile. The less risk you want to take, the more weighting you will give to buying property and holding for the long term. If you are willing to take more risk, you could potentially make more money through shares.

These case studies are not intended to be a substitute for independent advice. Once you have worked out your own investment goals and have some idea of possible strategies, we strongly recommend that you seek advice from a qualified financial planner or property investment adviser.

Round 22

ADVANCED INVESTMENT OPPORTUNITIES

We wrote this book to act as a guide for those who are new to, or just beginning to invest in, property and shares. We have discussed many of the fundamentals that relate to buying property and shares.

This chapter introduces some of the choices investors have once they have mastered the basics of direct investment in property and shares. We strongly encourage all investors to gain a thorough understanding of direct investment in property and shares before they embark on the riskier (and potentially more rewarding) advanced investment opportunities. You can mitigate some of your investment risks by arming yourself with this specialist knowledge and gaining an understanding of the potential benefits and pitfalls of these advanced investment strategies before you start investing.

★ ★ ★ ★ ★ ★ ★ PROPERTY ★ ★ ★ ★ ★ ★ ★

Property investors can make money in a number of ways: buy and hold for the long term, build to retain or sell, or renovate and rent or sell, for instance. These approaches are common and used extensively. However, some investors like to think outside the square and deal in some advanced investment strategies. In this section, we outline two of these strategies: property options and joint ventures.

Options

Have you ever wondered how new housing estates and suburbs are created? Developers rarely buy hectares of land through cash sales and tie up those precious funds while they spend years creating a new suburb.

Instead they buy on terms using an option. An option is a legal instrument that gives the buyer the right, but not the obligation, to buy land on certain terms at some future point in time. The seller cannot sell to anyone else while the option is in operation and is bound to sell to the buyer on those terms should the buyer elect to buy. (A type of option was outlined in Round 19 — the Popi.) The option commonly has a time period set in which the buyer must decide whether to buy. If the buyer elects not to buy and the time period expires, the option expires.

In exchange for the seller having their land tied up for the period of the option, the buyer pays a fee to the seller, called an option fee. If the buyer elects to buy, the option fee often becomes part of the deposit. If the buyer doesn't buy, the seller keeps the option fee.

Example

Consider that Farmer Joe owns a large parcel of land on the outskirts of town. A developer thinks that the property would be an excellent location for a new housing estate. The developer approaches Farmer Joe to do a deal. Rather than the developer buying the property outright on cash terms, then taking the risk of gaining approval to re-zone it from farming to residential (which may be refused), followed by developing roads and infrastructure and ultimately selling the allotments, the developer might offer Farmer Joe an option.

The developer pays Farmer Joe $200 000 as an option fee for the right to buy the land at any time in the next two years for the sum of $2 million. The developer uses that two-year period to apply for re-zoning; seek necessary consents from councils and other agencies; get plans drawn up; liase with home builders to

(continued)

Options are not just reserved for developers seeking to create new suburbs.

Many astute investors use options for smaller scale developments, such as subdividing a larger allotment into say two, three or four smaller parcels of land.

If used correctly, an option is a very powerful strategy.

Joint ventures

Joining forces with a family member, friend, colleague or even a business partner for property investment or development can be extremely beneficial. Often someone else has the skill set you don't. They may have the funds and you don't. They may have building experience and you don't. Alternatively, you may own land but have no funds to build on it or develop it.

Finding others to complement your skill set and objectives can mean the difference between getting started and not doing anything.

When two or more people join forces to undertake a project, it is called a joint venture.

Commonly we see two people join forces to buy an investment property, subdivide a suburban allotment into two, and build a house on each allotment for each investor.

Beyond that, a land owner can join forces with a builder to build on the land. The owner contributes the land to the deal and the builder uses his expertise and trade contacts. They might profit share 50–50, or some other percentage, depending on how much each party has contributed to the deal.

A joint venture can be as varied and broad as one's imagination permits.

As with any arrangement involving money, the potential for a dispute is very real. People have differing expectations, and that can lead to tension. Accordingly, it is essential that any joint venture be in writing and prepared by a solicitor.

A joint venture is in essence a business marriage and you can't rely on the honeymoon lasting forever. The joint venture needs to record how the parties are going to work together, their respective roles and contributions, how profits will be allocated and how they will separate once the project is over. If done properly, a joint venture can be a wonderful and beneficial experience, as well as financially rewarding.

★ ★ ★ ★ ★ ★ ★ ★ SHARES ★ ★ ★ ★ ★ ★ ★ ★

A big advantage that share investment offers is that there are several advanced investment strategies and derivative products that are readily available to investors to use to protect their investment portfolio during volatile periods or to leverage their returns.

This section introduces several advanced investment strategies. Should you wish to learn more about these strategies, you should consult a qualified adviser, or enrol in a reputable education course.

Short selling

There is only one way to make money from an investment: selling the investment at a higher price than you bought. But did you know that you can also make money as the market falls? One way to do this is through short selling.

In simple terms, short selling involves borrowing shares from a broker (that someone else owns and has made available for short selling purposes), then selling them while prices are high and when you expect the market to fall. Then when the market falls, you buy back the shares and return them to the broker, while you keep the profit. You make a profit from short selling because you have still sold an investment at a higher price than you buy it for—the only difference is that you sell the shares *first* (to open the transaction) and then buy them back later to close (also known as covering) the transaction. The shares are then returned to the broker.

Example

Assume ANZ is trading at $28.55 and your analysis is that it is likely to fall to $25.00. You decide to borrow 1000 ANZ shares from your broker to short sell. The broker will require collateral, usually cash or shares, and you may be required to pay borrowing fees too.

You sell the borrowed shares at $28.55 each. A few weeks later, the market falls to $25.00, at which point you buy back the shares, and return the shares to the broker. You have made the following profit:

- sold (short) 1000 ANZ shares at $28.55: $28 550 received into your account

- bought (to close) 1000 ANZ shares at $25.00: $25 000 paid out of your account

- your profit is the proceeds of the sale less the amount you paid to close the position, that is: $28 550 − $25 000 = $3550 (not including costs).

Short selling is available only over a selected number of shares (usually the top 200), and your broker may require you to have a margin account in order to use this strategy.

Short selling can be a very risky strategy, and it should only be used if you are comfortable with the risks. If your analysis is incorrect, and the share goes up, or worse, the company is taken over, you stand to lose a lot of money.

Example

In the earlier example, if ANZ went higher instead after a few weeks to $31.00, and you decided to close out of your trade, then you would have made the following loss:

- sold (short) 1000 ANZ shares at $28.55: $28 550 received into your account

- bought (to close) 1000 ANZ shares at $31.00: $31 000 paid out of your account

- your loss is the proceeds of the sale less the amount you paid to close the position, that is:. $28 550 − $31 000 = $3550 (not including costs).

Exchange traded options (ETOs)

Share options are derivative products, meaning that their price is *derived* from the underlying share price and its movements. The following is a simple discussion about these products.

Exchange traded share options (ETOs) have basically the same features as the property options mentioned earlier: they are contracts that give the buyer a right to buy or sell a share at a specific price, called the strike price, and by a specific date at which the contract may be exercised, or acted on. The seller of the option has specific obligations to the buyer if the buyer chooses to exercise their rights, as we will describe later.

ETOs are traded on the ASX alongside shares, so they can be bought and sold through your broker. The price that ETOs trade at is referred to as the premium or option price.

They are issued over most of the top 100 shares. Most of the liquidity, however, is found in options over the top 20 shares, meaning there is more likely to be sufficient volume for you to trade with. Each share ETO contract represents a parcel of 100 of the underlying shares.

There are two types of ETOs—call options and put options:

- A call option gives the buyer of the option a right to buy the underlying shares at an agreed price (called the exercise, or strike price) at any time up to the expiry date. Call option premiums increase in value as the underlying share price increases.

- A put option gives the buyer of the option a right to sell the underlying shares at an agreed price (called the exercise, or strike price) at any time up to the expiry date. Put option premiums increase in value as the underlying share price decreases.

ETOs that are issued over a share have different strikes or maturity prices (described later in this chapter) and different expiry dates (ranging from options that have less than a month to expire, to others that still have as much as 12 months or more before expiry).

Each different option series is identified with a unique six letter code, such as ANZSU9, where the first three letters represent the underlying share.

The option price itself is determined by the market. It will depend on:

- whether the option contract has intrinsic value—determined by the share price relative to its exercise price

- time value—how much time is left to the expiry of the option

- volatility—how volatile the share price has been recently.

When the option buyer and the option seller agree on a price for the option, the trade takes place, just like it does for a share.

We will look at four examples of how investors typically use options, and then two examples of how traders would use options.

Investors: lock in a buy price now for shares you want to buy later

In this case, you will buy call options.

If you think that the price of the shares you want to buy will increase, and you don't want to, or cannot, buy those shares now, you can buy call options over those shares instead.

When you buy a call option, you enter into a contract that gives you the right (but not the obligation) to buy the underlying shares (from the call options seller, who has the opposite view of the share price that you do) at an agreed (strike or exercise) price, on or before the agreed expiry date of that option. You pay the seller of the call options a premium to secure this right.

This effectively locks in a buy price now for the shares you want to buy later, when you expect they will be more expensive.

Example

It is now February and ANZ is trading at $28.55. Assume you wish to buy 1000 shares of ANZ at $28.50 sometime on or before July, but you think that by then ANZ shares will rise and be trading as high as $35.00. You choose to lock in your buy price now by buying the $28.50 July call options through your broker that are trading at $0.91 per option. If you wish to buy 1000 shares in ANZ later on, you need to buy 10 call options because each option contract represents 100 shares (so 10 option contracts × 100 shares per contract = 1000 shares).

Buying 10 option contracts will cost you $0.91 × 10 × 100 = $910 (plus brokerage and fees). The premium you pay to the option seller is not a deposit: it is an additional cost that secures the buy price for you at $28.50.

If, by July, ANZ is trading at $35.00 as you expected, you can exercise your call option and have the right to buy ANZ at $28.50. The call option seller now has to sell you their 1000 shares at $28.50.

With the share trading at $35.00, you have an immediate unrealised profit of $5.59 per share! Your break-even cost per share before brokerage costs is $29.41, that is, $28.50 (the share purchase price) + $0.91 (price of the option).

If by July, ANZ is trading at $20.00, your call option is worthless to you, and so you will not exercise your option to buy the shares because you can buy the shares on the market for less than the option contract price. You have lost your premium of $0.91 per option (total of $910).

Investors: protect (hedge) your investment portfolio from price falls

To do this, you would buy put options.

If you think that the price of the shares you hold will fall, but you don't want to sell your shares—because you may become liable for capital gains tax (CGT), for example—you can buy put options over those shares to protect them.

As the buyer of a put option, you enter into a contract that gives you the right (but not the obligation) to sell your shares at an agreed (strike) price, on or before the agreed expiry date of that option. You pay a premium to the seller of the put options that locks in a sell price now for your shares (*if* you choose to exercise your option) before the contract expiry date.

Here's an example of how this strategy works.

Example

It is now February and ANZ is trading at $28.55. You own 1000 shares purchased a long time ago at $21.00. If you think that the ANZ share price will fall to $20.00, you can either sell your shares now, or protect your shares by locking in a sell price at say, $28.00. You do this by purchasing 10 put options with a $28.00 strike price.

If, by July, ANZ is trading at $20.00 as you thought, you simply exercise your right to sell your 1000 ANZ shares at $28.00, and the put option seller now has to buy your 1000 shares at $28.00.

If on the other hand, ANZ is trading at $35.00 in July, then your put option will be worthless to you because you could sell your shares at the market price of $35.00 if you wish to. But just as insurance is purchased to be there when you need it, the put option was always intended to be used only if the price fell.

These two strategies require you to pay money to buy the options. There are other (riskier) ways of using options that actually earn you money, that is by being a seller of put and call options.

Investors: if you are prepared to commit to buy shares at a lower price than they currently are

To use this strategy, you will sell put options.

Assume ANZ is trading at $28.55 in February. You want to buy 1000 ANZ shares, but think that the market will fall to around $28.00. You could place an order to buy 1000 shares at $28.00 and wait for the price to fall to that level. Or you could sell 10 put options with a $28.00 strike and a July expiry, earning $1.35 in premium for each option (you need 10 options for 1000 shares so the total cost of the option is $1350), and then wait for ANZ to fall to or below $28.00 in the hope that your put options get exercised.

If ANZ then fell to $25.00, for example, it is likely that the put option buyer would exercise their right to sell their shares to you at the $28.00 strike price. You have an obligation to buy 1000 shares at $28.00, and do so because you had planned to buy ANZ at $28.00 anyway — except that it has actually cost you *less* than $28.00 to buy the shares. Why? Because you can consider that the $1.35 premium per option you received has reduced the average buy price to $26.65!

If ANZ didn't fall below $28.00, and by July had rallied further to $35.00, the put option you sold would be worthless — meaning you keep the entire premium that the put option buyer has paid you. You can then repeat the cycle by selling another 10 put option contracts and pocket more premium.

This is a very risky strategy that most brokers will not let you do. You will also be required to provide sufficient cash to the broker as collateral that you will be able to pay for the shares should you be exercised.

In theory this strategy makes sense. And it does if you remove the emotional aspect. But the reality is that if their sold options are exercised, some investors feel disenchanted when faced with the prospect of having to buy shares at a substantially higher price than the market price!

Investors: to generate additional income from your shares

Selling call options could achieve this goal for you. This strategy is used when you believe that the share price is likely to fall or to trade within a sideways trading range for some time.

One of the most common (and most successful) investment strategies is called covered call writing. It involves using the shares you already own as collateral and selling call options over them, with the potential obligation that if you are exercised, you have to sell your shares at the agreed exercise price.

Example

It is February and ANZ shares are trading at $28.55. You own 1000 shares in ANZ that you purchased a while ago at $21.00. You think that ANZ has found a temporary top and is unlikely to go higher in the short term.

You decide to sell 10 call options (fully covered by your 1000 shares in ANZ) at $28.50, with a May expiry. The premium at the time is $1.00 per option contract—so you receive $1000 (less brokerage and fees) for entering into the contract.

If your analysis is correct and, at expiry in May, ANZ's price is less than $28.50, the call option you sold expires worthless— meaning that you keep your shares as well as the entire premium the buyer gave you. You can then repeat the process if you still feel that ANZ is likely to remain subdued in price.

If, on the other hand, ANZ goes higher and at expiry is trading at $30.00, your call option will be exercised. You therefore have an obligation under the contract to sell your ANZ shares to the call option buyer, who has exercised their option at $28.50. The equivalent selling price is $29.50 if you include the premium that you received.

There are many more complex option strategies that investors can use to trade a particular view of a specific share. Investors can use different combinations of bought and sold options, and at different strikes and different expiry dates. Each of these has a unique risk versus reward profile, as well as differing probabilities of success. It pays to keep things simple though, and the four strategies we have discussed are the most common, and the most consistently successful when it comes to using options.

Traders: to profit from price rises

To use this strategy, the trader will buy call options.

Call options increase in value as the price of a share increases. Options are derivatives of shares, and buying an option contract is equivalent to buying 100 shares. This implies that options have a leveraged effect, and therefore options will usually magnify the price move of the underlying shares in percentage terms. Because of the leverage that options provide, traders can use them to trade short-term price rallies.

Example

If ANZ is trading at $28.55 in February, and you think that it is likely to increase to $35.00 by July, you could trade this by buying 1000 ANZ shares now for a cost of $28 550. Or you could buy 10 × $28.50 July call options for $0.91, a total cost of $910 (plus brokerage and fees).

If you are right, and ANZ is trading at $35.00 in July, your call options will be worth at least $6.50 each. This is because, if you wanted to, you could buy ANZ shares at $28.50 with that option, and if you sold it straight away at the market price of $35.00 the intrinsic value is $6.50 (an increase of 614 per cent)! As a trader though, you will probably just sell your call options and book your profit.

If you are wrong, and ANZ falls or stays approximately the same price close to the expiry of your option, then your option will probably be worthless.

Traders: profit from price falls

To use this strategy, the trader will buy put options.

Put options increase in value as the price of a share falls. As we have seen, options provide leverage that makes it attractive to trade short-term price falls.

Example

If ANZ is trading at $28.55 in February, and you believe that it is likely to fall to $25.00 by July, you could trade this view by buying 10 × $28.50 July put options for $1.00, a total cost of $1000 (plus brokerage and fees).

If you are right, and ANZ is trading at $25.00 in July, your put options will be worth at least $3.50 (an increase of 250 per cent)! You can then simply sell the put options and bank your profit.

If you are wrong, and ANZ increases in price or stays approximately the same price close to expiry of your option, then your option is likely to be worthless.

Investment warrants

A warrant is a derivative product, issued by a bank or financial institution, that is similar to an option in that it gives a buyer the right to buy or to sell the underlying share for a particular price. Just like options, warrants can be used by investors to leverage their investment returns, to diversify their portfolios or to hedge (protect) the value of their shares—or even to earn extra income.

In the early 2000s, short-term traders actively traded call and put warrants (trading warrants). Since the advent of CFDs, however (see later in this Round), most traders now trade with CFDs because they don't have expiry dates, and are easier to trade and understand.

Investment warrants, however, have remained popular with astute investors. These derivatives comprise an equity and a loan component, where the loan component eventually must be repaid.

There are two main types of investment warrants that investors use:

- *Ordinary instalment warrants.* Buying these is a little like owning shares. They provide investors with all the potential benefits of capital growth, dividends and franking credits that shares do.

- *Self-funding instalment warrants.* These warrants use the dividends being received from the underlying share to reduce the loan amount, potentially creating a positively geared investment. As an investor, you remain entitled to the franking credits attached to the share.

Investors use warrants in two main ways: to get some cash or to borrow in their self managed super fund.

Cash extraction

This strategy involves converting your existing shares into instalment warrants by lodging them with a warrant issuer. It is equivalent to taking out a mortgage over your shares. The warrant issuer provides you with cash as a loan in exchange for taking collateral over your shares. The biggest advantage of this strategy is that you maintain exposure to the shares you own, earning your dividends and franking credits as normal, but now you have additional cash with which to diversify and grow your portfolio. You also do not incur a tax liability, as you are not selling down your shares.

Borrowing in super funds

Superannuation legislation prohibits super funds from borrowing to invest. However, instalment warrants are a way of doing just that, by borrowing to invest in shares in your super fund. You buy warrants for only a proportion of the cost of the shares, and the shares' dividends repay the loan, meaning you can grow your super fund much more quickly.

Contracts for difference (CFDs)

A CFD is an agreement between a buyer and a seller to exchange the difference in value of a contract, between when the contract is opened and when it is closed. You don't actually buy or sell the underlying share: you are merely trading the price difference.

There are two types of CFDs—market maker CFDs and direct market access CFDs.

CFDs are mainly used by short-term traders who wish to trade a particular view of the share or market. Their advantages are:

- leverage
- easy to understand—trading in CFDs is virtually the same as buying or selling shares
- both rising and falling markets can be traded.

Investors are starting to use CFDs to hedge their portfolios as an alternative to using put options. This is because CFDs track the underlying share prices cent for cent and also they don't have a fixed expiry date.

Example

Let's assume that we had a view that ANZ was to fall to $20.00 from $28.55. We could buy 10 × $28.00 put options at $1.00 (costing you $1000) or we can short sell 1000 CFDs at $28.55 (which will give you $28550 on which you will earn a small amount of interest). Short selling CFDs is very similar to short selling shares.

If ANZ falls to $20.00, the options should be worth at least $8 (for a profit of over $7000!) and the CFDs will be worth $20000 (for a profit of $8550).

 ## Peter's property insights

There are many ways to make money in property. The advanced strategies described in this chapter can create opportunities for you to accelerate your wealth (or your journey to poverty!). A property option can either secure potential profit or, if things don't work out, waste your money. A joint venture can provide the opportunity to share profits with others that would not be possible on your own. Joint ventures also increase your business risk, as other parties are involved in the deal.

Zac's share insights

While it can be tempting to want to get involved in advanced and complex strategies with your share investments, the rule should always be to keep it simple. Education is the key, and understanding fully what the risks and benefits really are. Having a qualified and experienced adviser is critical too if you want to try these strategies.

 ## Conclusion

Before you embark on any advanced investment strategy, ensure you have mastered the basics first. Then educate yourself to gain knowledge and understanding of the advanced strategies. Finally, seek qualified advice from finance or property professionals, and speak to investors who have successfully used these strategies.

CONCLUSION: AND THE WINNER IS . . .

You have almost finished reading the book and you're wondering 'Which is better, property or shares?' Before we reveal who the winner is, let's summarise how each asset performed, based on the criteria that were mentioned at the start of the book.

Capital growth

In general, shares as an asset class will outperform property as an asset class. However, this doesn't mean that every share will outperform every property. There are many things to consider. When it comes to shares, you should aim to buy undervalued, quality shares. That is, you should buy into companies with strong management, a healthy balance sheet, a good business model and the potential to grow earnings. The timing of your purchase and subsequent sale of shares is critical. For property, you need to ensure that you buy the right type of property in the right location. A property with a valuable land component in close proximity to the city or the sea is what you should be looking for.

Income

It's too hard to pick a winner in this instance, so we've called it a draw. There are shares that provide great income, just as there are properties that earn a relatively high rent. Overall, property and shares are both good assets if you are seeking a moderate to high income.

Tax effectiveness

Both property and shares are winners here. Owning Australian stocks has the great advantage that their dividends can be franked, which means that 30 per cent of the tax has already been paid by the company issuing the dividend. If your investments are held in a self managed superannuation fund (SMSF) and you are retired, you will receive the franking credits back as additional income — tax-free! Property's advantage is the depreciation allowances that can significantly lower an investor's tax liability. New property or recently renovated or upgraded property will provide the best depreciation benefits. But be careful! You should never buy a particular property or shares *just* for their tax benefits. Tax effectiveness should be a bonus, not the sole purpose for buying the asset.

Degree of control

Property is the winner here. This is one of the main reasons investors buy property. Property investors have a greater degree of control over their asset than investors who own shares. If the value of a share is plummeting, or if their dividend is less than they wanted, what can a share investor do? The answer is not much. However, what can a property investor do to lift the value of their asset or increase their rent? For a start, the property investor can improve their property by upgrading or renovating. Even a simple clean and tidy-up can improve the overall return on a property.

Volatility of returns

Figure 3.1 (see p. 34) in Round 3 illustrates this perfectly. At a glance, it is obvious that the returns on shares are much more volatile than returns on property. The price of shares can rise and fall dramatically over a relatively short period of time. The same cannot be said for property. Most property is owned by the people that live in it, and they are very reluctant to sell just because there is a rumour that the property market is about to slump or because property prices are already dropping. If you are looking for that 'sleep well at night factor', property is the answer. This factor is particularly appealing to risk-averse investors.

Frequency of returns

This is not a big factor, but property wins here. Rental income can be paid weekly, fortnightly or monthly, whereas share investors usually receive dividends every six months. Unlike property returns, your share dividend payments can vary: if the company has a bad year there is a risk that it will reduce its dividend payments to shareholders, if not suspend them altogether. This is a risk particularly for companies that are involved in cyclical sectors, such as the mining companies.

Finance

Borrowing money to buy property and using the real estate itself as security is much cheaper than borrowing money to buy shares if all you have as security is the share portfolio you're buying. In early 2013, the cheapest variable mortgage interest rates were around 5.5 per cent, whereas the cheapest margin loans had interest rates of over 8 per cent. In addition, the loan-to-value ratio (LVR) on a share portfolio is lower than the LVR you could get on a home loan, and property has no margin calls.

Property wins here.

Leverage

This was almost the knockout blow that decked shares. The ability to have greater leverage to buy property can make a *huge* difference to your wealth creation. If you look at the leverage example given in Round 2, $40 000 cash could buy you a share portfolio with a total value of $160 000. This assumes a LVR of 75 per cent. On the other hand, $40 000 could secure you a property worth $400 000, on an LVR of 95 per cent (allowing $20 000 for purchasing costs). That is a *huge* difference. What would you prefer? Your $40 000 buying you an asset worth $160 000 or one worth $400 000? Property is the clear winner here.

Liquidity

Shares win by a mile! One of the greatest advantages of owning shares is that you can turn them into cash very quickly. Another benefit is that if you only need a small amount of money, you can sell just some of your shares; but generally speaking you can't sell a room of your house. Sure, you may be able to subdivide your property and sell part of that, but if you need, say $50 000 urgently, it may be rather difficult to achieve because it will take time to get the approvals in place. Try to quickly sell property! First you have to get the property ready for sale; then you have to market the property; and even if you sell it relatively quickly, you still have to wait until settlement to get your hands on the money. Assuming that you are willing to sell at market value, it might be up to three or four months before you can turn property into cash, whereas it will only take three or four days to turn shares into cash.

Entry, holding and exit fees

Entry fees (including stamp duties and conveyancing costs) are approximately 6 per cent of the purchase price to buy the property. When you are holding the property, expect that approximately 25 to 30 per cent of the gross rent will cover your expenses. When you sell, budget for approximately 4 per cent of the selling price to pay for costs, including sales commission. Compare that with buying shares, which attract no stamp duty; you pay as little as $9.95 to make a trade with a discount stockbroker; and management or administration fees of between 1 per cent and 2 per cent of the portfolio. If entry, holding and exit costs were the only consideration, investors would never buy property. Shares win here.

Ease of getting started

To buy even the cheapest property in Australia, you will still need a sizeable deposit. Whether some of that money comes from a government incentive or all of it comes from the investor, you need thousands, and more likely tens of thousands of dollars, just as a deposit to buy the property. Then you have to borrow the remainder, which would be hundreds of thousands of dollars or more. Compare that with buying shares. As little as $500 will be sufficient to help you start building a share portfolio to which you can add over time. It is far more affordable to buy a share portfolio than a property. Shares win.

Information

There is far more detailed and reliable research and market price transparency information in relation to shares than there is for property. Not only is there a plethora of data on the sharemarket and its performance, but there is also a lot of research available about almost every company listed on the Australian Securities Exchange (ASX). This includes information in annual company reports. This volume of information does not exist for properties. Most of the paperwork in property is in the contract, which deals with the legal issues. In addition, there is no regulation over who can provide property investment advice, whereas shares are classified by ASIC as a financial product, meaning that only licenced financial advisers can provide you with financial advice. If you're looking for fast, reliable and detailed information before you invest, shares are the winner.

Diversification

Shares are a clear winner. As property costs so much, it is very difficult to buy two or more properties in order to diversify and reduce risk. This is much easier with a share portfolio. With just a few thousand dollars, you can invest in numerous companies in a variety of sectors. For risk-averse investors, this is a big attraction. Shares win.

Legal issues

Most of the paper work that a property investor will come across is the legal documentation involved in buying and selling property. If you don't want to get involved in signing copious amounts of documents and involve lawyers or conveyancers in the deal, stick with shares; it's much simpler! Shares win.

Hassles

Looking for a relatively hassle-free investment? Buy shares. Even if a property investor has their property professionally managed, they will still need to deal with (and pay for) repairs, maintenance, council rates, water rates and other taxes and, possibly the biggest hassle, 'the tenant from hell'. There are ways to avoid bad tenants and many of the hassles associated with being a property owner but, in the end, share investment is much less trouble than property investment. Shares win.

Make money from falling markets

You can't make money from property when property prices are falling. Other than buying in at a cheap price, there's not much chance of making a profit on the downward slide of the property market. However, you can make money in a falling sharemarket by short selling, and achieve it in a relatively short period of time. Shares win.

Advanced investment opportunities

There are many more advanced investment opportunities to make money in the sharemarket than by investing in property. Options are common to both property and shares, but you have a variety of alternatives when it comes to shares, such as warrants and contracts for difference (CFDs)—and the list goes on. If you are looking for some variety in your investment life, seek out the advanced investment opportunities. Shares win.

Summary

There are both advantages and disadvantages inherent in investing in either property or shares. The great disadvantages of shares are the lack of leverage and the high volatility, whereas shares are much better than property when it comes to liquidity and diversification issues. Property has the advantage of providing the 'sleep well at night' factor for the risk-averse investor, but owning property can be more complicated than owning shares.

Wouldn't it be great if you could have an investment portfolio that allowed for:

- maximum capital growth
- high income
- regular income
- tax effectiveness
- some degree of control
- minimum volatility
- cheap finance options
- maximum leverage
- liquidity
- a small amount of start-up money
- cheap fees
- decision making based on fast, detailed and reliable data
- diversification across sectors
- minimum hassles and legal issues
- making some money in a falling market
- spreading your wings to try more advanced investment strategies.

The bad news is that there is no *one* asset that can provide you with everything. The good news is that all of this can be achieved by buying *both* property and shares. The ability to use the advantages of both asset classes, while at the same time minimising some of the disadvantages of each, is possible when you buy and hold some property and some shares.

We are not saying that you should have 50 per cent of your money in property and 50 per cent in shares. The weighting of property versus shares will depend on a variety of factors, particularly your risk profile as we described in Round 7. If you want to have your cake and eat it too, you need both property and shares.

Peter's property insights

Even though I am predominantly a property investor, I also own shares. I know my superannuation is mainly invested in the sharemarket, but I also directly invest in shares. Some of the reasons I invest in shares include that I can sell some of my portfolio if I have to, and I also like exposure to some of the potentially fast-growing sectors and companies. Property is still my favourite asset, but I also want have shares, as I want the opportunity to cash in some of the assets if I need to and I like the prospect of making lots of money very quickly.

Zac's share insights

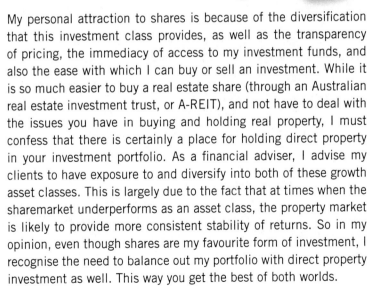

My personal attraction to shares is because of the diversification that this investment class provides, as well as the transparency of pricing, the immediacy of access to my investment funds, and also the ease with which I can buy or sell an investment. While it is so much easier to buy a real estate share (through an Australian real estate investment trust, or A-REIT), and not have to deal with the issues you have in buying and holding real property, I must confess that there is certainly a place for holding direct property in your investment portfolio. As a financial adviser, I advise my clients to have exposure to and diversify into both of these growth asset classes. This is largely due to the fact that at times when the sharemarket underperforms as an asset class, the property market is likely to provide more consistent stability of returns. So in my opinion, even though shares are my favourite form of investment, I recognise the need to balance out my portfolio with direct property investment as well. This way you get the best of both worlds.

Conclusion

Table 23.1 provides a summary of the battle to determine which is best, property or shares. We have explained how each has their own advantages and disadvantages. One is not better than the other, it just depends on you as an investor, and which you are more comfortable with. A truly balanced portfolio should have a mix of both shares and property.

Table 23.1: summary of the winners in a comparison of investing in shares and property

Round	Winner	Judges' comments
Capital growth	Shares	Just by a whisker!
Income	Draw	Depends on the particular asset
Tax effectiveness	Draw	Franking credits are great for shares Depreciation is a winner for property
Degree of control	Property	Property wins hands down
Volatility of returns	Property	Property is a much safer investment
Frequency of returns	Property	More regular income from property
Finance	Property	Property is a big winner here
Leverage	Property	This is property's biggest advantage
Liquidity	Shares	This is a great advantage for shares
Entry, holding and exit fees	Shares	Very cheap compared with property
Ease of getting started	Shares	Less money needed to get into the sharemarket
Information	Shares	Much more reliable share information available

(continued)

Table 23.1: summary of the winners in a comparison of investing in shares and property *(cont'd)*

Round	Winner	Judges' comments
Diversification	Shares	Big advantage for shares
Legal issues	Shares	Shares are much simpler to buy, own and sell
Hassles	Shares	Fewer hassles with shares, and no tenants to deal with
Make money from a falling market	Shares	Can make money in a rising *and* falling sharemarket
Advanced investment opportunities	Shares	More opportunities available in shares
Overall winner	Property and shares	You need both!

May your investment journey be prosperous and your goals accomplished.

GLOSSARY

appraisal A report that includes an estimation of the sale price of a property. Appraisals are compiled by real estate salespeople and agents, generally at no charge. They cannot be used in court if there is a dispute.

appreciation The increase in value of assets.

asset An investment which is expected to provide you with a return, whether it is capital growth, income or both.

Australian real estate investment trust (A-REIT) An REIT listed on the Australian Securities Exchange. *See also* real estate investment trust.

Australian Securities and Investments Commission (ASIC) The government organisation that acts as a corporate regulator and oversees the operations of companies and financial markets in Australia.

balance sheet An important financial summary of a company at a point in time, particularly at the end of a financial year, which forms part of the company's annual report. It shows the company's assets, liabilities and capital.

bear market A market in which share prices are generally falling over time.

blue-chip share A company that is considered to have the strongest fundamentals compared with the rest of the sharemarket. These are often companies in the top 50 by market capitalisation. These are usually seen as relatively safe and secure share investments.

body corporate A body made up of all the owners of a group of units, flats or apartments in a strata or community title property. Its task is to manage the common property and oversee the common areas of the property, such as car park, stairs, gardens, driveways.

bull market A market in which share prices are generally rising over time.

capital All money or assets that are available to invest or that have already been invested to produce a return.

capital growth An increase in the value of an investment over time.

capital gains tax (CGT) The tax payable when an asset is sold. This is based on the difference between the original purchase price and the sale price, including purchase and sale costs.

capital gains tax discount A discount of 50 per cent on the CGT payable that is available to investors, providing the asset has been owned for at least 12 months (and provided various other conditions have been met).

cash flow The movement of cash into and out of an account.

Clearing House Electronic Sub-register System (CHESS) An electronic book-entry register of the holdings of listed shares.

compounding Commonly described as interest earned on interest. Compounding can accelerate wealth creation where interest is earned, but can also accelerate losses where interest is payable.

conveyancer A professional that deals with the legal paperwork required when buying and selling property. They make arrangements for settlement, which includes finalising transfer documents, paying government duties and taxes, and liaising with the bank if you need to borrow money and the bank is using your certificate of title as security for a mortgage.

cooling-off period A length of time given to a prospective buyer to consider their impending property purchase. The length of time varies between the states and territories. Some states have no cooling-off period. There is no cooling-off provision when buying at auction.

correction A temporary fall in a company's share price (usually of less than 10 per cent) over a period of time.

debt A financial obligation owed by the borrower (the debtor) to the lender (the creditor). In other words, it is money that is owed.

depreciation The decrease in the value of assets.

depreciation schedule A list of items in an investment property that can be depreciated and claimed as a tax benefit. Items include carpets, hot-water systems and air conditioning.

derivatives Financial products, such as options, warrants and futures. Their value is linked to the price of the underlying share. When you buy a derivative you do not buy the share itself.

dividend The income that you receive from a share investment. Dividends are usually paid twice a year, but they are paid at the company's discretion. *See also* franking credits.

dividend yield The return on a share investment in percentage terms, calculated as the total dividends divided by the share price.

due diligence The research that an investor conducts before buying an asset in order to decide whether it will be a suitable investment.

earnings per share (EPS) The amount of revenue a company has generated divided by the number of shares on issue.

equity (property) Equity is the difference between the value of what you owe and the value of what you own. In other words, it represents the portion of the asset you own as compared to the portion that the lender owns.

equity (shares) Also termed shareholders equity, this is a term used to describe the net financial interest that an investor has in a company. It is calculated as total assets minus total liabilities.

ex-dividend This is the event at which the value of a dividend that will be paid to a shareholder is extracted from the share price. Investors who own the share before this date will be entitled to receive the dividend, and those who buy the share on or after that date will not be entitled to receive the dividend.

fixed rate loan A loan where the interest rate is fixed for a period of time, which can vary from one year to 15 years.

franking credits Also called imputation credits. This is a tax credit for the tax paid by a company on earnings that have been distributed as dividends to shareholders. To prevent double taxation on the dividend income you have received, you use these credits to reduce your total tax payable.

fundamental analysis The method of valuing shares by considering financial and economic data, such as cash flow, earnings, market share, debt, business model, management, competitive advantage and future expectations of these criteria.

gearing The term used to describe borrowings to purchase an investment. *See also* negative gearing; neutral gearing; positive gearing.

index A statistical calculation that is used to value and measure the performance of an asset.

inflation The increase in the cost of a basket of goods and services as measured by the consumer price index (CPI).

initial public offer (IPO) The process by which a company issues new shares to the public for the first time when it intends to list on the stock exchange.

interest The cost of borrowing money.

interest-only loan A loan where only the interest is paid, and the principal remains unpaid at the end of the loan.

leverage *See* gearing.

liability *See* debt.

line of credit loan A line of credit is a loan that is similar to a credit card, where you are able withdraw funds as required. Sometimes regular, minimum, interest-only repayments are required to be paid.

liquidity The ease of converting the asset to cash.

LMI (lender's mortgage insurance) A premium paid by the purchaser if the loan is more than 80 per cent of the value of the property. This insurance covers the lender if the borrower defaults on the loan.

low-doc loans Loans where minimal documentation is required by the applicant. Often used by self-employed people. The interest rate charged is often higher than for a full-doc loan.

LVR (loan-to-value ratio) The value of the loan as a percentage of the value of the asset.

margin call May occur when an investor holding a margin loan experiences a significant decline in the value of their shares. This causes the ratio of the value of the shares and the value of the loan to increase, and your broker will require you to reduce your loan to the minimum loan to value ratio. To do this you can deposit additional cash to reduce the loan, or you can sell some shares.

margin loan A loan that is provided to investors to purchase shares, where the shares themselves are used as collateral. Investors are required to maintain a margin between the loan value and the value of their shares at all times. *See also* margin call.

market capitalisation The total market value of a company's issued shares. It is calculated as the number of shares on issue multiplied by the share price.

median A statistical measure often used to measure movements in property prices. The median price is derived by arranging property prices in ascending or descending order and then selecting the middle value. It is not an average. The median gives a better indication of typical property pricing in an area compared to the average.

mortgage A loan that is secured by property.

negative gearing The interest payable on an investment loan is greater than the income received.

net worth The difference between an investor's total assets and total liabilities.

neutral gearing The interest payable on an investment loan is equal to the income received.

off the plan Buying a property off the plan involves signing a contract for property which has yet to be built. This is often the practice for new developments of units and apartments.

overbought Where a share price has risen too steeply in a short amount of time.

oversold Where a share price has fallen too steeply in a short amount of time.

positive cash flow Income from an asset (including tax benefits) is greater than all the expenses (including interest, rates and taxes, repairs, and so on).

positive gearing The income from an investment is greater than the interest payable on the investment loan.

price-to-earnings ratio (P/E ratio) The relationship between a company's share price and its earnings per share. The lower the P/E ratio when compared with its competitors, the cheaper a company's share price is in relative terms.

principal and interest loan A loan where both interest and principal are repaid over the life of the loan.

real estate investment trust (REIT) A listed property trust that buys property (generally commercial property) and manages it on behalf of the investors.

rental return The annual rental income as a percentage of the value of the property (also called the rental yield or yield).

return The income you receive for having invested in an asset. At times, returns can be negative.

return on assets A financial calculation that shows how efficiently a company is using their assets to generate revenue. It is calculated as earnings divided by assets.

return on equity A financial calculation that shows how efficiently a company is using shareholder money to generate returns for their investors. It is calculated as earnings divided by shareholder equity.

return on investment (property) Commonly referred to as the yield. Return on investment (ROI) is calculated as the profit as a percentage of the total investment.

return on investment (shares) A measure of how well a share investment has performed, calculated as capital gain divided by the original cost.

risk The potential that an investment will lose money.

self managed superannuation fund (SMSF) A type of trust that exist with the sole purpose of funding the beneficiaries' retirement.

shareholder equity Represented on a company's balance sheet as the difference between a company's assets and liabilities (also known as its net assets).

stamp duty A state government charge incurred when transacting in property.

stock exchange A market on which shares are traded between buyers and sellers.

strata title Most flats, units, apartments and townhouses that have some common areas are on strata title. All the dwellings are on a separate title, but there will be some common property that is shared by all owners, such water and sewage pipes, driveway, stairwell and garden.

subdivision A parcel of land that is divided into smaller allotments.

superannuation An investment structure that is intended to be used to accumulate assets to fund your retirement.

vacancy rate The number of vacant investment properties as a percentage of the total number of investment properties in an area.

valuation (property) The definitive value of the property. It is based on recent comparable sales in the area. It is conducted by a qualified valuer for a fee. Valuations are often required when you are borrowing money, finalising a divorce settlement or finalising a deceased estate. Valuations can be used as evidence in a court of law to help resolve a dispute.

valuation (shares) The value of a company that is calculated by research analysts based on a variety of mathematical models, including expected future earnings of the company and its potential for growth.

variable rate loan A loan in which the interest rate fluctuates.

vendor An owner selling their property.

volatility The variation in the potential level of expected returns of an investment.

yield The income as a percentage of the value of the asset.

INDEX

accountant 111, 115, 116
—property questions for 231, 234, 236
—share questions for 236, 238, 239–240
active investment style 128
advanced investment opportunities 154–69, 276
advertising costs 105, 106
advice and advisers 6, 63, 114, 119, 204, 222–223 *see also* brokers
—questions to ask 231–241
AFR Smart Investor Magazine 61
analysis, shares
—dividend growth rate 76
—dividends per share (DPS) 76
—earnings growth rate 76
—earnings per share (EPS) 76
—fundamental 72–77, 146
—growth 75–76
—income 73–75
—risk 76–77
—technical 146
—value 72–73
asset classes 1–5, 8, 79–80
Australian Bureau of Statistics (ABS) 53, 62
Australian Financial Review website 58
Australian financial services licence (AFSL) 236–237
Australian Investors Association (AIA) website 59

Australian Property Investor (API) 60
Australian Prudential Regulation Authority (APRA) 129
Australian real estate investment trusts (A-REIT) 124–126, 127
Australian Securities and Investments Commission (ASIC) 57, 58, 129, 206, 230, 236–237
Australian Securities Exchange (ASX) 29–31, 57, 59, 121, 260
Australian Stock Exchange (later Australian Securities Exchange) 30, 57
auctioneer 116
average days on market 66

bank/banker 112
—property questions for 232
—share questions for 237
basic loan 151
benefits of investment
—property vs shares 20–21
—property 11–15
—shares 15–20
beta statistic 76
body corporate fees 102, 103, 104, 105, 106
bonds *see* fixed interest investments; yield curve, bond
borrowing money 149–160 *see also* margin calls; margin loans; margin lenders
—property 14, 82, 150–157, 273
—shares 157–159, 273

boutique investment firms 119
brokers, stock 107–108, 110, 118
    204, 210, 213–214
    —questions for 237–238, 239
bubble, economic 41
building inspector 112
    —questions for 232
business cycle 39–51
    —contraction 44, 45–47
    —correction 44, 45
    —depression 45
    —expansion 44–45
    —growth 44, 45
    —peak 44, 45
    —property and 48–49
    —recession 44
    —recovery 44–45
    —sector investment 51
    —shares 47–48
    —stages 43–47
buy-back programs 108
buyer's agent 112

call options 260, 261–262,
    264–265, 266
capital, source of investment 242–245
capital gains tax
    —property 186–187, 236
    —shares 189, 190, 239–240
capital growth 271
    —property 3–4, 11–12, 95–96,
    271
    —shares 4–5, 15–16, 142, 271
capital losses 15–16
cash flow growth rates 75
cash investments 2–3, 79, 149
CHESS 30, 121–122, 189, 191, 201
    —sponsored registrations 202–203

combining property and shares
    276–277, 279–280
company investment structure
    166–167, 169
confidence, investor 39, 99–100
contracts, property 232–233
contracts for difference (CFDs)
    267, 269
control, level of
    —property 13, 272
    —shares 272
conveyancer 106, 112–113
    —questions for 232–233
cooling-off rights 196–197
costs of investment 101–110
    —property 14, 101–106, 109,
    185–186, 274
    —shares 17, 18, 107–109, 110,
    159, 274
custodian 121

debt investments 5 see also fixed
    interest investments
decision to invest, points to consider
    6–7
Defence Housing Australia (DHA)
    scheme 219
defensive investments 1, 80 see also
    cash investments; fixed interest
    investments
Delisted website 59
depreciation 13, 185–186, 234
derivatives market 29–30 see also
    options; exchange traded options;
    contracts for difference
development, property 88, 140–141,
    256–257
discharge mortgage registration fees
    105, 106

discretionary trust 168, 170
diversification 7, 19, 21, 22, 37, 84,
    88, 125, 126, 128, 129, 131, 158,
    212, 214, 237, 252, 267, 268, 275,
    276, 277, 278, 280
dividends 4, 5, 17
    —franking 74
    —franking credits 17, 74,
        192–193, 253
    —growth rates 76
    —per share (DPS) 76
    —stability 74
    —yield 74
divorce settlement, managing
    247–248

earnings growth rates 76
earnings per share (EPS) 76
economic clock 42–43
economy, national *see also* gross
    domestic product
    —cycles 40–51
exchange traded funds (ETFs)
    130–131, 211, 212, 215
exchange traded international
    securities 211–212
exchange-traded options (ETOs)
    260–267

Fairfax Media websites 54
family trust 168, 170
financial adviser/planner 119
    —share questions for 236,
        237–238, 239
financing investments 149–160 *see
    also* borrowing money
    —property 150–157
    —shares 157–159

Fincorp Investment Ltd 226–227
fixed interest investments 3, 79, 252
    see also yield curve, bond
fixed rate loan 152
franking *see* dividends
fundamental analysis of companies
    72–77, 146

gearing 157, 158, 159, 168, 170, 187,
    228, 229 *see also* borrowing money
    —positive 179, 182, 186, 268
    —negative 109, 178, 179, 182,
        186, 187, 245
GICS industry code 70, 98–99
global financial crisis (GFC) 37, 41,
    230
goals, investment 6, 10, 22, 41, 63,
    82, 111, 128, 134, 135, 137, 138,
    145, 148, 149, 159, 161, 171, 237,
    242, 243, 244, 245, 246–247, 248,
    249, 250, 251, 252, 253, 264, 280
Google Maps 54–55, 62
government searches 101, 103, 105
gross domestic product (GDP) 39,
    40, 45, 46
    —Australia 40–41
growth analysis, shares 75–76
growth investments 1, 2, 83 *see also*
    property; shares
GST 102, 104, 106, 108, 147

handyman 115–116
hedge funds 119
hedging 20, 21, 263, 267
home
    —saving for 243, 244–245
    —equity, using 160
honeymoon loans 153

house and land packages 199–200
hybrid trusts 168

income *see* return on investment
income analysis, shares 73–75
indexes, stock 97–99
individual name structure
    162–164, 169
insurance 104
interest only loan 150–151
introductory loan 153
information
    —property 53–57, 60–61, 62, 275
    —shares 19, 57–59, 61–62, 275
investment *see also* goals; property;
    shares; strategies
    —active 143–145
    —basics 1–8
    —cycles 39–51
    —emotions and 142
    —institutional 119
    —options 11
    —passive 143–145
    —reasons for 142
    —retail 118
    —schemes 217–220
    —scams 216, 220–224, 225–229
    —style 128
investors using options, share 261–266
Invest to Gain website 59
IPO (initial public offering) 5, 108
issuer sponsored registrations of
    shares 202–203

joint names/tenants investment
    structure 111, 162, 163, 164, 170,
    184, 197
joint ventures, property 256–257

land sales scams 222
land tax 104
Land Titles office registration fee
    101, 103
lawyer 113 *see also* conveyancer;
    legal matters
    —questions for 232–233
legal matters 195–205
    —property 195–200, 275
    —shares 19, 200–204, 275
lender's mortgage insurance (LMI)
    102
leverage 18–19 *see also* borrowing
    money
    —property 15, 21, 273
    —shares 15, 21, 158, 258, 266,
    267, 269, 273, 276, 277
line of credit (LOC) loan 152–153
liquidity 8, 18, 277
    —property 4, 18, 274, 276, 279
    —shares 18, 21, 31, 97, 130, 131,
    211, 212, 260, 274, 276, 279
listed investment companies (LICs)
    120, 131–132, 133
listed investment trusts (LITs) 131–132
loans, types of 150–159 *see also*
    borrowing money; margin calls;
    margin lenders; margin loans
loans *see* borrowing
loan to value ratio (LVR) 14, 157,
    159, 178, 273
low documentation loans 154

Madoff, Bernie 225–226
managed funds 210–211, 215
managed investments 124–133
    —property 124–127
    —shares 127–132

management expense ratios (MERs) 130

margin calls 14, 159, 228 *see also* margin loans

margin lender 119, 157
— questions for 234

margin loans 157–159

market capitalisation 97

market depth 68, 69

markets *see also* stock markets
— history of 23–38
— participants 111–123
— performance, historical 32–36
— property 23–27
— shares 4, 5–7, 29–31, 108, 127–31

market participants and facilitators 111–123
— property 111–117
— shares 117–122

market volume 68

median house price 66

mezzanine finance 223–224

mortgage broker 113

mortgage offset accounts 155
— questions for 233

National Rental Affordability Scheme (NRAS) 219–220

no documentation loans 154

no frills loans 151

off-market share purchase scams 225–226

Opes Prime Group 227

options, property 255–256

options, share *see* call options; exchange traded options (ETOs); put options

overseas investment 206–215
— property 206–209
— shares 210–214

partnership 163–165

passive investment style 128

P/E ratio 73

pest inspector 113–114
— questions for 232

Peter's property insights 7, 21, 37, 49–50, 62, 76, 88, 100, 109–110, 122, 132, 147, 159, 170, 180, 194, 205, 229, 252, 270, 278

platform administrators 120–121

Ponzi schemes 225–226

PriceFinder website 56

price quotes, shares 67–72
— terms 68–69

principal and interest loan 150

professional package for loans 154

property *see also* development; renovation; syndicates, property; tenants
— advanced opportunities 254–257, 276
— asset class 3–4
— buying 111–115, 184, 196–199, 231–234
— choice of 81
— commercial 93–94
— condition of 199
— demand for 14
— disclosure of particulars 196
— fixtures and fittings 197
— getting started 274–275
— holding 4, 115–116, 184–186, 234–235, 274
— improving 13, 88, 138–139

—investment in 134–137
—performance over time 32–34, 36
—price 66, 82, 24–27
—real value 135–137, 235
—research 206–207
—residential 93
—schemes 217–222
—selling 105–106, 116–117, 186–187, 235–236, 274
—settlement 198
—structure, investment 170, 184
—summary 279–280
—trading 138–139, 147
—transfer of title 195–196
—vacancy and vacancy rate 61, 65, 66, 80, 81, 94
property manager 13, 103, 104, 110, 111, 115, 116, 207, 208, 214, 217, 218
—questions for 234–235
property options for pensioners and investors (Popi) 221–222
pump and dump scams 224
put options 260, 263, 264, 267
pyramid schemes 226

quantity surveyor 114, 185

realestate.com.au website 56
real estate agent 105, 106, 117, 233, 235
Real Estate Institute of Australia (REIA) 56
real estate investment trusts (REIT) 124–125, 206
real estate salesperson 116, 233, 235

reasons to invest 9–22 see also decision to invest
recession 39, 41
record keeping
—property 187–188
—shares 188–189, 238
redraw facility 156–157
registry, share 70, 121–122, 189, 202–203, 225
renovation, property 88, 138–139
rentals see also tenants
—gross yield 66
—vacancy rate 66
repairs and maintenance 103–104, 115–116
research 52–63, 120
Reserve Bank of Australia (RBA) 41
retirement 229 see also self managed superannuation funds
—amount needed 135–137
—managing investment volatility 251–252
—preparing for 248–251
—saving for 245–246
return on investment 90–100 see also dividends
—capital growth 3–5, 11–12, 15–16, 91, 92, 93–99, 142, 271, 272, 273
—income 16, 90, 91, 271, 267, 276
—property 3, 4, 11–12, 19–20, 93–96, 142, 264–266, 271
—shares 4–5, 15–16, 17, 19–20, 96–99, 142, 158, 264–266, 271, 272, 273
—yield 91–92

risk 2–3, 7 *see also* margin calls
—analysis 76–77
—attitude to 80
—borrowing 149
—business 82–83
—controllable 81–82, 84, 89
—counterparty 86
—currency 85, 208–209
—economic 82
—fund manager 130
—inflation 84–85
—interest rate 82, 85
—investment 79–89
—legislative 83, 85
—management 37, 81, 88
—market 85
—non-controllable 82–83,
    84–86, 89
—overseas investment 207–209,
    213, 214
—performance 86
—profile 80, 87–88, 243, 244,
    246, 247, 248, 249, 250,
    251, 252
—property 3–4, 80–83 126
—reward relationship
    79–80, 86
—shares 4–5, 83–86
RP Data 55, 57

sales growth rates 75
savings plans 243–244
scams, investment 216, 220–230
—avoiding 222
—identifying 220–221
—property 222–224
—shares 224–228
sector investment roadmap 50, 51

self managed superannuation funds
    (SMSFs) 170, 172–183, 252
—activities 174–175
—administration 181–182
—borrowing in 179, 268
—costs 181–182
—defined 173–174
—investments 175–177
—permitted receipts 175
—purchasing property 177–179,
    182
—purchasing shares 179–181
—sole purpose rule 174–175
—statistics 172–173
—tax benefits 177–179, 182
Share Dividends website 59
shareholders rights and obligations 201
    see also dividends; shares
sharemarkets *see* stock markets
share price charts 71–72
share registry *see* registry, share
shares *see also* analysis; contracts for
    difference; dividends; exchange
    traded funds; exchange traded
    options; margin calls; managed
    funds; margin lenders; margin
    loans; stock market; warrants,
    investment
—advanced opportunities
    258–269, 276
—asset class 4–5
—benefits of investment 15–20
—blue-chip 15, 21, 32, 157, 226
—business influences 99–100
—business sector 98–99
—buying 189–190, 236–238
—exit strategy 142
—getting started 274–275

—holding 108–109, 142–143,
190, 238–239
—income from falling markets
19–20, 267, 276
—investment in 142–145
—leverage 18–19
—ownership 200–201
—performance over time 31,
32–35
—price quotes 67–72
—risk 4–5, 79–80, 83–86
—selling 142, 144, 191–192,
239–240
—settlement 18, 201–203
—structure, investment 170, 188
—summary 279–280
—trading 146–147, 170,
266–270
short selling 258–260
Smart Property Investment (*SPI*) 60–61
SNR (statistically not reliable) 67
sole trader structure 163, 164, 169, 170
sources of information 52–63
—magazines 60–62
—property 53–57, 60–61, 62
—shares 57–59, 61–62
—websites 52–59
split loan 152
stamp duty 18, 101, 103
standard variable loan 151
statistics, understanding 64–78
—property 64–67, 77
—shares 67–76, 77–78
stockbrokers *see* brokers
stock markets *see also* markets
—Australian 4, 29–31
—foreign 4
—history of 27–31

—primary/secondary 5–6, 108
—reason for 5–7
Storm Financial 228
strategies, investment 243, 244, 245,
246–247, 248, 249, 250, 252
structures for investment 161–172
—considerations 161–162
—comparison of features 169
superannuation *see also* retirement;
self managed superannuation
funds
—scams 226–227
—strategies 250–251
Sydney Futures Exchanges 29, 30
syndicates, property 126–127

taxation 184–194
—capital gains (CGT) 186–187,
189, 190, 192, 236, 239–240
—franking credits 192–193
—property 13, 109, 184–188
—shares 16–17, 188–194, 272
tenants 19, 21, 22, 66, 81, 90, 94,
103, 104, 115, 208, 220, 276, 280
tenants in common 184, 197
testamentary trusts 170
timeframe, investment 86–87,
253, 229
timing, investment
—property 49, 81, 82
—shares 50, 142–143, 253
traders, share 118, 146–147, 170,
266–267
TradingEconomics website 59
trading vs investing 134–148
—property 134–141
—shares 141–147
—tax implications 188–189

trusts, property 124–126
trust structure 167–170, 169
— types 168, 170

unit trusts 131, 168

valuation, share 73
value analysis, shares 72–73
valuer, property 114–115
valuer
— property questions for 233–234
vendor discount 66
volatility 2, 13–14, 37, 63, 79–80, 87,
  251–252, 253, 262, 272, 277
— property 2, 13–14, 20, 34, 35,
  79, 100, 110, 272, 279
— shares 2, 17, 20, 34, 37, 35, 37,
  38, 50, 62, 76, 79, 84, 89, 158,
  229, 237, 251–252, 253, 258,
  261, 272, 276, 279

warrants, investment 267–268
website sources 52–59
— property 53–57
— shares 57–59
work hours, reducing 249

Yahoo! Finance 58
yield curve, bond 46–47
Your Investment Property (YIP) 61

Zac's shares insights 7, 21–22, 37–38,
  50, 62–63, 77–78, 88–89, 100,
  110, 122–123, 133, 147–148,
  159–160, 170, 182–183, 194, 205,
  239–240, 253, 270, 278

Printed in Australia
22 Jan 2025
LP040350